Reflexive Translation Studie

C000258784

Literature and Translation

Literature and Translation is a series for books that address literary translation and for books of literary translation. Its emphasis is on diversity of genre, culture, period and approach. The series uses an open access publishing model to disseminate widely developments in the theory and practice of translation, as well as translations into English of literature from around the world.

Series editor: Timothy Mathews is Emeritus Professor of French and Comparative Criticism, UCL.

Reflexive Translation Studies

Translation as Critical Reflection

Silvia Kadiu

First published in 2019 by
UCL Press
University College London
Gower Street
London WC1E 6BT

Available to download free: www.ucl.ac.uk/ucl-press

Text © Silvia Kadiu, 2019

Silvia Kadiu has asserted her right under the Copyright, Designs and Patents Act 1988 to be identified as author of this work.

A CIP catalogue record for this book is available from The British Library.

This book is published under a Creative Commons 4.0 International license (CC BY 4.0). This license allows you to share, copy, distribute and transmit the work; to adapt the work and to make commercial use of the work providing attribution is made to the authors (but not in any way that suggests that they endorse you or your use of the work). Attribution should include the following information:

Kadiu, S. 2019. *Reflexive Translation Studies*. London, UCL Press. https://doi.org/10.14324/111.9781787352513

Further details about Creative Commons licenses are available at http://creativecommons.org/licenses/

ISBN: 978-1-78735-253-7 (Hbk.)
ISBN: 978-1-78735-252-0 (Pbk.)
ISBN: 978-1-78735-251-3 (PDF)
ISBN: 978-1-78735-254-4 (epub)
ISBN: 978-1-78735-255-1 (mobi)
ISBN: 978-1-78735-256-8 (html)
DOI: https://doi.org/10.14324/111.9781787352513

To my father

Contents

Preface

This book presents a creative translation practice which I hope will inspire students, practitioners and scholars to experiment with the boundaries of translation beyond conventional acceptations of the term as a transfer of meaning from one language to another. My approach in this volume uses the movement of crossing at play in translation as a way of engaging with existing theory, while reflecting on that translating experience and unfolding in response a view of what translation is or could be about. Its premise is that translation theory – the way we perceive, describe or think about translation – is inevitably interwoven with practice. Here, theorising takes place during the translating process itself, in the act of undertaking a translation and attempting to articulate our experience of it, of facing a translation dilemma and reflecting on possible solutions.

In this framework, translation is conceived as a productive process which enables an experiential, tangible mode of thinking. Engaging critically with a piece of theory by translating it constitutes a creative gesture. It presupposes that the text chosen for translation demands further exploration and interrogation, and that recontextualising it through translation may bring to light new perspectives on translation. Ultimately, this book celebrates the critical and creative power of translation, its potential for questioning established concepts and creating new ones in the process. Its invitation to apprehend texts through translation extends beyond translation studies, to students and scholars across the humanities, as well as to practitioners and thinkers beyond academia.

Using translation as an instrument for critical reflection may prove constructive in a variety of ways. In the context of this volume, my focus is on translating theoretical texts from English into French and vice versa. However, I would like to invite readers to look beyond the confines of my practice and consider the range of possibilities that engaging with any given material – text, film, painting – through translation (transcreation, adaptation, ekphrasis) may instigate in their own discipline or field.

Acknowledgments

This book grew out of my doctoral research at UCL and could not have been written without the support of Timothy Mathews and Theo Hermans. Their comments have inspired me in countless ways, and I am deeply grateful for their continuing guidance over the years.

My warm thanks go also to all those friends, university colleagues and family members who have advised, corrected or encouraged me during the various stages of developing this work. I am especially thankful to Geraldine Brodie, Stephen Hart, Thomas Connolly, Jane Fenoulhet, Nicolas Froeliger, Lance Hewson, Françoise Wuilmart and Alba Simaku. I would like to extend my gratitude to the Centre for Multidisciplinary and Intercultural Inquiry and the School of European Languages, Culture and Society at UCL, as well as to the Arts and Humanities Research Council, for their support with this project.

I am also grateful to Taylor & Francis Group and SUNY Press for permission to reproduce material from Lawrence Venuti's *The Translator's Invisibility* (2008) and Antoine Berman's *The Experience of the Foreign*, translated by Stefan Heyvaert (1992).

Finally, I wish to thank my husband, Matthieu Dadou, for his unwavering support and enthusiasm at every stage of completion.

List of tables

Introduction:
Genesis of a reflexive method in translation

Translation theories calling for reflexivity

The rapid development of translation studies as a discipline since the 1990s, 'a period that experienced a boom in translation theory,'[1] has seen a proliferation of theories calling for greater reflexivity in translation, which raise issues of visibility, creativity and ethics. Four Western scholars in particular – all of whom also had or still have careers as practising translators – have been prominent in emphasising the need for a reflexive practice of translation: Lawrence Venuti, Susan Bassnett, Henri Meschonnic and Antoine Berman. This book presents a creative way of exploring their theories. It examines the thinkers' approaches to translation in both form and content, offering critical readings of their theories as well as practical translations of the texts that articulate them.

In *The Translator's Invisibility*,[2] Lawrence Venuti argues that increased awareness of a translation's conditions of production is necessary for an ethical translation practice, since translation involves a degree of ethnocentric violence that tends to erase the cultural specificity of the source text. For Venuti, a translation that highlights its own status as translation is ethical in that, instead of attempting to dissimulate the domesticating forces at play in translational activity, it draws attention to, and raises awareness of, the cultural differences between source and target texts.[3] In his view, the translator has an ethical obligation to indicate the otherness of the foreign text when importing it into the target culture.

In her essay 'Writing and Translating',[4] Susan Bassnett focuses on a different aspect of reflexivity in translation: the question of creativity. For her, translating is a form of writing which triggers a dialogic interaction between author and translator, an intimate relation in which the translator becomes aware of her own creative voice.[5] In

Bassnett's approach, reflexivity is not a matter of making a text's status as translation visible, but of recognising the inspirational and creative impulse prompted by translation. According to Bassnett, translating is a conscious and reflexive form of writing, a playful and poetic activity, comparable to theatrical performance.

In *Ethics and Politics of Translating*,[6] Henri Meschonnic also insists on the creative aspect of translation. In Meschonnic's view, translating is above all an inventive, poetic and transformative enterprise, during which language and life interact. For Meschonnic, theory and practice cannot be separated in translation because translation always involves a reflexive decision-making process, which manifests in return the translator's relation to language and to translating.[7] Except when it is automated, translation, in his view, always expresses a theoretical position: the translator's perception of language and engagement with the world.

Similarly, in *Toward a Translation Criticism*,[8] Antoine Berman argues that translators and translation scholars should reflect on translation in a way that combines theoretical considerations with the experience of translation. For Berman, reflecting on the act of translating, and developing a self-reflexive theory of translation, is crucial for liberating translation from its ethnocentric impulse and from the repressed status from which it has suffered in the past.[9] In Berman's work, an ethical approach to translation is inseparable from a reflexive study of translation – that is, from disciplinary self-reflexivity.

In their own way, each theorist suggests that self-awareness is a key requirement for an ethical practice of translation. By advocating the visibility of the translating subject (Venuti), the translator's right to creativity (Bassnett), the supremacy of human translation (Meschonnic) and an autonomous study of translation (Berman), they seek to liberate translation from its ethnocentric violence (Venuti), from the demands of fidelity (Bassnett), from mechanical representations of language (Meschonnic) and from its dependence on other disciplines (Berman). In championing reflexivity, their ultimate aim is to empower translation, both as a professional practice and as an academic discipline.

The purpose of this book is to explore whether reflexivity, as presented by each of these scholars, can bring about the empowerment that they seek. To what extent can reflexivity foster an ethical practice of translation? Can reflexivity provide an effective translation methodology? And what can reflexive translation strategies tell us about the role, scope and nature of reflexivity in translation? The experimental approach I develop to address these questions is itself both reflexive and self-reflexive. Using translation as an instrument for critical reflection, the method I showcase here consists of translating translation theory by folding it back on the text that formulates it. Operating simultaneously on theoretical and practical levels, it inquires into reflexivity through reflexivity, reflecting on reflexive translation theories by translating them according to their own guiding principles.

A reflexive method in translation

The reflexive practice presented in this book is inspired by Jacques Derrida's deconstructionist approach in 'Des Tours de Babel'. In this text, Derrida attempts an intralingual translation of Walter Benjamin's 1923 essay 'The Task of the Translator', to reflect on Benjamin's translation theory.[10] In discussing and trying to enact specific aspects of Benjamin's essay, Derrida also develops and showcases his own philosophy of translation: the idea that translation is impossible yet necessary. Derrida chooses to translate Benjamin's theory in a Benjaminian way both to explore and to actualise this double bind of translation, which consists in the simultaneous necessity and impossibility to translate, exemplified by the word 'Babel', an untranslatable proper noun meaning at the same time father, God and confusion.

Reflecting on the polysemy of the term 'Babel', Derrida undertakes an intralingual translation of Maurice de Gandillac's French translation of Benjamin's text into French – an endeavour that he presents as follows:

> This singular example [the word Babel], at once archetypical and allegorical, could serve as an introduction to all the so-called theoretical problems of translation. But no theorization, inasmuch as it is produced in a language, will be able to dominate the Babelian performance. This is one of the reasons why I prefer here, instead of treating it in the theoretical mode, to attempt to translate in my own way the translation of another text on translation.[11]

For Derrida, theorisation is unable to dominate the Babelian performance (the polysemy of the word Babel, which makes its translation both necessary and impossible), because this performance is itself embedded in a language. To think about translation, Derrida prefers to engage in translation, choosing to describe translation by practising translation.

My approach in this book is comparable. The experimental translations that I propose as possible interpretations of the translation theories examined offer practical ways of exploring theories which suggest that reflexivity is the only way of developing an ethical translation. The sample translations presented in each chapter serve to illustrate the main concepts of the reflexive theory under scrutiny, as well as my response to it, by providing concrete examples of what a reflexive translation may look like in each case. These translations are conceived as a creative and critical form of engagement with key contemporary translation theories. They question the capacity of reflexivity to counteract the power relations at play in translation, and problematise affirmative claims about (self-) knowledge in translation.

The reflexive method is rooted in the idea that stating is performing an act. First theorised in the 1950s by the English philosopher John Langshaw Austin, the concept of performativity establishes that words do something in the world, something which is not just a matter of generating consequences. According to Austin, in speech acts, words are actions in themselves: they are 'performed' and make a difference in the world.[12] Common examples of speech acts include promising, naming and declaring. Extending his definition of performativity to all utterances, Austin suggests that any statement may function as performative, since it may be doing by saying something. The reflexive method in translation is performative in that it proposes to enact the source text by simultaneously doing and saying what it says/does. Saying and doing, word and spirit, form and content are co-dependent in this approach.

The idea that form and content are inseparable is largely recognised in literary translation, and poetry especially.[13] When it comes to translations of theoretical texts, however, the emphasis so far has mostly been on the way concepts travel,[14] rather than on how form and content interact in the process of the transfer from one context to another. Embracing the idea that form and content, saying and doing, text and metatext interconnect in translation, my reflexive approach in this book offers an analysis of the particular operation of reflexivity involved in the translation of translation theory: the fact that the medium of expression (translation) is enmeshed with the object of the discourse (translation). For, when translating translation theory, the translator finds herself performing the activity discussed in the source text itself: her task as a translator mirrors the practice described in the text she translates.

Translating translation theory

The translation of translation theory is a relatively neglected area of inquiry in translation studies. In recent decades, however, a growing number of studies have emerged that reflect on the expansion of the discipline. Some report the rise of university programmes,[15] others highlight the proliferation of new journals and publications in the field,[16] while others still describe which translation theories are taught as part of these programmes,[17] or attempt to map the ways in which research interests in the discipline have shifted throughout the years.[18] Despite the growing interest in meta-disciplinary questions, however, comprehensive accounts of the translations of translation theory remain scarce.

Jacques Derrida's 'Des Tours de Babel' and Lawrence Venuti's 'Translating Derrida on Translation' are two of the very few examples of article-length writings reflecting on the practice of translating translation theory. In fact, even these two texts are not, so to speak, reflections on translating translation theory *per se*. 'Des Tours de Babel' is a reflection on translation which presents itself as an act of translation, rather than a reflection on translating theory, while 'Translating Derrida on Translation' starts off as a reflection on translating Derrida's 'What is a "Relevant" Translation?' but rapidly digresses into a discussion of translation in cultural studies.[19]

At the time of writing, there is no single volume specifically devoted to the translations of translation theory, no study that attempts to theorise this particular practice of translation. Everything that has been written so far on the subject appears in scattered form, either as prefaces to actual translations of theoretical texts on translation (see Françoise Massardier-Kenney on translating Berman's *Pour une critique des traductions*)[20] or in author interviews (see Pier-Pascale Boulanger on translating Meschonnic's *Éthique et politique du traduire*).[21] Interestingly, these writers, too, highlight the performative aspect of their work – the fact that they translated texts by mirroring the translation theories developed in those texts themselves.

In the introduction to her English translation of *Pour une critique des traductions*, for example, Massardier-Kenney makes clear that her approach to translating Berman's book was deliberately informed by Berman's own translation theory: 'The principles I used to translate Berman's text,' she points out, 'were those proposed by Berman in the text itself.'[22] Throughout her preface Massardier-Kenney explains her translational choices with reference to Berman's ideas of translation. However, she does not explicitly state why applying Berman's theory would be more appropriate than translating his text in another way, as though for her a performative approach was unquestionably the best way of translating Berman.

Similarly, in an interview with René Lemieux and Caroline Mangerel,

Boulanger supports her approach to translating Meschonnic by saying that 'Meschonnic must be translated according to his own conception of translation.'[23] In the introduction to her translation of *Éthique et politique du traduire*, she further explains:

> In order to keep the reader's attention, I could have worked to flatten the reading bumps to correct, smooth English, but this would have constituted domestication, which contradicts Meschonnic's idea of translating. He clearly outlines what should be translated in a text when he says that 'we must invent discourse equivalences in the target language: prosody for prosody, metaphor for metaphor, pun for pun, rhythm for rhythm' (see p.71). So I decided to apply Meschonnic's theory of translating to translating Meschonnic's theory. This decision implied doing to English what he did to French, resisting conventional forms in the translation as he does in his writing.[24]

In saying that translating Meschonnic faithfully meant following his own vision, Boulanger implies that when translating translation theory, a performative approach is always preferable.

Joseph F. Graham's translation of Derrida's 'Des Tours de Babel' provides another example of a performative perspective on translating translation theory. In a note to his English version of Derrida's text, Graham indicates that the principles guiding his translation of Derrida's essay were also those found in the text itself:

> There was consolation for so much effort to so little effect in that, whatever we did, we were bound to exhibit the true principles of translation announced in our text. And so this translation is exemplary to that extent. To the extent that we were guided in translation, the principles were also those found in the text. Accordingly, a silhouette of the original appears for effect in many words and phrases of the translation.[25]

In this note, Graham suggests that despite its shortcomings, his English translation of 'Des Tours de Babel' remains faithful to the French original because it exemplifies the central idea articulated by Derrida in this piece: the impossibility yet necessity to translate.

Translating translation theory seems intuitively to call for a reflexive approach. It triggers an uncanny mirroring effect, as the translator finds herself performing the activity that the theorist discusses in the text to translate. Translating translation theory thus brings about the possibility of new forms of fidelity in translation. In the context of such practice, the demand of fidelity to the source text appears to apply simultaneously to form and content, as though translating the original differently than according to its own guiding principles would mean betraying it. When translating translation theory, the ideas articulated in the source text tend to dictate the way it ought to be translated, seemingly leaving the translator no other choice but to translate the text reflexively by attempting to apply the theorist's vision to the text itself.

Reflexivity, performativity, deconstruction

In this monograph, translating a theoretical text in the light of its own theory is developed into an instrument of critical and self-critical inquiry. The ambition is both to explore the applicability of translation theories advocating greater reflexivity and to inspect the unique form of reflexiveness involved in the translation of translation theory. Studying the reflexive experience prompted by the activity of translating translation theory is essential to understanding the nature of performativity in translation. As an extreme manifestation of the fusion of form and content, signifier and signified, theory and practice, translating reflexively brings into question a defining aspect of fidelity in translation – the opposition letter vs. spirit which has preoccupied thinkers of translation for centuries. By moving beyond this opposition, the operation of reflexivity at play in translating translation theory provides the grounds for a tangible exploration of the possible applications of a performative approach to translation.

What does it mean to simultaneously do and say a text by translating it? To what extent is such a practice feasible? And what would its benefits and limits be? The reflexive method showcased in this book is deliberately deconstructive in nature. Following Derrida's own deconstructionist approach, it strives 'to undo a construction with infinite patience, to take apart a system in order to understand all its mechanisms, to exhibit all its foundations, and to reconstruct on new bases'.[26] Using translation to think about translation, the reflexive method aims to untangle the structures of the texts translated by exposing their internal contradictions, furthermore building on these aporias to develop a critical and self-critical mode of theorising reflexivity in translation.

In this perspective, the reflexive method offers a practical exploration of a deconstructionist approach to translation. Derrida's writings have been widely influential in translation studies. His essays 'Des Tours de Babel' and 'What is a "Relevant" Translation', which subvert traditional views of translation as a secondary, inferior form of expression, have become canonical texts, foregrounding the importance of critical inquiries in the discipline.[27] However, his contribution to translation is often considered too abstract or inapplicable.[28] Moreover, translation scholars invoking his work as a source of inspiration tend to focus on the notion of untranslatability,[29] rather than on the necessity to translate. Thereby they occlude the fact that for Derrida deconstruction itself is an operation of translation and transformation – a process that 'consists of transference, and of a thinking of transference, in all the senses that this word acquires in more than one language, and first of all that of the transference between languages'.[30]

In this book, I experiment with the reflexive method and explore it as a possible application of a deconstructionist approach to translation. Unlike interpretations which give priority to the concept of untranslatability in Derrida's work, my own approach advances the notion that Derrida's deconstructionist philosophy is in fact unthinkable without a creative, experimental practice of translation. My analysis of the particular form of reflexiveness involved in the translation of translation theory seeks to provide new insight into the articulation of reflexivity in translation, and ethics of translation beyond that. For in various ways, the four theorists discussed in this book associate reflexivity with ethics, and my intention ultimately is to question the scope and limits of an ethical practice of translation based on the opposition between reflexive and non-reflexive approaches.

Reflexive, self-reflexive, self-critical

Reflexivity is an important but slippery topic, which may conjure up a variety of concepts. In some social theories, reflexivity refers to an essential human capacity; in others, it is a system property; in still others, it is a critical, or self-critical, act. In 'Against Reflexivity as an Academic Virtue and Source of Privileged Knowledge',[31] Michael Lynch identifies six main categories of reflexivity (mechanical, substantive, methodological, meta-theoretical, interpretative and ethno-methodological), four of which are themselves subdivided into further sub-categories.

Lynch's classification of reflexivity, which I have summarised in the table below, provides a good overview of its complexity:

Table 0.1: Summary of Michael Lynch's classification of reflexivity[32]

Category	Subcategory	Description	Examples
Mechanical reflexivity	Knee-jerk reflexivity	A habitual, automatic or thoughtless response	In behaviourist psychology, a pattern through which a stimulus evokes a response.
	Cybernetic loopiness	A circular process involving feedback loops.	Models using mechanistic imagery, but emphasising a humanistic sense of reflexivity as *self-reflection*.
	Reflections ad infinitum	An infinite regress of reflections.	Halls of mirrors, the Möbius strip, Escher's hand drawing itself.
Substantive reflexivity	Systemic-reflexivity	Modes of social inquiry relying upon expert knowledge.	Risk benefit analysis, economic forecasts, opinion polling, etc.
	Reflexive social construction	Subscription to the reality of socially constructed facts.	The way consensual beliefs give rise to objective social institutions (e.g. value of currency).
Methodological reflexivity	Philosophical self-reflection	The Enlightenment ideal of self-knowledge.	Self-inspection and rejection of appearances in favour of deeper foundations of certainty.
	Methodological self-consciousness	The attempt to correct biases that distort or confound access to the object of study.	Researchers considering their relations to the groups they study.
	Methodological self-criticism	Self-criticism aiming to enhance epistemic value.	Confessional ethnography, anti-objectivistic styles of discourse analysis and textual criticism.
	Methodological self-congratulation	A self-exemplifying sociology of science.	Applying the same indices of 'maturation' in the natural sciences to the study of their own specialty.
Meta-theoretical self-reflexivity	Reflexive objectivation	An objectivation of the social field.	Critically revaluing what members of a given field take for granted.
	Standpoint reflexivity	A reflexive critique of dominant discourse.	Subjecting one's own framework to criticism.
	Breaking frame	An exposure and realisation of the conjurer's tricks.	Film or painting calling attention to the illusionist techniques deployed to create a sense of reality.
Interpretative reflexivity	Hermeneutic reflexivity	A style of interpretation based on the reader's active interpretation.	A sociologist's self-critical interpretation (vs. ordinary interpretations, unconscious of the forces influencing them).
	Radical referential reflexivity	A pre-occupation with, and sceptical treatment of, *representation*.	An analysis problematising or deconstructing positive claims about knowledge without distinction or exemption.
Ethnomethodological reflexivity		The reflexivity of accounting practices and accounts.	An ethnographic description (which explains the features of a specific setting, but uses the setting itself to make sense of the description).

Each of the types of reflexivity listed by Lynch involves some form of 'recursive turning back': a return, a repetition or a folding back. However, what the turning back does, how it does it and what its implications are vary from category to category, as well as within a given category.

Furthermore, the boundaries between these various aspects of reflexivity are not clear-cut, but fuzzy, interdependent. Ethnomethodological reflexivity, for example – the correlation between a fact and its description – is simultaneously methodological and substantive, for it involves both philosophical self-reflection and subscription to the reality of socially constructed facts. Interpretative reflexivity, on the other hand, which includes reading, thinking, contemplating or making sense of an object or text, is prominent in most categories, including substantive, methodological and meta-theoretical reflexivity. The main challenge of dealing with the notion of reflexivity lies first and foremost in identifying and clarifying its multiple and shifting meanings, the nuances surrounding its various uses and its overlap with other key notions such as reflection, self-reference and self-reflexivity.

The distinction between reflexivity (folding something back on itself) and self-reflexivity (pointing to or reflecting upon oneself) is particularly unstable and hazy. The process of translating translation theory is at once reflexive and self-reflexive. The mirroring, self-reflexive effect prompted by the act of performing the activity discussed in the source text seems to instigate a performative, reflexive approach that incites translators to fold the theory they translate back on itself. Hence, in most cases, my use of the term 'reflexivity' also encompasses the notion of *self-reflexivity*. Later in the book, however, the distinction between these two concepts will emerge more clearly as a result of the sample translations I present in each chapter.

The texts discussed in this monograph each address a different aspect of reflexivity in translation. Venuti's argument in favour of a foreignizing practice that strives to secure the visibility of a translation's status as translation falls within the categories of *breaking frame* (an exposure and realisation of the translator's tricks) and *standpoint reflexivity* (a critique of the ethnocentric discourse prevailing in Anglo-American culture). Bassnett's approach to translation as a subjective engagement with the source text relies on *hermeneutic reflexivity*, a style of interpretation based on the translator's creative reading of the text to translate. The opposition poetics vs. mechanics underlying Meschonnic's theory is founded on the distinction between *hermeneutic reflexivity* (the translator's subjective interpretation of the source text) and *mechanical reflexivity* (a thoughtless, automatic response to a stimulus).

And Berman's call for disciplinary self-reflexivity is a form of *reflexive objectivation*, which consists in critically revaluing the role of translation studies in the articulation of translation and ethics.

My own approach, and use of translation as a critical instrument, is inscribed in a reflexive and self-critical praxis that interrogates affirmative claims about knowledge and self-knowledge in translation. The reflexive method is unstable and continuously changing, mirroring the object under scrutiny even while critically challenging it. Translating reflexively will mean different things in relation to the different texts examined. It requires redefining reflexivity in each context of use, determining what it signifies for each of the theorists and what it brings into play for their respective theories. Overall, this approach attempts to characterise the various expressions of reflexivity in translation, their complex articulation with ethics, and the extent to which reflexivity is possible, preferable or even avoidable in each case.

The treatment of reflexivity in this book thus operates concurrently on three levels: (1) thematically, in the object of analysis (the reflexive translation theories analysed); (2) methodologically, in the method of analysis (folding a theory back on itself); and (3) self-critically, on a meta-disciplinary level (reflecting on the benefits and limits of the reflexive method adopted). The multiple layers of reflexivity at play – within the text, in the translating process and from a scholarly perspective – are often difficult to untangle and therefore constantly challenge the researcher's own self-awareness. These challenges will themselves be examined and discussed throughout this work.

What is translation theory?

In his seminal paper entitled 'The Name and Nature of Translation Studies', James Holmes describes the then-emerging discipline known as translation studies as being concerned with 'the complex of problems clustered round the phenomenon of translating and translations'.[33] He identifies two main branches in the discipline: on the one hand, 'pure research', which includes 'translation theory' (the establishment of general principles to explain or predict translation phenomena); and on the other hand, 'applied translation studies', in which the findings of pure research are applied in 'actual translation situations, in translation training, and in translation criticism'.[34] In Holmes' categorisation, then, translation theory is a subcategory of research within the wider discipline of translation studies.

However, the use of the term has created some confusion in the field, for several scholars have employed it to refer to the discipline of translation studies as a whole. Anton Popovič, for example, defines translation theory as a 'discipline engaged in the systematic study of translation',[35] while Peter Newmark describes it as 'the body of knowledge that we have and have still to have about the process of translating'.[36] As Mark Shuttleworth and Moira Cowie point out, though, such definitions gradually came to represent the minority in the discipline, as the term became more and more used in the sense of Holmes's categorisation, taking on a meaning which is closer to that of 'theory' in the natural sciences: 'a specific attempt to explain in a systematic way some or all of the phenomena related to translation'.[37]

In the *Encyclopedia of Applied Linguistics*, Maria Tymoczko defines translation theory, following definition 4 of 'theory' in the *Compact Oxford English Dictionary*, as 'a scheme or system of ideas or statements held as an explanation or account of a group of facts or phenomena', which she opposes to the 'loose or general sense' of definition 6, 'an idea or set of ideas about something; an individual view or notion'.[38] According to Tymoczko, translation scholars do not consistently maintain a distinction between these different meanings. For her, the term 'translation theory' should only be used to refer to 'the development and testing of hypotheses'.[39] Natural scientific approaches like Tymoczko's are more and more debated, however – notably by translation theorists who make a deliberate choice to use the term 'theory' in the general sense of individual views or notions.

Jean Boase-Beier, for instance, defines theory as 'a partial description (mental or perhaps written down) of a segment of reality', which, she stresses, quoting Iser, is especially true in the humanities, where theories 'do not embody laws that make predictions, but rather search for metaphors adequate to the description of the phenomena in question in order to understand them'.[40] For Boase-Beier, translation theories are partial, descriptive accounts which represent different ways of seeing and practising translation. Deconstructionist scholar Joseph F. Graham goes even further, challenging the very idea that elaborating an all-encompassing theory of translation is possible. Translations, he suggests, comprise an indefinite and fuzzily distinguished set of problems that differ sufficiently from each other to undermine any single theoretical framework.[41]

In this book, the term 'translation theory' is intentionally used in the broad sense of individual views or notions about translation, so as to account not only for the experiential, subjective and partial nature of the theories that I consider, but also my manner of considering them. The texts examined in subsequent chapters are acknowledged works of theory through which the authors present their own perspectives on translation phenomena – perspectives that centre primarily on their personal experience of translation, or perception of what translation is or should be about. In response to these texts, my reflexive practice presents a performative, process-driven form of theorising through which I compose my own approach to translation.

My use of the word 'theory' is close to Anthony Pym's. In *Exploring Translation Theories*, Pym draws on the Greek etymology of the term 'theory' (*theā*, view + *horan*, to see), stressing its analogy with the word 'theatre' to define translation theory as 'the scene where the generation and selection process takes place'.[42] In Pym's approach, translators are theorising all the time as part of their practice, since they generate translations by formulating various alternatives and then choosing between them to determine their definitive translation. While translating, translators constantly think 'what translation is and how it should be carried out'.[43] They theorise translation internally as part of the translating process, thus developing a certain view of how to practise translation.

In this work, theorising may thus refer to: 1) the decision-making process at play in translation (the mental formation of an individual perception of translation through translation); 2) the formulation of metaphors and/or explanations designed to describe translation (the written account through which an individual perception is expressed); 3) the operation of inquiring about the applicability of specific theories (the adoption and development of a critical positioning in response to existing statements about translation). My overall approach is qualitative rather than quantitative in nature. Its aim is not to provide a general account of reflexivity in translation (its regularities, tendencies, frequencies, distributions), nor to quantify how typical or widespread it is (how much of it there is), but to reflect on the various manifestations of reflexivity in translation through the actual practice of this activity.

Reflexive translation studies

In the past decades, translation studies has increasingly focused on the ethical dimension of translational activity, emphasising reflexivity to assert the role of the researcher in understanding and highlighting the ethical issues at stake.[44] The main ambition of these translation theories has been to counteract the power relations at play in translation (between minor and dominant languages, for example) by making visible the transformative dimension of translation itself. The main idea underlying this line of thought is that, in order to highlight manipulation in translation (such as a stereotypical representation of the source culture), research must itself be reflexive and think about the conditions of its own emergence. This is necessary because, like the translator, the researcher is 'constantly faced by choices, choices he can make only on the basis of his individual grasp (knowledge, sensibility, experience…) of the two languages and cultures involved, and with the aid of his personal tastes and preferences'.[45] The selection and interpretation of concepts, metaphors and theories is not only determined by their empirical, objective applicability; it is also influenced by the researcher's feelings, personal ideologies and motives. Reflection and self-reflection upon these conditions of research is therefore key to the empowering capacity of that reflection itself.

Several scholars have emphasised the need for increased reflexivity in conducting research on translation. At the outset of the discipline, James Holmes registers a moment of disciplinary self-awareness. According to him, '[t]ranslation studies has reached a stage where it is time to examine the subject itself'.[46] More recently, Theo Hermans has suggested that the self-observations that come with the maturation of every discipline '[oblige] us to reconsider not just what we know, but how we know'.[47] Like Hermans, Mona Baker stresses the importance of the role of the researcher in shaping the course of the research, and the subsequent need for increased attentiveness to the researching self.[48] In adopting a reflexive methodology while simultaneously investigating the viability of the reflexive approach adopted, I am seeking here to serve as a step towards a better comprehension of the researching self in translation studies.

Reflexivity in research is built on an acknowledgement of the ideological and historical pressures forming researcher and researched alike. In its attempt to identify, acknowledge and act upon the constraints of a research project (location, subjects, process, theoretical context, data, etc.), reflexivity has important ethical implications. According to scholar Jay Ruby, failure to acknowledge the interests implicit in a critical agenda, or to assume value-free positions of neutrality, results in a 'dishonest position'.[49] The failure to acknowledge the interests implicit in any critical agenda is considered unethical because a project that affirms its neutrality perpetuates existing norms instead of attempting to reflect and act upon them. In the same way as 'a theory of translation should attempt to empower translators-to-be and raise their conscience as writers concerning the responsibility they will face in the seminal role they will play in the establishment of all sorts of relationships between cultures',[50] the aim of translation scholars 'should be research and training that produces readers of translations and translators who are critically aware'.[51]

The reflexive methodology I adopt to explore the scope and confines of reflexive translation theories thus invites me, as a researcher, to also think reflexively about my own approach. The goal, however, is not so much to highlight my subjectivity as a researcher as to explore the extent to which such subjectivity can be highlighted at all. Focusing on the question of whether reflexivity can produce self-awareness, the sample translations I showcase and discuss in this book question the very possibility that one can ever be fully aware of, or make visible, the conditions at play in the production of a translation. To what extent can reflexivity be achieved in translation research? Can a researching translator ever be aware of the range of motivations behind her own translation choices? Finally, to what extent can research methods based on reflexivity be considered more ethical than non-reflexive approaches? If it is true that translation and research on translation can never be fully reflexive and self-reflexive, then the question of an ethics of translation needs to be reformulated beyond the concepts of visibility, self-awareness and intention which underlie current approaches to translation ethics.

Translation theory in translator education

Translation theory plays a central role in translator education, and many scholars have underlined the benefits of theoretical instruction in translator training throughout the development of the discipline.[52] Translation theory is essential, according to these scholars, because it gives translators more options to choose from when they translate;[53] makes them aware of problems they may not have anticipated,[54] and provides them with a metalanguage for explaining their choices.[55] In other words, it helps them to make better-informed decisions.

Interestingly, many of the texts taught on such courses are themselves texts in translation. In Lawrence Venuti's anthology *Translation Studies Reader*,[56] for example, which is widely used in translator training programmes in the UK, we see that 13 out of the 32 theoretical texts listed (40%) have been translated into English from a foreign language. This proportion is even larger in Rainer Schulte and John Biguenet's *Theories of Translation*,[57] an anthology of essays containing 61% of translated texts (13 out of 21). A look at the mandatory reading list of any postgraduate translation studies programme in the UK shows that many of the key texts taught as part of the curriculum are translations from foreign languages.

Analysing the nature of the shifts and challenges at play in translating translation theory is important for understanding the impact that translation may have on the dissemination of such texts and the academic response to them. Like any translation activity, translating theory involves interpretation and transformation, and perhaps even implies a degree of conscious or unconscious manipulation. A translated piece of theory will inevitably be different from the original. It will have a different effect on the way readers interact with it and interpret it. Students' interpretation of a theoretical text is also likely to influence their perception of translation and their behaviour as translators when they enter the professional world.

If students interpret Derrida's concept of untranslatability as a deliberate gesture of resistance to translation, for example, they may be inclined subsequently, as literary translators, to retain 'untranslatable' words in the original language, words that have no established equivalent in the target language. If, on the other hand, they apprehend untranslatability as an inevitable dimension of the process of translating itself, they may be less likely to highlight the 'untranslatability' of these words and hence decide to translate them in a more creative or experimental way.

Raising these issues in the context of translator education is crucial in allowing both students and trainers to address the fact that the theory on which their training is based might itself be a translation. As Dilek Dizdar perceptively notes in the *Handbook of Translation Studies*, the 'reflexive turn' in the discipline, which foregrounds 'the untenable nature of a value-free and detached point-of-view', requires that we 'recognise that theory itself is ambivalent and contingent'.[58] The reflexive method developed in this book aspires to encourage students and trainers to adopt a critical attitude towards the texts that they study or teach in translation, and thereby hopes to make a practical contribution to fostering critical thinking in translator education.

Contents and structure

This volume is divided into four chapters, each of which centres on the work of a prominent translation theorist and the specific aspect(s) of reflexivity conjured up by his or her approach.

Chapter 1 deals with Lawrence Venuti's concept of foreignization and its ethical significance in translation. In this chapter I explore the scope and limits of Venuti's foreignizing approach by presenting and discussing a sample translation of the opening pages of *The Translator's Invisibility* into French. I suggest that the ethics of visibility championed by Venuti cannot be secured or sustained, and showcase a reflexive translation practice which, unlike foreignization, productively thematises its own shortcomings.

Chapter 2 centres on Susan Bassnett's essay 'Writing and Translating', and her description of reflexivity in translation as an intimate dialogue between author and translator. In response to Bassnett's dialogic metaphor, I provide an example of a performative translation of her text in the form of a colour-coded open letter addressed back to the author. Building on Bassnett's subjective and personal approach, reflexivity in this chapter is conceived as the responsive enactment of a prior utterance.

Chapter 3 focuses on my comparative experimentation with human and machine translations of an extract from Henri Meschonnic's *Éthique et politique du traduire*. Putting side by side machine translation outputs and human versions of Meschonnic's text, this chapter questions the hierarchy poetics vs. mechanics underlying Meschonnic's claim that reflexivity is inherent to human translation – and ultimately shows that automation is itself traversed by reflexivity and uncertainty.

Chapter 4 explores Antoine Berman's approach to reflexivity in translation through analysis of my back translations of excerpts from selected works by Berman: *The Experience of The Foreign*, 'Translation and the Trials of the Foreign' and *Toward a Translation Criticism*. These translations exemplify the challenges of an ethics of translation based on self-awareness, and tentatively redefine reflexivity as an experience of uncertainty and self-opacity.

Notes

1   Edwin Gentzler, *Contemporary Translation Theories* (Clevedon: Multilingual Matters, 2001), 187.
2   Lawrence Venuti, *The Translator's Invisibility* (London and New York: Routledge, 1995/2008).
3   Venuti, *The Translator's Invisibility*, 1–20.
4   Susan Bassnett, 'Writing and Translating', in *The Translator as Writer*, ed. Susan Bassnett and Peter Bush (London: Continuum, 2006), 173–183.
5   Bassnett, 'Writing and Translating', 179.
6   Henri Meschonnic, *Éthique et politique du traduire* (Paris: Verdier, 2007).
7   Henri Meschonnic, *Ethics and Politics of Translating*, trans. Pier-Pascale Boulanger (Amsterdam and Philadelphia: John Benjamins, 2011), 61.
8   Antoine Berman, *Toward a Translation Criticism*, trans. Françoise Massardier-Kenney (Kent: Kent State University Press, 1995/2009).
9   Antoine Berman, *The Experience of the Foreign*, trans. Stefan Heyvaert (New York: SUNY Press, 1984/1992), 1.
10 Jacques Derrida, 'Des Tours de Babel', trans. Joseph F. Graham, in *Difference in Translation*, ed. Joseph F. Graham (Ithaca: Cornell University Press, 1985), 165–207.
11 Derrida, 'Des Tours de Babel', 175.
12 John Langshaw Austin, *How to Do Things with Words* (Oxford: Clarendon Press, 1962/1975), 139.
13 See James S. Holmes, *Translated! Papers on Literary Translation and Translation Studies* (Amsterdam: Rodopi, 1988), 18.
14 For example: Şebnem Susam-Saraeva, *Theories on the Move* (Amsterdam and New York: Rodopi, 2006).
15 For example: Monique Caminade and Anthony Pym, *Annuaire mondial des formations en traduction et en interprétation* (Paris: Société des Traducteurs Français, 1995), 4.
16 For example: Jeremy Munday, *Introducing Translation Studies* (London: Routledge, 2001), 6.
17 See Akiko Sakamoto, 'Translators Theorising Translation: A Study of Japanese/English Translators' Accounts of Dispute Situations and its Implications for Translation Pedagogy' (PhD diss., University of Leicester, 2014), 40–51.
18 For example: Sara Rovira-Esteva, Pilar Oreroa and Javier Franco Aixelá, 'Bibliometric and Bibliographical Research in Translation Studies', *Perspectives: Studies in Translatology* 23, no. 2 (2015): 159–160.
19 Lawrence Venuti, 'Translating Derrida on Translation: Relevance and Disciplinary Resistance', *Yale Journal of Criticism* 16, no. 2 (2003): 237–262.
20 Françoise Massardier-Kenney, Introduction to *Toward a Translation Criticism*, trans. Françoise Massardier-Kenney (Kent: Kent State University Press, 2009), 1–21.
21 Pier-Pascale Boulanger, 'Traduire Meschonnic en anglais', interview by René Lemieux and Caroline Mangerel, *Trahir*, no. 4 (2013): 1–7.
22 Massardier-Kenney, 'Introduction', xi.
23 Boulanger, 'Traduire Meschonnic en anglais', 6 (my translation).
24 Pier-Pascale Boulanger, Introduction to Henri Meschonnic, *Ethics and Politics of Translating*, trans. Pier-Pascale Boulanger (Amsterdam and Philadelphia: John Benjamins), 30.
25 Joseph F. Graham, ed., *Difference in Translation* (Ithaca: Cornell University Press, 1985), 205.
26 Didier Cahen, 'Derrida and the Question of Education: A New Space for Philosophy', in *Derrida and Education*, ed. Gert J.J. Biesta and Denise Eguéa-Kuhenne (London & New York: Routledge 2001), 13.
27 Dilek Dizdar, 'General Translation Theory', in *Handbook of Translation Studies Volume 3*, ed. Yves Gambier and Luc van Doorslaer (Amsterdam and Philadelphia: John Benjamins, 2012), 58.
28 Jean-Louis Kruger, 'Translating Traces: Deconstruction and the Practice of Translation', *Literator* 25, no. 1 (2004): 48–9.
29 For example: Emily Apter, *Against World Literature: On the Politics of Untranslatability* (New York: Verso, 2013).
30 Jacques Derrida, *Memoires: For Paul de Man*, trans. Cecile Lindsay, Jonathan Culler and Eduardo Cadava (New York: Columbia University Press, 1989), 14–15.
31 Michael Lynch, 'Against Reflexivity as an Academic Virtue and Source of Privileged Knowledge', *Theory, Culture and Society* 17, no. 3 (2000): 26–54.

32 Lynch, 'Against Reflexivity as an Academic Virtue and Source of Privileged Knowledge', 26–34.
33 James S. Holmes, 'The Name and Nature of Translation Studies', in *Translated! Papers on Literary Translation and Translation Studies*, ed. James S. Holmes (Amsterdam: Rodopi, 1972/1988), 67–80.
34 Holmes, 'The Name and Nature of Translation Studies', 71.
35 Anton Popovič, 'Aspects of Metatext', *Canadian Review of Comparative Literature* 3, no. 3 (1976): 23.
36 Peter Newmark, *A Textbook of Translation* (New York: Prentice-Hall International, 1988), 19.
37 Mark Shuttleworth and Moira Cowie, *Dictionary of Translation Studies* (Manchester: St. Jerome, 1997), 185.
38 Maria Tymoczko, 'Translation Theory', in *The Encyclopedia of Applied Linguistics*, ed. Carol A. Chapelle (Oxford: Blackwell Publishing Ltd., 2013), 1.
39 Tymoczko, 'Translation Theory', 1.
40 Jean Boase-Beier, 'Who Needs Theory?', in *Translation: Theory and Practice in Dialogue*, ed. Antoinette Fawcett, Karla L. Guadarrama García and Rebecca Hyde Parker (London: Continuum, 2010), 26.
41 Graham, *Difference in Translation*, 29.
42 Anthony Pym, *Exploring Translation Theories* (London and New York: Routledge, 2010), 1.
43 Pym, *Exploring Translation Theories*, 1.
44 See Dizdar, 'General Translation Theory', 56–58.
45 Holmes, *Translated! Papers on Literary Translation and Translation Studies*, 54.
46 Holmes, 'The Name and Nature of Translation Studies', 79.
47 Theo Hermans, 'Paradoxes and Aporias in Translation and Translation Studies', in *Translation Studies: Perspectives on an Emerging Discipline*, ed. Alessandra Riccardi (Cambridge: Cambridge University Press, 2002), 22.
48 Mona Baker, 'The Pragmatics of Cross-Cultural Contact and Some False Dichotomies in Translation Studies', in *CTIS Occasional Papers*, ed. Maeve Olohan (Manchester: UMIST, 2001), 11–12.
49 Jay Ruby, 'Exposing Yourself: Reflexivity, Anthropology and Film', *Semiotica* 3, no. 1–2 (1980): 154.
50 Andrew Chesterman and Rosemary Arrojo, 'Shared Ground in Translation Studies: Concluding the Debate', *Target* 14, no. 1 (2002): 159.
51 Lawrence Venuti, *The Scandals of Translation: Towards an Ethics of Difference* (London and New York: Routledge, 1998), 30.
52 See Sakamoto, 'Translators Theorising Translation: A Study of Japanese/English Translators' Accounts of Dispute Situations and its Implications for Translation Pedagogy', 37.
53 Mona Baker, *In Other Words: A Coursebook on Translation* (London: Routledge, 1992), 2.
54 Christiane Nord, 'Training Functional Translators', in *Training for the New Millennium: Pedagogies for Translation and Interpreting*, ed. Martha Tennent (Amsterdam: John Benjamins, 2005), 2.
55 Pym, *Exploring Translation Theories*, 4.
56 Lawrence Venuti, ed., *The Translation Studies Reader* (London and New York: Routledge, 2004).
57 Rainer Schulte and John Biguenet, eds., *Theories of Translation: An Anthology of Essays from Dryden to Derrida* (Chicago and London: University of Chicago Press, 1992).
58 Dizdar, 'General Translation Theory', 58.

Chapter 1
Visibility and Ethics

Lawrence Venuti's foreignizing approach

> From the moment the circle turns, that the book is wound back upon itself, that the book repeats itself, its self-identity receives an imperceptible difference which allows us to step effectively, rigorously, and thus discreetly, out of the closure. Redoubling the closure, one splits it. Then one escapes it furtively, between two passages through the same book, through the same line, following the same blend (…). This departure outside of the identical within the same remains very slight, it weighs nothing, it thinks and weighs the book *as such*. The return to the book is also the abandoning of the book.
>
> G.W.F. Hegel[1]

Lawrence Venuti's seminal work, *The Translator's Invisibility*, opens with a quotation by American translator Norman Shapiro, which Venuti indirectly uses to criticise the idea – implied by Shapiro – that a good translation should not draw attention to itself but be transparent like 'a pane of glass'.[2] For Venuti, Shapiro's approach, which is symptomatic of the regime of fluency prevailing in the Anglophone world, is problematic because by concealing the transformative component of translational activity, the transparent translation erases the foreignness of the foreign text and the translator's inscription in the translated text. Coining the concept of foreignization, Venuti advocates instead an approach to translation which seeks to resist fluency and highlights the fact that the text produced in the target culture is a translation.

Venuti's approach relies on two forms of reflexivity: *standpoint reflexivity*, a reflexive critique of dominant discourse (the expectation of fluency in the Anglo-American publishing industry), and *breaking frame*, an exposure of the conjurer's tricks (the domesticating work of self-effacing translators). Foreignization is a pivotal concept in Venuti's theory in that it establishes a direct link between visibility and ethics. A good translator, for Venuti, must strive to make himself visible within the translated text in order to raise awareness that the text created is not an original. The main contribution of the foreignizing approach to translation studies lies precisely in this promise to generate and secure an ethical translation practice.

Foreignization finds its roots in the idea that translation involves a degree of ethnocentric violence which tends to erase the cultural specificity of the source text. By recreating the foreignness of the original work in the target language, a foreignizing translation, Venuti claims, makes visible its condition as a translation and thereby counteracts the violent erasure of cultural difference at the core of any translating process. In this perspective, a foreignizing translation is ethical because, instead of attempting to dissimulate the ethnocentric violence at play in translation, it draws attention to it.[3] In Venuti's theory, indicating the otherness of the foreign text when importing it into the target culture is a necessary precondition for ethical translating.

But does visible translating necessarily produce an ethical translation? What happens, for example, if the indication of a translation's status as translation is itself manipulative, as is the case with pseudo-translations? Can the indication of a text's status as translation ever be secured? And if so, for how long can the reader's awareness be sustained? In the following pages, I give a brief overview of Venuti's foreignizing approach, before presenting a performative translation of the opening pages of *The Translator's Invisibility*. I then explore the scope and limits of foreignization as experienced during my attempt to translate Venuti's own text in a foreignizing way. I contrast Venuti's approach, and the translation strategies he describes as producing foreignizing effects, with a deconstructionist translation practice which 'values experimentation'[4] not so as to indicate the otherness of the foreign text, but in order to interrogate, and go beyond, its internal contradictions.

The concept of *foreignization*

First published in 1995, Lawrence Venuti's *The Translator's Invisibility* provides an account of the history of translation from the seventeenth century to the present day, and shows how fluency prevailed over other translation strategies to shape the canon of foreign literatures in

English. Since its publication, the book has provoked much controversy in translation studies, especially around the concept of foreignization, also referred to as 'foreignizing translation'. Drawing from the theory of German theologian and philosopher Friedrich Schleiermacher, and developed against the predominance of fluent translation strategies in the British and American book industries, foreignization involves, in Venuti's own terms, 'deviating enough from native norms to stage an alien reading experience'.[5] With this concept, Venuti's objective is to challenge domesticating practices that prioritise fluency and transparency, in order ultimately to enrich the translating culture and submit it to self-critical interrogation.

However, Venuti's concept has been accused of doing exactly the opposite. Loredana Polezzi, for example, has suggested that foreignizing translations may create an overly exotic Other which can thus 'contain the text within the boundaries of stereotypical representations of foreign cultures'.[6] Susan Bassnett has pointed out that a foreignizing approach can result in distancing the target language reader unnecessarily from the source language narrator or culture.[7] Jean Boase-Beier has highlighted the inherent contradiction of a practice which, by allowing the foreign text to become visible in the translation, 'causes exactly that invisibility of the translation against which Venuti argues'.[8] Further editions of Venuti's work, which clarify key terms and develop arguments in response to the aforementioned criticisms, were published in 2008 and 2017.

In the introduction to the third edition, Venuti goes to great lengths to address the contentious reception of his book, and to try to clear up any confusion surrounding his work. Unsurprisingly, his primary focus in these pages concerns the concepts of domestication and foreignization, and their ethical significance. While stressing that fluency is not in itself domesticating,[9] Venuti reiterates the need for a foreignizing translating practice that challenges the dominance of fluent translation strategies and calls attention to the fact that the text created in the target culture is not the original. 'Fluent translation,' he explains, 'allows a translation to pass for its source text, inviting readers to remain within the illusionism during and after their reading experience'.[10] The goal of a foreignizing translation is to break that illusion 'by disclosing its translated status as well as the translator's intervention'.[11]

Venuti's own practice as translator is inspired by Philip Lewis' concept of 'abusive fidelity', which is itself of Derridean influence. In 'Translating Derrida on Translation', the text in which he discusses his translation of Derrida's 'What is a "Relevant" Translation', Venuti explains that his ambition in translating Derrida's text was to:

implement what Philip Lewis has called 'abusive fidelity,' a translation practice that 'values experimentation, tampers with usage, seeks to match the polyvalencies and plurivocities or expressive stresses of the original by producing its own.' Abusive fidelity is demanded by foreign texts that involve substantial conceptual density or complex literary effects, namely poetry and philosophy, including Derrida's own writing. This kind of translating is abusive in two senses: it resists the structures and discourses of the receiving language and culture, especially the pressure toward the univocal, the idiomatic, the transparent; yet in so doing it also interrogates the structures and discourses of the foreign text, exposing its often unacknowledged conditions.[12]

In this passage, Venuti draws on Lewis' concept to justify his approach to translating Derrida, which he later goes on to describe as both 'resistant' to fluency (twisting the English language) and yet 'relevant' for an English reader (maintaining a level of intelligibility).

In fact, the concept of foreignization as a whole (the idea that the linguistic and cultural difference of the foreign text should be made visible within the translating language) can be read as an extrapolation of Lewis' notion of abusive fidelity (the notion that translations should not adopt the norms of the target culture but try to follow the source text closely, even if the result sounds strange to most readers). However, there is a noticeable difference between Lewis's and Venuti's approaches. While in Lewis's view irregularities should be pursued only at points of ambiguity or textual density, in Venuti's theory resistance is developed into an ethical safeguard. In other words, whereas for Lewis creating estranging effects should be sought only if it enables new forms of fidelity to the source text, for Venuti a foreignizing approach seems always preferable.

According to Venuti, in a foreignizing translation, the translator intentionally disrupts the linguistic and genre expectations of the target culture in order to introduce a perceptible difference within the target language itself. Discontinuities can be created by utilising marginal and minority forms, which may include close adherence to the source text structure and syntax, calques, archaisms, slang, jargon, dialects or any other linguistic form that disrupts the expectation of fluency in the target culture. These minor variables (minor in the sense of being marginalised and put into a minority position), which Venuti calls 'the remainder' – a term borrowed from Jean-Jacques Lecercle[13] – constitute a foreign element within the target culture which can be used to mark the foreignness of the translated text.

One of the examples Venuti gives is his own translation of works by the nineteenth-century Italian author Iginio Ugo Tarchetti:

> Nel 1855, domiciliatomi a Pavía, m'era alio studio del disegno in nuna scuola privata di quella cittá; e dopo alcuni mesi di soggiorno aveva stretto relazione con certo Federico M. che era professore di patologia e di clinica per l'insegnamento universitario, e che morí di apoplessia fulminante pochi mesi dopo che lo aveva conosciuto. Era un uomo amantissimo delle scienze, della sua in particolare – aveva virtú e doti di mente non comuní – senonché, come tutti gli anatomisti ed i clinici in genere, era scettico profondamente e inguaribilmente – lo era per convinzione, né io potei mai indurlo alie mie credenze per quanto mi vi adoprassi nelle discussioni appassionate e calorose che avevamo ogni giorno a questo riguardo.

> In 1855, having taken up residence at Pavia, I devoted myself to the study of drawing at a private school in that city; and several months into my **sojourn**, I developed a close friendship with a certain Federico M., a professor of pathology and clinical medicine who taught at the university and died of severe apoplexy a few months after I became acquainted with him. He was very fond of the sciences and of his own in particular – he was gifted with extraordinary mental powers – except that, like all anatomists and doctors generally, he was profoundly and incurably skeptical. He was so by conviction, **nor could I ever** induce him to accept my beliefs, no matter how much I endeavored in the impassioned, heated discussions we had every day on this point.[14]

The foreignizing approach adopted by Venuti in the above translation comes through in the inclusion of foreignizing elements, such as close adherence to the source text syntax (e.g. the adjunct positions in the first sentence), calques (e.g. *soggiorno* as *sojourn*) and the use of the archaic structure *nor could I ever* – elements that seek to disrupt the expectations of fluency in the target language and indicate the otherness of the translated text.

However, in discussing specific examples and case studies Venuti does not explain how the translation strategies he describes as producing a foreignizing effect will assuredly raise awareness of the text's status as translation, nor does he define how many foreignizing elements are required to create a foreignizing text, and therefore to secure an ethical translation. Venuti's concept raises intricate questions for practising translators. How much disruption is needed to foment a foreignizing translation? How far can one take foreignization without disengaging the reader? And how foreignizing should a translation be to be deemed ethical? In the next section of this chapter, I engage with these questions in a practical way, as I undertake a performative translation of the opening pages of *The Translator's Invisibility* into French. Following the reflexive method presented in the introduction to this book, I attempt to translate Venuti's text in a foreignizing way in order to explore the scope and confines of his foreignizing approach.

Enacting foreignization: example of a ~~foreignizing~~ translation

The excerpt below is taken from *The Translator's Invisibility*, Lawrence Venuti, © 2008, Routledge, reproduced by permission of Taylor & Francis Books UK.

~~Chapter 1: Invisibility~~
Chapitre 1 : Invisibilité

~~I see translation as the attempt to produce a text so transparent that it does not seem~~
Je vois la traduction comme une tentative de produire un texte tellement transparent qu'il n'aurait
~~to be translated. A good translation is like a pane of glass. You only notice that it's~~
pas l'air d'être traduit. Une bonne traduction ressemble à une vitre. On ne la remarque qu'à de
~~there when there are little imperfections — scratches, bubbles. Ideally, there shouldn't~~
petites imperfections — des éraflures, des bulles d'air. L'idéal serait de n'en pas repérer du tout. La
~~be any. It should never call attention to itself.~~
traduction ne devrait jamais attirer l'attention sur elle-même.

~~Norman Shapiro~~
Norman Shapiro

I The regime of fluency
I Le régime de la fluence

"Invisibility" is the term I will use to describe the translator's situation and
«L'invisibilité» est le terme que j'utilise pour décrire la situation et l'activité du
activity in contemporary British and American cultures. It refers to two mutually
translateur dans les cultures contemporaines britannique et américaine. Il renvoie à
determining phenomena : one is an illusionistic effect of discourse, of the
deux phénomènes au moins qui se définissent réciproquement: le premier est un effet
translator's own manipulation of the translating language, English in this case; the other
d'illusion du discours, de la manipulation du langage traduisant par le translateur, en
is the practice of reading and evaluating translations that has long prevailed in the United
l'occurrence l'anglais; l'autre est une pratique de lecture et d'évaluation des traductions
Kingdom and the United States, among other cultures, both Anglophone and foreign-
qui a longtemps prévalu en Grande-Bretagne et aux Etats-Unis, ainsi que dans d'autres
language. A translated text, whether prose or poetry, fiction or nonfiction, is
cultures, anglophones ou de langues étrangères. Un texte traduit, qu'il s'agisse de prose,
judged acceptable by most publishers, reviewers and readers when it reads
de poésie, de fiction ou d'un récit, est jugé acceptable par la plupart des éditeurs, des
fluently, when the absence of any linguistic or stylistic peculiarities makes it
commentateurs et des lecteurs s'il se lit de manière fluente, si l'absence de toute
seem transparent, giving the appearance that it reflects the foreign writer's
particularité linguistique ou stylistique produit une impression de transparence, d'avoir
personality or intention or the essential meaning of the foreign text — the
reflété la personnalité ou l'intention de l'écrivain étranger, ou le sens fondamental du
appearance, in other words, that the translation is not in fact a translation,
texte étranger–l'impression, en d'autres termes, que la traduction n'est en réalité pas
but the "original."
une traduction, mais le texte « original ».

The illusion of transparency is an effect of a fluent translation strategy, of the translator's
L'illusion de la transparence est l'effet d'une stratégie de traduction fluente, de l'effort
effort to insure easy readability by adhering to current usage, maintaining
du translateur d'assurer une lecture facile en se conformant à l'usage courant, en
continuous syntax, fixing a precise meaning. (...) What is so remarkable here is
maintenant une syntaxe continue, en fixant un sens précis. (...) Ce qu'il y a de remarquable
that this illusory effect conceals the numerous conditions under which the
en cela c'est que l'effet de transparence dissimule les nombreuses conditions dans
translation is made, starting with the translator's crucial intervention. The more
lesquelles la traduction est produite, à commencer par l'intervention décisive du translateur.
fluent the translation, the more invisible the translator, and, presumably, the
Plus la traduction est fluente, plus le translateur est invisible, et, dans cette perspective,
the more visible the writer or meaning of the foreign text.
plus l'auteur et le sens du texte étranger sont visibles.

~~The dominance of fluency in English-language translation becomes apparent in~~
La prédominance de la fluence dans les traductions vers l'anglais est visible dans les critiques de
~~a sampling of reviews from newspapers and periodicals. On those rare occasions~~
journaux et de revues. Aux rares occasions où les critiques abordent la question de la
~~when reviewers address the translation at all, their brief comments usually focus on~~
traduction, leurs commentaires souvent brefs se focalisent habituellement sur le style,
~~its style, neglecting such other possible questions as its accuracy, its intended~~
négligeant d'autres questions éventuelles, comme celles de sa justesse, du public ciblé, de sa
~~audience, its economic value in the current book market, its relation to literary~~
valeur économique dans le marché actuel du livre, de son rapport aux tendances littéraires de
~~trends in English, its place in the translator's career. And over the past sixty years~~
langue anglaise, de sa place dans la carrière du translateur. Et dans les soixante dernières
~~the comments have grown amazingly consistent in praising fluency while damning~~
années, les commentaires se sont étonnamment unifiés à louer la fluence et à condamner les
~~deviations from it, even when the most diverse range of foreign texts is considered.~~
traductions qui en dévient, même face à un assortiment de textes étrangers des plus divers.

~~Take fiction, for instance, the most translated genre worldwide. Limit the choices~~
Prenons le cas de la fiction, le genre le plus traduit dans le monde. Bornons-nous aux écrivains
~~to European and Latin American writers, the most translated into English, and pick examples~~
européens et d'Amérique latine les plus traduits en anglais, et prenons pour exemples des textes
~~with different kinds of narratives—novels and short stories, realistic and fantastic, lyrical~~
appartenant à différents types de récit – romans et nouvelles réalistes, fantastiques, lyriques,
~~and philosophical, psychological and political. Here is one possible list: Albert Camus's~~
philosophiques, psychologiques et politiques. Proposons la liste suivante : *The Stranger* d'Albert
~~*The Stranger* (1946), Françoise Sagan's *Bonjour Tristesse* (1955), Heinrich Böll's *Absent Without*~~
Camus (1946), *Bonjour Tristesse* de Françoise Sagan (1955), *Absent Without Leave* d'Heinrich
~~*Leave* (1965), Italo Calvino's *Cosmicomics* (1968), Gabriel García Márquez's *One Hundred Years of*~~
Böll (1965), *Cosmicomics* d'Italo Calvino (1968), *One Hundred Years of Solitude* de Gabriel García
~~*Solitude* (1970), Milan Kundera's *The Book of Laughter and Forgetting* (1980), Mario Vargas~~
Márquez (1970), *The Book of Laughter and Forgetting* de Milan Kundera (1980), *In Praise of the*
~~Llosa's *In Praise of the Stepmother* (1990), Gianni Celati's *Appearances* (1992), Adolfo~~
Stepmother de Mario Vargas Llosa (1990), *Appearances* de Gianni Celati (1992), *A Russian Doll* d'Adolfo
~~Bioy Casares's *A Russian Doll* (1992), Ana Maria Moix's *Dangerous Virtues* (1997), Michel~~
Bioy Casares (1992), *Dangerous Virtues* d'Ana Maria Moix (1997), *The Elementary Particles*
~~Houellebecq's *The Elementary Particles* (2000), Orhan Pamuk's *My Name is Red* (2001), José~~
de Michel Houellebecq (2000), *My Name is Red* d'Orhan Pamuk (2001), *The Double* de José
~~Saramago's *The Double* (2004), and Ismail Kadare's *The Successor* (2005). Some of these translations~~
Saramago (2004) et *The Successor* d'Ismail Kadare (2005). Certaines de ces traductions anglaises sont
~~enjoyed considerable critical and commercial success in English; others made an initial splash,~~
joui d'un succès critique et commercial considérable; d'autres ont fait sensation au début puis ont
~~then sank into oblivion; still others passed with little or no notice. Yet in the reviews they~~
sombré dans l'oubli; d'autres encore sont passées inaperçues ou presque. Pourtant dans les critiques

~~were all judged by the same criterion: fluency. The following selection of excerpts~~
elles ont toutes été jugées en fonction du même critère : la fluence. La sélection d'extraits ci-dessous,
~~comes from various British and American periodicals, both literary and mass-~~
dont certains sont tirés de textes rédigés par des critiques, romanciers et commentateurs réputés,
~~audience; some were written by noted critics, novelists, and reviewers:~~
provient de diverses revues britanniques et américaines, aussi bien littéraires que grand public :

~~It is not easy, in translating French, to render qualities of sharpness or vividness,~~
Il n'est pas facile de rendre les qualités d'acuité et de vivacité quand on traduit en français,
~~but the prose of Mr. Gilbert is always natural, brilliant, and crisp.~~
mais la prose de M. Gilbert est toujours naturelle, éclatante et piquante.

~~(Wilson 1946:100)~~
(Wilson 1946 : 100)

~~The style is elegant, the prose lovely, and the translation excellent.~~
Le style est élégant, la prose charmante et la traduction excellente.

~~(New Republic 1955:46)~~
(*New Republic* 1955 : 46)

~~In Absent Without Leave, a novella gracefully if not always flawlessly translated by Leila~~
Dans *Loin de la Troupe*, un roman grâcieusement, si ce n'est parfaitement, traduit par
~~Vennewitz, Böll continues his stern and sometimes merciless probing of the~~
Leila Vennewitz, Böll continue son sondage rigoureux et parfois sans merci de la
~~conscience, values, and imperfections of his countrymen.~~
conscience, des valeurs et des imperfections de ses compatriotes.

~~(Potoker 1965:42)~~
(Potoker 1965 : 42)

~~The translation is a pleasantly fluent one: two chapters of it have already appeared in~~
C'est une traduction qui est agréablement fluente : deux de ses chapitres sont déjà
~~Playboy magazine.~~
apparus dans le magazine *Playboy*.

~~(Times Literary Supplement 1969:180)~~
(*Times Literary Supplement* 1969 : 180)

~~Rabassa's translation is a triumph of fluent, gravid momentum, all stylishness and~~
La traduction de Rabassa triomphe par son élan fluent et gravide, plein d'élégance et
~~commonsensical virtuosity.~~
virtuose de bon sens.

~~(West 1970:4)~~
(West 1970 : 4)

~~His first four books published in English did not speak with the stunning lyrical precision~~
Ses quatre premiers livres publiés en anglais n'avaient pas l'impressionnante précision
~~of this one (the invisible translator is Michael Henry Heim).~~
lyrique de celui-ci (le traducteur invisible est Michael Henry Heim).

~~(Michener 1980:108)~~
(Michener 1980 : 108)

Foreignization in practice

Performing foreignization

Choosing to perform foreignization – instead of simply commenting on it – serves several purposes. Exploring the possible effects of foreignization by attempting to produce a foreignizing translation is a uniquely hands-on approach, one which allows me to examine the intricacies of Venuti's theory within the tangible constraints and challenges of an actual translation. Furthermore, attempting to create a foreignizing translation in order to think about foreignization facilitates a form of critical engagement with the text which is productive rather than dismissive. In these pages, interrogating the scope and confines of foreignization through translation is testament both to the far-reaching influence of Venuti's theory in translation studies and to its unexplored potential beyond the realm of literary translation – including in wider disciplinary contexts, such as the one wherein my own approach is anchored.

My performative translation of the opening pages of *The Translator's Invisibility* centres primarily on the concept of foreignization, a pivotal notion in Venuti's overall translation theory, and the basis for the ethical translation practice he promotes. This focus on foreignization is inevitably selective, and reflects in part Venuti's own view that both translation and translation criticism are necessarily interpretive in nature.[15] However, the primacy given to the concept of foreignization in my interpretation of Venuti's work is not exclusive. It is conceived in articulation with other key elements in his theory (including the notions of visibility, fluency and heterogeneity), as well as in relation to the main translation strategies he describes as capable of producing a foreignizing effect.

In an attempt to disturb the French reader and to create a foreignizing effect, in my translation of Venuti's text I have chosen to translate the term 'translator' using the archaic French word *translateur*, instead of the modern French term *traducteur*. Phonetically closer to the English term 'translator', the word *translateur* is itself interesting because it carries negative connotations of transparency that echo the very invisibility of the translator that Venuti takes issue with in his book. According to French dictionary *Le Littré*,[16] uses of the Old French word *translateur* between the sixteenth century and eighteenth century show that, as the word was gradually replaced by the modern French term *traducteur*, it was sometimes employed to refer to someone who translates too faithfully, someone who imitates the original text too slavishly. Two instances of this negative connotation can be found in the literature.

The first example appears in Joachim Du Bellay's *Défense et illustration de la langue française*, where the French poet contrasts the paraphrasing activity of the *translateur* with the imitating role of the *traducteur*:

> Encores seroy' je bien d'opinion que le scavant translateur fist plus tost l'office de paraphraste, que de traducteur.[17]

> It is my opinion that the learned **translateur** works more as a paraphraser, than as a **traducteur**. [18]

It is important to note that, in this context, imitation is perceived as a creative form of translation (one which, by imitating the style of the original text, contributes to expanding the target language), whereas paraphrasing refers to a practice which simply restores the meaning of the source text, its content.

The second example can be found in Jean-François Marmontel's *Œuvres complètes*, where Marmontel opposes the translational activities of the *traducteur* and the *translateur* in the following terms:

> S'il s'éloigne trop de l'original, il ne traduit plus, il imite ; s'il le copie trop servilement, il fait une version et n'est que translateur.[19]

> If he [the **traducteur**] distances himself too much from the original, he does no longer translate, he imitates; if he copies too slavishly, he only provides a version and is a mere **translateur**.[20]

The word's negative connotation as it appears in these two examples – *translateur* as someone who copies too slavishly, but does not challenge the boundaries of the target language – echoes Venuti's criticism of the translator's invisibility in modern English-language cultures, and thereby epitomises the main argument developed by Venuti in his book: the fact that translators should be more visible.

Selecting an unusual, archaic word like *translateur* (archaisms being one of Venuti's most discussed foreignizing techniques) to translate such an important concept in Venuti's theory allows me to perform a translation of Venuti's text in the strong sense, in that it enables me to both say and do what the source text says. Using the archaic term *translateur* instead of the modern French word *traducteur* makes the invisible translator (*translateur* vs. *traducteur*) literally visible (stand out) in my translation, and as such, it allows me to translate Venuti's theory performatively, by enacting it. Through such enaction, however, my performative translation also highlights the limits of the foreignizing approach, as I shall explain later in this chapter.

Degrees of foreignization

The purpose of foreignization, according to Venuti, is to point to the foreignness of the source text, so that it is immediately visible to target readers that they are reading a translation. 'Discontinuities at the level of syntax, diction, or discourse', he explains, 'allow the translation to be read as a translation [...] showing where it departs from target language cultural values, by showing where it depends on them.'[21] My translation of Venuti's text raises the question of whether the use of the word *translateur* can in itself increase awareness of the text's status as a translation – since the word *translateur* could, for example, be a concept that a French theorist or poet (like Du Bellay or Marmontel) has created in a French cultural context in order to refer to a specific type of translator: one who translates too faithfully or too slavishly. How can I make sure that the use of an archaic term like *translateur* will draw attention to the text's status as translation, and be perceived as such by a French readership?

In the second edition of *The Translator's Invisibility*, Venuti clarifies his foreignizing approach, emphasising the need to include minority forms within the target language itself. In his later book *The Scandals of Translation*, Venuti continues to insist on the concept of foreignizing translation (or minoritising translation, as he also calls it), but further focuses on its ability to cultivate a varied and 'heterogeneous discourse'.[22] According to Venuti, foreignization can only be achieved by contrast with, and differentiation from, the nature and register of other words in the text. Venuti shows, for example, how his own translations seek to create a foreignizing effect by juxtaposing archaisms such as 'scapegrace' and modern colloquialisms such as 'con artist' and 'funk', or by using British spellings in an American text, to jar the reader with a heterogeneous discourse. Foreignization, Venuti argues with these examples, must occur through differentiation within the target language itself.

In trying to perform, and enact, this particular aspect of Venuti's concept, in my translation of Venuti's text I have translated the word 'translator' not only as *translateur* but also as *traducteur*, depending on the context in which the word is used. For example, when the term 'translator' appears as part of a quotation from Michener, I chose to translate it as *traducteur* instead of *translateur*, so as to contrast Michener's rather conventional use of the term with Venuti's criticism of the translator's invisibility. Contrary to Venuti, in Michener's quotation the term 'invisible' has a positive quality, and works to build an argument in favour of fluency and transparency:

> His first four books published in English did not speak with the stunning lyrical precision of this one (the invisible translator is Michael Henry Heim).

> Ses quatre premiers livres publiés en anglais n'avaient pas l'impressionnante précision lyrique de celui-ci (le **traducteur** invisible est Michael Henry Heim).[23]

By using form (the combined use of the words *translateur* and *traducteur*) to reflect the content of Venuti's argument in favour of a heterogeneous discourse, my performative translation of Venuti's text raises several questions.

If, as argued by Venuti, alternation of foreignizing and fluent strategies is necessary to create an overall foreignizing effect, then how much foreignization and how much fluency are needed? Is the juxtaposition of the terms *translateur* and *traducteur* sufficient to create a foreignizing effect? And to what extent can I be certain that even the most heterogeneous use of language will highlight the text's status as translation? Although he explicitly argues in favour of foreignization against fluency, Venuti does not recommend a specific degree of foreignization. This is something that the translator needs to negotiate and define according to the specific demands of her project: how far can one take foreignization; up to what point is it acceptable, and how foreignizing can a translation be? Each of the translator's choices works as an element of response to these questions, which ultimately build into an overall reply in the form of the translated text itself.

My own experimental translation of Venuti's text indicates that reflexivity – that is, awareness of the text's status as translation – is not possible without making visible the act of translating itself. Even a mixed use of archaic and modern words like *translateur* and *traducteur* does not suffice to ensure that a French audience will know that my text is a translation, for these words could very well be variations on the concept of 'translator' created in French by a French-speaking theorist: *translateur* to refer to a foreignizing translator vs. *traducteur* to designate a fluent translator, as in the two aforementioned examples from Du Bellay and Marmontel.

Venuti makes clear that foreignization is a decision that takes place within the target language. For him, a 'foreignizing translation signifies the differences of the foreign text, yet only by disrupting the codes that prevail in the translating language'.[24] However, assuming that linguistic heterogeneity will in itself create reflexivity does not take into account the fact that an utterance can be heterogeneous, regardless of whether it is a translation or not. This oversight is particularly striking in the context of Venuti's work, since he frames his overall approach within a deconstructionist view of language:

> Translation is a process by which the chain of signifiers that constitute the foreign text is replaced by a chain of signifiers in the translating language which the translator provides on the strength of an interpretation. Because meaning is an effect of relations and differences among signifiers along a potentially endless chain (polysemous, intertextual, subject to infinite linkages), it is always differential and deferred, never present as an original unity.[25]

But if we consider, following Derrida and his concept of *différance*[26], that all language (not just translation) is differential, then it is impossible to make the status of a translation visible based simply on difference. If within any given language words are always differing (are different from one another) and deferring (their ultimate meaning being always postponed), no foreignizing effect, even the most estranging or defamiliarising one, can suffice to signal a text's status as translation. With the concept of foreignization, Venuti shows that his whole approach to translation depends on the fantasy of a secure border between source and target texts.

Perhaps one of the best-known examples used by Venuti to illustrate a successful foreignizing effect is Matthew Ward's translation of Albert Camus' novel *The Stranger*, and more specifically its opening line, 'Maman died today', which retains Camus's use of the French word *maman*. According to Venuti, the context makes clear to the English reader that *maman* means 'mother' in Ward's version. But it means much more besides to English readers, Venuti claims, because it not only signals the childlike intimacy of the narrator's relationship, but also tells readers that they are reading a translation, a version of the French work not to be confused with the original text. However, like the alternation of the words *traducteur* and *translateur* in my translation, the use of word *maman* cannot in itself signify the foreignness of the original and raise readers' awareness of the status of the translated text as translation, because the context does not exclude the possibility that the word might in fact refer to the mother of a French character in an English-language novel.

To draw attention to the text's status as translation, the translator would have to either add a footnote explaining the strategy adopted, or merely rely on the readers' use of paratextual elements (such as the author's name, reference to the translator on the title page, etc.). In both cases, however, the very principle of foreignization (the idea of making the foreignness of the original visible *within the translated text itself*) would be negated, and there would still be no guarantee that awareness of the text's status as translation would be sustained during the reading process. In the third edition of *The Translator's Invisibility*, Venuti vehemently insists on the fact that, in his theory, the term 'foreignizing' does not describe specific translation choices or strategies, but rather the ethical effect of translated texts, which – he reiterates – is 'to alter the way in which a translation is customarily read by disclosing its translated status'.[27] Venuti's focus on the effects of foreignization, as opposed to the techniques devised to achieve them, highlights a crucial element of his argument: the fact that the effectiveness of foreignization depends essentially on readers' perception of the translated text – a perception that the translator can hardly control or secure.

In fact, Ward's translation of *The Stranger*'s opening line is characteristic of a wider linguistic issue, which is formulated by Derrida in the following terms: 'How is a text written in several languages at one time to be translated?' Taking the example of the sentence 'And he war' in James Joyce's *Finnegans Wake*, Derrida wonders how *war*, which may refer either to the English *war* for battle or to the German *war* for *was*, could be translated into another language. Derrida's example is interesting in relation to foreignization because it further emphasises that language can be heterogeneous, estranging and defamiliarising regardless of whether it is a translation or an original. The effect of Joyce's play on the plurilingual homophony of the word 'war' could indeed be described as estranging, or even foreignizing, despite the fact that it is not a translation. More generally, how can we convey the foreignness of a plurilingual text, concept or word when translating it into a different language? What does foreignness mean in a plurilingual context? And how can heterogeneous uses of language in translation (such as borrowings, slang or foreign words) be differentiated from heterogeneous uses of language in other forms of writing (including plays on words, plurilingual expressions or ambiguous words)?

In his conference presentation entitled 'What is a "Relevant" Translation?', Derrida addresses these questions in relation to the word *relevante*, both a French and English term, an adjective borrowed from the English, which is not yet used in French, but which, nevertheless, is marked by the meanings of the French verb 'relever,' as well as those of the French noun 'relève'.[28] Immediately placing his presentation 'within the multiplicity of languages',[29] Derrida thus exemplifies his (now famous) saying that if we 'only ever speak one language', it is 'never (...) only one language',[30] highlighting that what unites historic languages is the heterogeneity of language itself. In Derrida's presentation, the plurilingualism of the word *relevante* challenges the notion of natural, transparent language, and serves to illustrate the long and complex cultural history of any given language. If any use of language may be heterogeneous, regardless of whether it is a translation or not, then a foreignizing translation, one that aims to make its own status as translation visible, must, in order to differentiate itself from the heterogeneity that characterises other forms of language, do more than create a heterogeneous discourse.

Beyond foreignization

Venuti is aware of the contradictions underlying the concept of foreignization, and in particular the fact that, since it cannot strictly operate within the translating language itself, a foreignizing translation also involves domestication: 'foreignizing translation still requires the translator to draw on the resources of the translating language and culture and is therefore implicated in the ethnocentrism that lies at the very heart of translation'.[31] Nevertheless, despite his acknowledgement that foreignization can never fully escape domestication, since ethnocentric violence is 'inherent in *every* translation process',[32] Venuti still argues in favour of foreignizing translations, because even though they are just as 'partial in their interpretation of the foreign text' as are domesticating translations, they 'tend to flaunt their partiality instead of concealing it'.[33]

The main ethical effect of a foreignizing translation, according to Venuti, is its capacity to point to itself, and thereby to make visible the ethnocentrism at play in translation – the fact that translation cannot offer unmediated access to the foreign. However, if, as I have argued, the techniques presented by Venuti as having a foreignizing effect (archaisms, calques, slang, etc.) cannot in themselves make visible a text's status as translation, then no translation, however foreignizing or defamiliarising it might be, can highlight the ethnocentrism at play in translation processes without also pointing to the ethnocentric violence underlying its own creation. Whereas for Venuti foreignization must be conveyed within the translating language itself, my experimentation with foreignization shows that reflexivity – that is, awareness of the text's condition as translation – is possible only if we make visible the act of translating itself, by showing the original text that is being translated.

To be reflexive and point to the act of translating, my performative translation of Venuti's text makes the difference of the foreign text literally visible by displaying the foreign text as crossed out and replaced by the translated text:

> ~~'Invisibility' is the term I will use to describe the translator's situation~~
> « L'invisibilité » est le terme que j'utilise pour décrire la situation et
> ~~and activity in contemporary British and American cultures.~~
> l'activité du translateur dans les cultures contemporaines britannique
> et américaine.

My interlinear translation thus performs Venuti's concept of foreignizing translation, but does so by transgressing it, in the etymological sense of going beyond it, crossing it. It performs Venuti's concept insofar as it highlights the ethnocentric violence at play in translation by striking off the original and thereby marking its absence. But it also transgresses the concept in that it makes visible the difference of the foreign text, not through a play of differences within the translating language itself (an impossible ambition, as I have argued), but by pointing to the translation's relation to the original:

> ~~Original~~
> *Translating*
> Translation

In my translation, the original is still there, visible, but only to the extent that it has been crossed out, deleted – thereby suggesting that in translation the foreign text can only be made visible as absence.

In the context of this translation, the concept of foreignization can only be performed in accordance with a notion of the performative that, in Derrida's words, 'must be dissociated, by an act of deconstruction, from the notion of presence with which it is generally linked'.[34] My experiment in foreignization shows that a performative translation of Venuti's text is inevitably transgressive, since to achieve foreignization (increase awareness of the text's status as translation) one must go beyond foreignization (point to the act of translating itself). While for Venuti, a foreignizing practice should aim to release 'the remainder by cultivating a heterogeneous discourse, opening up the standard dialect and literary canons to what is foreign to themselves, to the substandard and marginal',[35] my own experience of foreignization suggests that the 'otherness' of the foreign text cannot be made visible without simultaneously releasing the violent act of erasure and substitution that the translating process operates.

A 'relevant' translation of Venuti's text, such as the one I have proposed in this chapter, enacts the concept of foreignization by simultaneously challenging it, by pushing it beyond its limits. Relevant, here, is to be understood in the Derridean sense, as operating a conserving-and-negating lift, an effect of substitution and difference – an operation inscribed in the double meaning of Hegel's concept of *Aufhebung*, a German word 'that signifies at once to suppress and to elevate', and which Derrida translates as 'la relève'.[36] My sample translation enacts the idea that a relevant translation (in this case, raising to conscious levels a translation's status as translation) both suppresses and extends the original. It suggests that in order to thoroughly enact and perform a theoretical text into another language or form, the translator must also call it into question and challenge it. Central to my ~~foreignizing~~ translation is the idea that a performative practice of translation also includes a critical element.

Venuti's own translation of Derrida's essay 'What is a "Relevant" Translation?' comes across as rather conventional and fluent. In this translation, Venuti does not seem to employ many of the devices he mentions in *The Translator's Visibility* as producing a foreignizing effect. Looking at the first few lines, for example, one may be surprised by the transparency of his version:

> How dare one speak of translation before you who, in your vigilant awareness of the immense stakes – and not only of the fate of literature – make this sublime and impossible task your desire, your anxiety, your travail, your knowledge, and your knowing skill?

> How dare I proceed before you, knowing myself to be at once rude and inexperienced in this domain, as someone who, from the very first moment, from his very first attempts (which I could recount to you, as the English saying goes, off the record), shunned the translator's metier, his beautiful and terrifying responsibility, his insolvent duty and debt, without ceasing to tell himself 'never ever

again': 'no, precisely, I would never dare, I should never, could never, would never manage to pull it off'?[37]

Except perhaps for the use of Middle English terms such as 'travail' and 'metier', Venuti's translation sounds rather natural and hardly draws attention to its own status as translation.

Interestingly, the most reflexive element in this passage (the one that most clearly points to the text's status as translation) is not one constructed by Venuti, but Derrida's parenthetical intervention: '(which I could recount to you, as the English saying goes, off the record)'. Underlining the linguistic and cultural specificity of the expression 'off the record', Derrida's comment indirectly points to the fact that the text is written in another language than English. Given that it appears in an English context here, this indication suggests that the English version we are reading is unlikely to be a text originally written in English. The reflexive effect in this case is not the result of a foreignizing technique, but is inscribed in the phrasing of the original text itself, and made visible through the process of translating and its recontextualising work.

In this example, reflexivity is made possible not by reconstructing the otherness of the foreign text and attempting to make it present through differentiation, but through a recontextualising of the text's plurilingualism, which makes it visible only by showing its effacement and hinting at its absence. When translated into English, the plurilingual character of the expression 'which I could recount to you, as the English saying goes, off the record' is erased, and therefore becomes graphically invisible; however, it is this very effacement which signals the text's potential status as translation, by underlining the fact that in an English context mentioning the cultural specificity of the expression 'off the record' is irrelevant – unless the text was not originally written in English. Derrida's example is a further illustration that a text's potential to highlight its own status as translation also depends on making visible the work of recontextualisation that translation activates, as effacement of the original and re-enactment of it in a different context.

Conclusion: from foreignization to ~~foreignization~~

The reflexive approach engaged in translating Lawrence Venuti's translation theory uncovers crucial aspects of reflexivity in translation. Showing that a reflexive practice of translation based on visibility cannot be secured nor sustained, this experimentation in foreignization suggests that to perform foreignization one may need to exceed foreignization itself. In my sample translation, enacting another text by simultaneously saying and doing what the text says requires going beyond it, crossing its limits. It means stretching the boundaries of Venuti's concept, but only to realise its own potential as an approach that seeks to point to the ethnocentric violence at play in all translational activity. In this sense, my ~~foreignizing~~ translation is at once abusive and faithful, transgressive and performative, enacting Venuti's concept while in the same moment emphasising its limits. Like Philip Lewis's notion of 'abusive fidelity', this performative experiment in foreignization occasions a redefinition of fidelity in translation which accounts for the fact that, while displacement may itself manifest faithfulness, it inevitably exceeds the translator's will or control.

From a critical perspective, the reflexive practice deployed in this chapter shows that ironically folding a text's theory back on itself is an impossible task, one that cannot be accomplished without also transforming the concepts translated, without also introducing a difference. Hence, in this framework, folding a theory back on itself does not mean repeating the source text's theory by reproducing it identically, but going beyond it by embracing its internal contradictions. My engagement with reflexivity in this chapter showcases a performative practice whereby translation is not understood as 'the transport of a semantic content into another signifying form',[38] but as the re-enactment of a text in a different context. In this approach, meaning itself is a performative and contextual event, which cannot be extracted from, or exist outside, the specific context of its creation. In Derridean terms, '[it] must await being said or written in order to inhabit itself, and in order to become, by differing from itself, what it is: meaning'.[39] Performing a translation of a theoretical text thus becomes a form of critical interrogation whereby attempting to enact a text (like *The Translator's Invisibility* and its key notion of foreignization) contributes to creating a new concept: ~~foreignization~~.

In such practice, translating reflexively is a form of writing 'under erasure' (*sous rature*), an approach first developed by Martin Heidegger and later expanded by Derrida to indicate a word's inaccuracy or difference by crossing it out. In fact, writing 'under erasure' is a typographical expression of the fact that key terms and concepts in a text may be paradoxical or self-undermining. In my ~~foreignizing~~ translation, this difference (the concept's non-identity to itself) is the locus of a theoretical stance through which I – as a translator – create and express my own approach to foreignization. My contribution as a translator is precisely this 'abuse' (or difference), 'whereby the translation goes beyond – fills in for – the original'.[40] In addition, since writing is always a structure of signs under erasure, 'always already inhabited by the trace of another sign which never appears as such',[41] the technique of '*sous rature*' is used in my translation to signify that all meaning derives from difference, including (but not only) in translation. In fact, my ~~foreignizing~~ translation signals that, just like foreignizing translation, translating under erasure cannot secure reflexivity, visibility or awareness of a text's status as translation, since all writing (not just translation) takes place under erasure. As such, my experimental translation of Venuti's text presents a practice which, unlike foreignization, accounts for the productive failure of its own reflexive endeavour.

In the third edition of *The Translator's Invisibility*, Venuti appears to soften his approach, reorienting foreignization towards a more open, slightly less prescriptive practice. Not only does he acknowledge that the ethical effects of a foreignizing translation depend primarily on their recognition by the readers of the receiving culture, but the linguistic and cultural differences perceptible in a foreignizing translation are now described in ways that seek to avoid the idea of untroubled transfer.[42] In fact, Venuti suggests that, to be effective, a foreignizing translation requires that readers themselves make an effort and be trained to perceive the linguistic and cultural differences inscribed in the translated text.[43] For Venuti, foreignizing translation requires a level of comparative analysis which, as he recognises himself, excludes de facto readers who do not speak the source language or whose interest in the translated text may be limited to readerly pleasure. Ironically, since they may depend on a certain level of scholarly analysis to be recognised at all, the effects of foreignization are targeted at readers who are most likely already to be sensitive to, or willing to engage with, the ethical issues at stake in translation. The ethical impact of foreignization, too, is presented in more tentative terms, as the following extract from the third edition illustrates:

> What allows a foreignizing translation, furthermore, to limit and redirect its inevitable domestication is not its orientation toward or adherence to the source text, but rather the translator's command and application of certain linguistic and cultural resources in the receiving situation. It is the effects of those resources that potentially exceed mere domestication and become differential.[44]

Here, the use of the word 'potentially' is decisive, in that it hints at foreignization's incapacity to secure an ethical translation. If translation techniques are not in themselves foreignizing, and if a foreignizing translation cannot guarantee to draw attention to its own condition, then to what extent is it ethical?

Venuti still argues in favour of foreignization, insisting that the mere choice of source text can suffice to create a foreignizing effect. But in most instances the choice of text too is neither *only* foreignizing nor *only* domesticating. My own sample translation of *The Translator's Invisibility* into French, for instance, may be deemed simultaneously foreignizing and domesticating. Venuti's criticism of the dominant regime of fluency in the Anglophone world was undeniably a marginal argument when his book first came out in 1995. However, when transferred to a French context, Venuti's position as a minor voice becomes more uncertain. On the one hand, translating Venuti into French means promoting a marginal American voice, which also has the potential to confront implicit expectations of fluency in the French book industry. On the other hand, the concepts of domestication and foreignization are hardly marginal in the context of French translation theory, where they echo the ideas of at least two prominent French thinkers: Jean-René Ladmiral[45] and Antoine Berman.[46] In fact, Venuti's position on the international academic scene is rather ambiguous. His voice remains to a certain extent marginal, as it is still widely criticised by translators and scholars across the world. At the same time, *The Translator's Invisibility* has become a canonical text in translation studies, where it is extensively referred to and used as teaching material in translation programmes worldwide.

The intricacies of determining whether a translation is foreignizing or domesticating, as highlighted throughout this chapter, illustrate the difficulty of approaching translation through these two concepts without risking oversimplifying the challenges at play in translational activity, or reproducing the binary oppositions ('literal' vs. 'free' translation) that Venuti's approach claims to combat. Venuti expressly condemns interpretations of his work that treat the distinction between domesticating and foreignizing translation as a simple 'dichotomy' or 'binary opposition', suggesting that such readings eliminate its conceptual complexity.[47] Yet he seems oblivious to the fact that his very choice of terms, and the dualistic way they are presented in his work, may themselves have contributed to the interpretations he denounces. The most compelling element in the introduction to the latest edition of *The Translator's Invisibility* is perhaps Venuti's explicit call for innovative translation strategies, as well as for critical, partial and open engagements with his text. This chapter's response to Venuti's call has sought to provide a detailed illustration of what such critical engagement may involve in practical terms, as well as an example of an alternative reflexive translation practice which constructively thematises its own failures and limitations.

Notes

1 Georg Wilhelm Friedrich Hegel quoted in Gayatri Chakravorty Spivak, 'Preface', in Jacques Derrida, *Of Grammatology*, trans. Gayatri Chakravorty Spivak (Baltimore: Johns Hopkins University Press, 1976/1997), vii.
2 Lawrence Venuti, *The Translator's Invisibility: A History of Translation* (London & New York: Routledge, 2008), 1.
3 Venuti, *The Translator's Invisibility* (2008), 16.
4 Philip Lewis, 'The Measure of Translation Effects', in *Difference in Translation*, ed. Joseph F. Graham (Ithaca: Cornell University Press, 1985), 41.
5 Venuti, *The Translator's Invisibility* (2008), 15–16.
6 Loredana Polezzi, *Translating Travel: Contemporary Italian Travel Writing in English Translation* (Aldershot: Ashgate, 2001), 70.
7 Susan Bassnett, 'Bringing the News Back Home: Strategies of Acculturation and Foreignization', *Language and Intercultural Communication* 5, no. 2 (2005): 127.
8 Jean Boase-Beier, 'Who Needs Theory?', in *Translation: Theory and Practice in Dialogue*, ed. Antoinette Fawcett, Karla L. Guadarrama García and Rebecca Hyde Parker (London: Continuum, 2010), 30.
9 Lawrence Venuti, *The Translator's Invisibility: A History of Translation* (London & New York: Routledge, 2017), xv.
10 Venuti, *The Translator's Invisibility* (2017), xvii.
11 Venuti, *The Translator's Invisibility* (2017), xv.
12 Lawrence Venuti, 'Translating Derrida on Translation: Relevance and Disciplinary Resistance', *Yale Journal of Criticism* 16, no. 2 (2003): 252.
13 Jean-Jacques Lecercle, *The Violence of Language* (London & New York: Routledge, 1990).
14 Lawrence Venuti, *The Scandals of Translation: Towards an Ethics of Difference* (London & New York: Routledge, 1998), 15 (my emphases).
15 Venuti, *The Translator's Invisibility* (2017), x.
16 Émile Littré, *Dictionnaire de la langue française* (Paris: Hachette, 1863–1877).
17 Joachim Du Bellay, *Défense et illustration de la langue française* (Tours: Centre d'Études Supérieures de la Renaissance, 1549/2009), 20.
18 Du Bellay, *Défense et illustration de la langue française*, 20 (my translation and emphases).
19 Jean-François Marmontel, *Œuvres complètes* (Paris: Belin, 1787/1819), 193–194.
20 Marmontel *Œuvres complètes*, 193–194 (my translation and emphases).
21 Lawrence Venuti, 'Translation as Cultural Politics: Regimes of Domestication in English', in *Critical Readings in Translation Studies*, ed. Mona Baker (London & New York: Routledge, 2010), 75.
22 Venuti, *The Scandals of Translation*, 11.
23 Charles Michener quoted in Venuti, *The Translator's Invisibility*, 3 (my translation and emphases).
24 Venuti, *The Translator's Invisibility* (2008), 15.
25 Venuti, *The Translator's Invisibility* (2008), 13.
26 Playing on the polysemy of the French word *différer*, meaning both 'to differ' and 'to defer', Derrida coined the word *différance* to refer to the never-ending deferral and divergence at work in the chain of signification – the fact that signs of language can only function with reference to other signs which are absent as well as different (see Derrida, `Difference', in *Speech and Phenomena*, trans. David B. Allison (Evanston: Northwestern University Press, 1968/1973), 278–301).
27 Venuti, *The Translator's Invisibility* (2017), xv.
28 Jacques Derrida, 'What Is a "Relevant" Translation?', trans. Lawrence Venuti, *Critical Inquiry* 27, no. 2 (1998/2001): 175.
29 Derrida, 'What Is a "Relevant" Translation?', 176.
30 Jacques Derrida, *Monolingualism of the Other; or, The Prosthesis of Origin*, trans. Patrick Mensah (Stanford: Stanford University Press, 1996/1998), 27.
31 Venuti, *The Translator's Invisibility* (2008), 19.
32 Venuti, *The Translator's Invisibility* (2008), 17.
33 Venuti, *The Translator's Invisibility* (2008), 28–29.

34   Jacques Derrida, 'Living On/Borderlines', in *Deconstruction and Criticism*, trans. James Hulbert (New York: Continuum, 1979), 90.

35   Venuti, *The Scandals of Translation*, 11.

36   Derrida, 'What Is a "Relevant" Translation?', 196.

37   Derrida, 'What Is a "Relevant" Translation?', 174.

38   Jacques Derrida, *The Ear of the Other: Otobiography, Transference, Translation*, trans. Avital Ronell and Peggy Kamuf (New York: Schocken, 1982/1985), 120.

39   Jacques Derrida, *Writing and Difference*, trans. Alan Bass (Chicago: University of Chicago Press, 1967/1978), 11.

40   Lewis, 'The Measure of Translation Effects', 42.

41   Spivak, 'Preface,' xxxix.

42   Venuti, *The Translator's Invisibility* (2017), xiii.

43   Venuti, *The Translator's Invisibility* (2017), xvi–xvii.

44   Venuti, *The Translator's Invisibility* (2017), xiii.

45   Jean-René Ladmiral, *Sourcier ou cibliste* (Paris: Belles Lettres, 2014).

46   Antoine Berman, *L'épreuve de l'étranger* (Paris: Gallimard, 1984).

47   Venuti, *The Translator's Invisibility* (2017), xiii.

Chapter 2
Subjectivity and Creativity
Susan Bassnett's dialogic metaphor

I, as a responsible reader, am not (…) seeking to reveal an unchanging core of meaning, the text's 'secret' in the conventional sense of unrecoverable interior, but rather attempting to perform, here and now, an affirmation of its singularity and alterity – a different kind of secret that cannot simply be revealed. If this performative response is to do justice to the singularity of the text (…) it must itself be singular and inventive – not merely an act of obedience to a law.

Derek Attridge[1]

This chapter centres on Susan Bassnett's essay 'Writing and Translating'.[2] Published in a collection of articles exploring the interpretative role of the translator, Bassnett's intensely personal and subjective text describes her practice as a writer and translator. For her, translating and writing literary texts are intertwining experiences: translating is a reflexive activity through which the writing subject becomes aware of her own possibilities and voice as a writer. In her essay, reflexivity is not perceived as the result or effect of a given translation strategy or choice of text, but as a dialogic process through which the author and the translator interact.[3] In fact, Bassnett is not interested in reflexive writing strategies or in forms of translating which draw attention to themselves. Rather, by comparing translation to a dialogue, she seeks to highlight the correlation between writing and translating, in an effort to assert the creative power of translation.

Bassnett's text deals with reflexivity on three levels. Firstly, reflexivity is conceived as self-discovery and self-perception. Speaking about translating Alejandra Pizarnik, for example, she explains: 'I felt I was somehow engaged in a kind of dialogue with her, that by translating I could understand my own thoughts better.'[4] Translation in this context occasions a reflexive operation of self-exploration. Secondly, Bassnett describes translating as a singularly 'playful' activity through which one 'consciously and deliberately' engages with a text: an activity which 'can act as a regenerative force'.[5] Here, reflexivity lies in the conscious interaction with, and distance from, the source text, in the translator's capacity to create something different: a 'counter-poem'.[6] Thirdly, with its introspective tone and autobiographical quality, the essay is itself the locus of a self-reflexive process whereby the author looks back on her own approach to translating and writing in an attempt to better understand what constitutes the translating self.

Bassnett's overall approach to translation as a subjective engagement with the source text relies on hermeneutic reflexivity, a style of interpretation based on the translator's creative reading of the text to be translated. In this chapter I draw on Bassnett's essay to explore the idea of a dialogic interaction between author and translator shaped by her theory, and engage in a performative translation of her text into French, so as to interrogate the significance of her metaphor in the context of my own reflexive practice of translation. If translating is a reflexive form of writing that requires an active engagement with the source text, as Bassnett suggests, to what extent is it dialogic? What aspects of the relationship between author and translator are brought to light by the use of the 'dialogue' metaphor? What does a dialogic translation involve in practical terms? And to what extent is it reflexive?

In this chapter I give a brief overview of Bassnett's approach in 'Writing and Translating' and examine her essay in the context of a growing concern with subjectivity and creativity in translation studies. I then present a performative translation of her text in the form of an open letter addressed back to the author. My letter builds on Bassnett's description of reflexivity as a dialogic relation between author and translator to present performativity in translation as a responsive enactment of a prior utterance. In the following section I discuss the ways in which my translation of Bassnett's essay both enacts and questions her dialogic metaphor, and then reflect on my own theorisation of reflexivity in translation as a responsive and responsible enactment of a prior utterance. I argue that translation invokes a combination of sensorial and intellectual reactions that manifests in return the translator's subjective perception of the translated text, and seals at the same time her responsibility towards it.

Creativity in translation

Written as part of a volume of essays she edited with Peter Bush under the title *The Translator as Writer*, Susan Bassnett's 'Writing and Translating' presents a personal account of translation, describing its process as a form of writing which engages the translator in 'some kind of dialogue' with the author of the source text.[7] Bassnett's essay aims to show, through examples of her own experience of translating authors such as Pirandello and Pizarnik, that the intimacy involved in the translator's relationship with the author of the source text goes beyond the demand of fidelity with which it is usually associated. For Bassnett, translating is a creative activity that involves inspiration, transformation and rewriting. It is a dialogic process through which the translator discovers her own voice as a writer.

Bassnett's text forms part of what Paschalis Nikolaou and Maria-Venetia Kyritsi describe as an 'inward turn' in translation studies,[8] a movement within the discipline characterised by a growing interest in the creative, experiential and subjective aspects of translating. Closely related to the 'translator's turn' and its focus on the translator's consciousness, this greater emphasis on inner spaces goes hand in hand with a renewed attention to the translator's creativity – as illustrated by recently edited volumes such as Jean Boase-Beier and Michael Holman's *The Practices of Literary Translation: Constraints and Creativity*,[9] Eugenia Loffredo and Manuela Perteghella's *Translation and Creativity*,[10] Peter Bush and Bassnett's *The Translator as Writer*,[11] and Loffredo and Perteghella's *One Poem in Search of a Translator*.[12]

In the *Handbook of Translation Studies*, Carol O'Sullivan provides a brief synopsis of creativity in translation, stressing that in translation studies uses of the term usually seek to challenge the perception that translating is a derivative form of writing. Thus, she explains:

> Eugenia Loffredo and Manuela Perteghella have usefully pointed out that distinctions between 'original' and 'derivative' writing are themselves cultural constructs and increasingly untenable in a postmodern critical era (2006: 3–6); if translation is a mode of writing, then it cannot be separated from the broader concept of literary writing itself: both are 'creative writing'.[13]

Viewing translation as a creative practice is crucial to studies concerned with the translating 'self', notably those exploring how voice, style and subjectivity are formed through translation. As Nikolaou and Kyritsi underline in their introduction to *Translating Selves*, the conjoining of self and creativity within translation studies has led theorists themselves to depart from academic discourse and to adopt a more personal tone in theorising translation.[14] This is precisely what Bassnett does in 'Writing and Translating'. Often diverging from scholarly considerations, her essay mostly centres on her own creative and translation practice. In this text, Bassnett embarks on a personal process of self-discovery whereby she theorises translation primarily on the basis of her own experience and subjective perception of the translating task.

Bassnett's discussion of her literary experiments with Pirandello, Pizarnik and poetic writing not only seeks to reveal that literary translators often have unspoken parallel lives as writers, but also serves to highlight that 'in an adverse environment of sustained self-suppression required for the channeling of another literary voice, the experiential actuality is often one of dialogue and influence, of creative alchemy and meaningful ventriloquism'.[15] Using the reflexive method of folding a theory back on itself, I inquire into this proposition through a performative translation of Bassnett's essay which, following her own approach, invokes a personal and subjective engagement with the source text. In my translation, theorising becomes a creative form of writing, one that does not seek to provide an all-encompassing view of translation, but rather a personal account of a specific encounter with a text through translation.

Letter to Susan Bassnett: example of a creative critical translation

The critical translation below is a creative commentary on the following essay:

Susan Bassnett, 'Writing and Translating', in *The Translator as Writer*, edited by Susan Bassnett and Peter Bush (London: Continuum, 2006), pp. 173–183.

À Susan Bassnett

Objet : Lettre ouverte

Le 18 mai 2018,

Chère Susan,

Je t'écris en réponse à ton texte « Writing and Translating », paru dans l'anthologie d'essais intitulée The Translator as Writer, qui m'a beaucoup interpellée, non seulement en tant que traductrice et chercheuse mais aussi en tant que lectrice et amatrice de littérature.

Dans ce texte, tu nous dis que tu n'as jamais réussi à savoir exactement quand la distinction entre écriture et traduction est devenue hégémonique. Tout ce que tu sais, expliques-tu, c'est qu'une telle distinction existe et qu'elle semble avoir lieu depuis quelque temps déjà, conduisant le plus grand nombre à percevoir la traduction comme la fille maudite de l'écriture, quant à elle qualifiée d'« originale » ou de « créative », et considérée comme supérieure.

Ce que l'on oublie souvent, soulignes-tu, c'est que de nombreux écrivains sont également traducteurs, et que, contrairement à la croyance populaire, pour eux la distinction hiérarchique entre ces deux activités n'existe pas. Tout comme l'imitation, la traduction peut servir à l'apprentissage de l'art de l'écriture, car si les écrivains ont la capacité d'imaginer et de faire parler plusieurs personnages, ils devraient être en mesure de se forger leur propre voix.

Ton premier mémoire de recherche portait sur James Joyce et Italo Svevo, et l'intérêt pour le modernisme que ce projet éveilla en toi te conduisit dans les bras de Pirandello. Tu écrivis trois livres et plusieurs articles sur Pirandello, et traduisis un certain nombre de ses pièces pour la radio, le théâtre et l'édition, ainsi que des essais et des nouvelles. Cet intérêt pour Pirandello dura une bonne vingtaine d'années, puis disparut complètement. Avec ses contorsions intellectuelles et la structure complexe de ses phrases, ses intrigues à fin ouverte et son sens de l'humour sombre, Pirandello, celui qui t'avait intriguée pendant des années, perdit toute son importance.

Tu étais tombée amoureuse d'un auteur d'un style complètement différent, la poétesse argentine Alejandra Pizarnik. Traduire Pizarnik et traduire Pirandello furent des expériences complètement différentes, nous expliques-tu. Hormis la différence de style, de contenu et de genre, tu te vis aborder la tâche de manière tout à fait différente. Lorsque tu traduisais Pirandello, et lorsque tu traduis n'importe quelle œuvre complète d'ailleurs (qu'il s'agisse d'une pièce de théâtre, d'un roman, d'une nouvelle ou d'un essai), tu commences par écrire une version manuscrite, sur laquelle tu ne reviens souvent jamais. Pour toi, cette étape est indispensable, c'est une étape qui consiste à « matérialiser l'acte de lecture » par l'écriture. Écrire machinalement page après page fixe en quelque sorte la lecture de chaque phrase ; cela révèle les aspects problématiques du texte, les difficultés de compréhension et les passages qu'il faut retravailler. L'étape suivante, qui constitue d'après toi la tâche de traduction réelle (ou « translation proper » comme tu l'appelles dans ton texte, certainement en référence indirecte à l'expression de Roman Jakobson), est une étape d'écriture et de réécriture, qui consiste à formuler des phrases, utiliser des dictionnaires, des encyclopédies et des dictionnaires de synonymes. Il y a donc pour toi une distinction claire entre la traduction et d'autres formes d'écriture : traduire implique selon toi un travail d'écriture conscient et délibéré en plusieurs étapes. Cela comporte un aspect ludique, un enjouement qui ne se manifeste pas dans d'autres activités d'écriture, où le jeu (si on peut l'appeler ainsi) se produit intérieurement, avant même que l'étape d'écriture concrète ne commence. Bien que la traduction soit elle-même une forme d'écriture, sembles-tu suggérer ici, elle s'en distingue par le fait qu'elle opère une réflexivité particulière, un retour du texte sur lui-même, une distance du traducteur vis-à-vis de l'activité qu'il pratique – distance réflexive dont l'expérience serait exacerbée comparativement à d'autres formes d'écriture. Cette idée que la traduction est une activité intrinsèquement réflexive, c'est précisément ce que cette traduction de ton texte sous forme de réponse épistolaire se propose d'explorer. Ma démarche interroge la capacité d'un texte à en énoncer un autre, et les modalités selon lesquelles il pourrait le faire, par le biais d'une représentation formelle des problèmes que soulève une théorisation de la traduction comme forme d'écriture singulièrement critique et réflexive. Peut-on incarner, actualiser, exprimer formellement le discours d'un(e) autre sans s'en dissocier, autrement dit sans manifester du même coup son propre positionnement face au texte traduit? Cette question, et l'approche performative que j'adopte ici pour y répondre, ont un caractère volontairement ludique et ironique. Car il est bien question ici d'aborder la traduction comme performativité et performance, comme représentation, comme jeu d'acteur—c'est-à-dire comme dédoublement et redoublement de l'énoncé auquel le traducteur prête sa voix.

Traduire les poèmes de Pizarnik et traduire d'autres écrivains étaient des activités très différentes de ton point de vue. Pour Pizarnik, tu traduisais plusieurs poèmes d'une traite, presque toujours le weekend, aux heures perdues lorsque les enfants étaient occupés et que tu pouvais te détendre. Traduire Pizarnik était une sorte de récréation. Tu ne rédigeais pas de brouillons comme tu le faisais pour les autres écrivains, et avec le recul, tu te rends compte que le processus de traduction des textes de Pizarnik s'apparentait bien plus à une pratique d'écriture qu'à celle de la traduction. Tu te sentais en quelque sorte prise dans un dialogue avec elle, comme si en traduisant ses textes tu parvenais à mieux comprendre tes propres pensées. On pourrait presque dire que traduire Pizarnik équivalait à écrire du Bassnett – et ceci, malgré bien évidemment le grand fossé entre vos cultures, vos religions, vos éducations et vos expériences de vie.

En 2002, tu as publié un petit livre dans lequel tu essayais de mieux comprendre les motifs de l'écriture et de la traduction, la relation qui peut s'établir entre l'écrivain et le traducteur, les notions d'influence et de transmission qui sous-tendent la traduction. Tu l'as intitulé Exchanging Lives (« Échange de vies »). Il s'agit d'un recueil divisé en quatre parties : tes traductions de Pizarnik avec le texte original espagnol sur les pages opposées, un mélange de traductions et de poèmes que tu avais rédigé et présenté sous forme de dialogue. La quatrième partie était consacrée à ce poème épitaphe intraduisible de Pizarnik :

Alejandra alejandra
debajo estoy yo
alejandra

Et de ton contre-poème :

Susan susanna
lying below
susanna

Auquel j'ajoute le mien :

Silvie silvia
Sous latente
silvia

dans lequel tes deux noms d'usage dans les deux différentes sphères linguistiques font écho à la double signification du mot « lying », de même que l'utilisation du mot « debajo » par Pizarnik évoque des significations multiples—et de même que dans ma version, l'emploi de mes deux noms d'usage en français et en anglais rappellent la duplicité phonologique du mot « latente », qui peut aussi s'entendre

« l'attente ». Il te semblait, et je te rejoins là-dessus, que la meilleure traduction que tu pouvais proposer de la structure serrée du poème si court de Pizarnik était d'en donner ta propre alternative. Surgit encore une fois, à travers cette volonté de détacher la traduction des préoccupations de stricte équivalence, la question du statut du texte traduit dans son rapport à l'original. Tes choix manifestent une approche phénoménologique de la traduction conçue non pas comme un processus visant à reproduire une signification soi-disant objective de l'œuvre originale, mais comme un acte de lecture personnel au sein duquel le traducteur exprime ses propres réactions face à sa rencontre subjective et intime avec le texte source. En ce sens, ta traduction, que tu appelles ici de façon suggestive un « contre poème », fonctionne (pareillement à cette lettre) comme une réponse au texte qu'elle propose d'incarner.

Tu n'as pas retraduit Pizarnik depuis que tu as fini le manuscrit d'*Exchanging Lives*. La réception du livre fut mitigée : certains commentateurs ont aimé l'idée de deux écrivains pris dans une sorte de dialogue à travers la traduction, d'autres se sont plaints des « inexactitudes » dans les textes traduits. Je fais, quant à moi, partie d'une troisième catégorie de commentateurs : ceux qui se demandent ce que l'idée de « deux écrivains pris dans une sorte de dialogue à travers la traduction » veut dire concrètement—question que la présente traduction tente d'explorer par la pratique, en actualisant formellement ta vision de la traduction comme dialogue intime entre auteur et traducteur. La forme épistolaire, combinée ici avec l'interpellation directe « Susan » et l'utilisation du pronom personnel « tu » qui témoigne d'un registre de discours informel, fonctionne comme une mise en application réflexive de la notion d'intimité que tu décris dans ton essai. Par ailleurs, dans ma version l'alternance des pronoms personnels « je » et « tu » met en jeu la dimension dialogique qui sous-tend selon toi l'interaction entre auteur et traducteur dans l'acte traductif. Le style d'écriture du traducteur serait, de ton point de vue, influencé par celui de l'auteur, inévitablement imprégné de la voix qu'il traduit, inéluctablement transformé par le rapport dialogique que constitue le processus de traduction. Ce point essentiel, qui est aux fondements de ton appel en faveur de la revalorisation du traduire comme forme d'écriture créative, est représenté dans mon texte par la fusion ponctuelle des pronoms personnels « je » et « tu » en un « nous » silencieux et indivisible.

La multiplicité des voix à l'œuvre dans cette traduction performative se divise principalement en trois catégories: adresse directe par l'interpellation « tu » ; emploi de la première personne du singulier « je » ; superposition des voix auctoriale et traductive à travers un « nous » implicite. Ces catégories soulignent trois aspects essentiels de la dynamique complexe entre « je » et « tu » à l'œuvre dans le processus traductif : d'une part, le traducteur parlant au nom de l'auteur, dont il articule les mots dans une autre langue et à qui il confère explicitement la provenance du discours; d'autre part, le traducteur assumant sa voix de traducteur comme réponse au discours de l'auteur et devenant lui-même agent du discours, c'est-à-dire un auteur à part entière ; et enfin, une superposition des voix de l'auteur et du traducteur qui résulte en une sorte de polyphonie invisible, en une fusion des voix, où instances auctoriale et traductive se confondent.

Bien qu'incarnant tous ces aspects importants de ta théorie, ma performance de ton texte soulève aussi plusieurs questions. En essayant de mettre en application l'interaction dialogique entre auteur et traducteur par exemple, la forme épistolaire montre en retour que le type de texte auquel on a affaire dans une traduction n'est justement pas un dialogue, puisque l'auteur ne peut pas y répondre, et que cet auteur n'y est d'ailleurs pas à proprement parler l'agent de l'énonciation. L'utilisation de la seconde personne rend compte de cette contradiction en montrant que l'auteur est l'agent d'un discours dont il est dépossédé. En effet, l'emploi du « tu » indique que, même si l'énoncé en question t'est explicitement attribué (« tu nous dis que tu »), tu (en tant qu'auteur) es en réalité absente, car ce n'est pas toi qui parles, mais moi qui te fais parler sur le mode du discours indirect. Cette traduction met ainsi en scène l'appropriation de la voix auctoriale par le traducteur, qui de ce fait rend impossible l'utilisation du « je » par l'auteur. En tant qu'auteur, tu ne peux pas me répondre, à moins bien sûr que j'en décide autrement et choisisse de te faire répondre de manière fictive—mais cela ne serait qu'une autre manière de continuer à te faire parler, à affirmer ma position auctoriale, à conserver le pouvoir de parler en ton nom.

L'emploi des pronoms personnels « je » et « tu » dans cette lettre suggère qu'une conception dialogique de la traduction ne peut être qu'imaginaire et métaphorique—sauf si l'auteur et le traducteur entreprennent véritablement de traduire ensemble. De plus, en s'efforçant d'actualiser l'intimité du rapport entre auteur et traducteur que tu décris, la forme épistolaire défie, par la même occasion, la possibilité même de cette intimité. Par-delà son registre discursif informel et son ton familier, cette lettre souligne délibérément sa propre incapacité à construire une expérience totalement intime car, en tant que lettre ouverte, c'est-à-dire en tant qu'écrit expérimental destiné à être lu par d'autres lecteurs que toi, Susan, elle est constamment hantée par la figure de cet autre lecteur, qui n'est pas toi. Représentant et contestant à la fois la possibilité d'une intimité dans l'activité traductive, ma réponse à ton texte suggère que le processus traductif n'est ni totalement dialogique, ni entièrement privé, mais au mieux un mise en scène de ces concepts. Ma version épistolaire substitue ainsi à ta théorisation de la traduction comme dialogue intime entre auteur et traducteur une performance de la traduction comme réponse à un énoncé antérieur, effectuant par-là littéralement une réponse à ta théorie.

Amicalement,

Silvia

Légende

Adresse directe à travers l'emploi du pronom personnel « tu » (« nous expliques-tu », etc.)

Voix du traducteur exprimée notamment par l'utilisation du pronom personnel « je » (« je t'écris en réponse à », etc.)

Superposition des voix (aucun recours aux pronoms personnels)

Commentaire (expression de l'opinion personnelle du traducteur)

Citation dans la langue de l'original (mise en abyme de l'intertextualité, qui accentue l'effet polyphonique)

Citation en langue étrangère dans l'original (mise en abyme du plurilinguisme, qui accentue l'aspect multilingue)

Traduction de citation (traduction d'un texte cité par l'auteur)

Interventions para-textuelles (explication de mots étrangers, références à d'autres textes, etc.)

Traduction indirecte (traduction d'une citation sous forme de discours indirect)

Genre épistolaire (conventions du genre épistolaire)

Contre-signature (contre-signature du texte qui scelle l'appropriation de l'énoncé par le traducteur)

Creative critical translating

Dialogic translation?

My performative translation of 'Writing and Translating' into French focuses primarily on the dialogic metaphor developed by Bassnett in this essay. This metaphor is the locus of the reflexive translation practice she describes in this piece – translating as an empowering form of writing that prompts awareness and creativity. My translation attempts to perform her perception of translation as an intimate dialogue in the form of an open letter, addressed back to the author. The epistolary form, combined with the direct interpellation 'Susan' and the use of the personal pronoun 'tu' (a rather informal and intimate address in French), functions as a reflexive application of the notion of intimacy described by Bassnett. Furthermore, the alternation of the first- and second-person pronouns 'je' and 'tu' aims to stage, in a rather extreme manner, the dialogic dimension of translation as verbal interaction between translator and author. In this essay, Bassnett also draws on her personal experience as a translator to show how much translation has influenced her own writing and style. This last, but central, argument in Bassnett's theory, which sets the ground for re-establishing the status of translation as a creative form of writing, is made visible in the numerous passages where, in my translation, the personal pronouns 'tu' and 'je', initially distinct, blend into an invisible, silent 'us'.

The various layers of my reflexive performance of Bassnett's theory can be summarised using the colour code below: direct address to the author (yellow); use of the first-person in addressing the author (orange); superposition of the author's and translator's voices (light blue). For example:

Chère Susan,

Je t'écris en réponse à ton texte « Writing and Translating », paru dans l'anthologie d'essais intitulée *The Translator as Writer*, qui m'a beaucoup interpellée non seulement en tant que traductrice et chercheuse mais aussi en tant que lectrice et amatrice de littérature.

Dans ce texte, tu nous dis que tu n'as jamais réussi à savoir exactement quand la distinction entre écriture et traduction est devenue hégémonique. Tout ce que tu sais, expliques-tu, c'est qu'une telle distinction existe et qu'elle semble avoir lieu depuis quelques temps déjà, conduisant le plus grand nombre à percevoir la traduction comme la fille maudite de l'écriture, quant à elle qualifiée d'« originale » ou de « créative », et considérée comme supérieure.

Ce que l'on oublie souvent, soulignes-tu, c'est que de nombreux écrivains sont également traducteurs, et que, contrairement à la croyance populaire, pour eux la distinction hiérarchique entre ces deux activités n'existe pas. Tout comme l'imitation, la traduction peut servir à l'apprentissage de l'art de l'écriture, car si les écrivains ont la capacité d'imaginer et de faire parler plusieurs personnages, ils devraient être en mesure de se forger leur propre voix.

These categories highlight three different aspects of the complex je/tu dynamics at play in translation: firstly, the translator speaking in the name of the author, enacting her words in another language and explicitly attributing ownership of these words to the author (yellow); secondly, the translator taking ownership of her voice as a translator, responding to the author's discourse and becoming herself an authoring agent, an author (orange); and thirdly, a superposition of the author's and translator's voices creating an invisible polyphony, a confusion of voices, where authoring and translating agencies become inseparable (light blue).

Even while it enacts crucial elements of Bassnett's translation theory, though, my performance of her text also challenges several of her central arguments. Indeed, in its attempt to stage the dialogic interaction between author and translator, for example, the epistolary form makes evident that the type of text we are dealing with in translation is not a dialogue at all, since the author cannot respond and is not even speaking in the first place. The use of the second-person address epitomises this contradiction, for it signals both the author's ownership and also her loss of her own utterance. In '[d]ans ce texte, tu nous dis que tu n'as jamais réussi à savoir exactement quand la distinction entre écriture et traduction est devenue hégémonique', for instance, the use of 'tu' makes clear that, while the utterance is explicitly attributed to the author ('tu nous dis que tu'), the author is in fact absent, for it is not the author who is speaking, but the translator who is making the author speak through indirect discourse ('tu nous dis que tu'). By using both first- and second-person pronouns, my translation performs an appropriation of the author's utterance, making it impossible for the author, Susan Bassnett, to say 'I'.

Bassnett cannot respond unless I decide to stage or imagine a possible response, which would be another way of continuing to make her speak, of retaining the authoring agency, of retaining the agency to speak in her name. Here, the use of the personal pronouns 'je' and 'tu' shows that a dialogic conception of translation can only be imaginary and metaphoric. Moreover, by its effort to enact the concept of intimacy developed in Bassnett's text, the epistolary form simultaneously questions the very possibility of full intimacy between author and translator in translation. Despite its direct address, informal register and intimate tone, my letter to Bassnett shows its own deliberate failure to build an entirely intimate experience because, as an open letter – that is, as an experimental letter designed to be read by other readers than Bassnett – it is constantly haunted by the figure of this other reader, a reader of my letter to Bassnett who is other than Bassnett. Staging yet defying the possibility of performing intimacy, my translation is at best a *mise en scène* of intimacy. Neither fully dialogic nor private, my epistolary version of Bassnett's text questions the idea of an intimate dialogue between author and translator, for which it substitutes a view of translation as a subjective response to an anterior utterance, thus literally performing a responsive translation.

Responsive translations

My approach to translation as a response to an anterior utterance is in part inspired by a relatively recent series of translation experiments collected in a book entitled *One Poem in Search of a Translator: Rewriting 'Les Fenêtres' by Apollinaire*. Edited by Loffredo and Perteghella, the volume consists of twelve translations into English of Guillaume Apollinaire's poem 'Les Fenêtres'. Translators from different backgrounds and working contexts (poets, professional translators, academics, visual artists, etc.) were asked to engage with the multimodal dimension of this poem, which is inspired by Robert Delaunay's 'Les Fenêtres' series of paintings. The final product showcases a broad spectrum of creative techniques, ranging from machine translations to inventive uses of colour and collage. Each translation is accompanied by a self-reflective commentary which provides insight into the complex process and experience of translating Apollinaire's text.

The choice of poem is itself self-reflexive: it 'embodies the notion of translation suggested by the "creative turn" which, after an initial resistance, achieves a liberation of the reading process by promoting the explosion of multiple readings elicited by the text'.[16] As Loffredo and Perteghella clearly outline in their preface, their experimental approach follows the footsteps of Clive Scott's 'experiential' view of translation as a reading experience, as 'the ultimate performance of reading'.[17] Reading, according to Scott, is not an interpretative activity (a 'post-textual' operation), but a phenomenological process (an 'in-textual' operation) whereby 'the reader actualises or embodies her individual experience of the text'.[18] In his view, 'it is translation's business to capture the perceptual experience of reading/performing one text into another'.[19] For Scott, as in the reflexive method I deployed to translate Bassnett, translation consists of reworking the source text into a reflection of the translator's own reading, an experience wherein what the words do on a sensorial level (their impact on the reader) cannot be separated from what they say (the way they are interpreted).

Drawing from Scott's phenomenological approach, Loffredo and Perteghella's experiment in *One Poem in Search of a Translator* relies explicitly on the idea of translation as an enactment of the translator's sensory response to a source text. The multiplicity of methods and media used to perform the translations testifies to the subjectivity and creativity at play when reading and responding to a text, emphasising that translating is as much to do with expressing how the source text affects the translator as with what it says, or what it means. In my experience of translating translation theory, reading – and translating, as a response to a previous utterance – is indeed inseparable from interpretation. In fact, my experimentation raises the question of whether it is ever possible to separate what a text does from what it says in any translation act. For while Loffredo and Perteghella, following Scott, emphasise the purely sensorial and experiential dimension of reading and translating, their project also suggests that the performance of a text is in reality inseparable from its analysis, from its context and from the enactment of its potential meaning.

As mentioned previously, Loffredo and Perteghella's choice of a poem which embodies the liberation of the reading process is itself self-reflexive, and suggests an engagement with the source text that exceeds the senses. Further, as 'paratextual spaces where translators act as "textual critics" intervening and discussing "alternative textual variants" or showing "the elusive nature of translation"',[20] the commentaries take the translations another step beyond the purely sensorial. Similarly, in my epistolary translation of Bassnett's text, using a colour code to map out the different voices, registers and levels of discourse deployed in response to her essay serves to symbolise the dynamic interaction of sensorial and interpretative elements at play in my approach to translation. The colours signify in both form (visually, each produces a different sensory effect) and content (analytically, each represents a particular mode of discourse), thus concretely highlighting the sensorial and critical aspects of my response to Bassnett.

If the translatorly readings proposed in *One Poem in Search of a Translator*, and in my response to Bassnett, are interpretative, they are not interpretative in a hermeneutical, explanatory sense, for they are not just the expression of a rational interpretation of the source text. In my experiment, the intellectual component of translation cannot be separated from its sensorial performance. Interpretation, in my approach, is simultaneously experiential and analytical, practical and theoretical, emotional and critical. In this way I follow Douglas Robinson, who, in the *Translator's Turn*, suggests that translating is an activity in which the rational and the emotional are intertwined, indivisible:

> That our understanding of language, our memories of language, our use and reuse of language, our language-related choices and decisions are all 'somatically marked'. That we have *feeling* for words and phrases, registers and styles, either when someone else is speaking or writing or when we are doing so ourselves, either when we are working in a single language or when we are engineering a transfer from one to another; and that all of our decisions about language, including what word or phrase would be best or what would be most 'equivalent', are channeled through these feelings.[21]

From this point of view, there can be no thinking without feeling. Just as in *One Poem in Search of a Translator* translating poetry and expressing one's sensory perception of it requires a degree of analytical engagement, so does critical interpretation involve an amount of sensuous interaction with the source text when translating translation theory.

Translating 'Writing and Translating' proves a particularly creative and sensory task given that in this text Bassnett deliberately employs a subjective tone, incorporating personal anecdotes and references into her poems, some of which she actually cites in her piece. Translating such a hybrid essay highlights the difficulty of enacting a text without also engaging with it theoretically and reacting to it on a sensory level – that is, without responding to it both analytically and aesthetically. My translation of Bassnett involved enacting a meaning in construction, a meaning that was being created during the very act of performing that translation. Responding, from this perspective, required interpreting in a performative way. It meant performing according to my own understanding and sensitivity. It meant interpreting in the two-fold etymological sense: 'to declare' (to make an utterance) and 'to explain' (to construct meaning).

Modern acceptations of the term reflect both these aspects: 'to translate orally' and 'to give or provide the meaning of'.[22] In the verb 'interpret', enactment and the creation of meaning are inseparable, as the ambiguous status of the 'I' in professional interpreting illustrates. In professional interpreting, the 'I' simultaneously enacts both authoring and translating instances, the initial utterance and its response, the act of speech and its interpretation. As Theo Hermans explains:

> the necessary illusion is one of transparency and coincidence (...). As the interpreter's voice falls in, coincides with and in so doing – paradoxically – disappears behind [the author's] voice, the physical experience of hearing two distinct voices speaking more or less simultaneously is suppressed, or sublimated, and in practice we consider the two voices to be wholly consonant.[23]

And yet, Hermans further clarifies, 'the translation never coincides with its source, it is not identical or equivalent in any formal or straightforward sense'.[24] In fact, the translation's non-identity to (or distance from) the original is precisely where the translator's response is located. It is the locus of a meta-text whereby the translating subject expresses her own relation to, view on and position toward the text she translates.

    Translating compels the translator to transform the original text. The translator's role as mediator – 'the extent to which translators intervene in the transfer process, feeding their own knowledge and beliefs into their processing of a text'[25] – makes non-intervention impossible. In fact, the decision to remain neutral and stay as close as possible to the source text is itself a form of positioning. As Theo Hermans suggests:

> Translation, as the retrieval and representation of an anterior discourse, can be viewed as a form of quotation. In this view the translator is a reporter who simulates, re-enacts, reproduces the reported discourse mimetically. That makes translation a form of direct speech, with as a consequence, limited to minimal reporter control over the reported words. However, even a simulation contains a deictic aspect, which we attribute to the simulator. The matter is complicated further, first by the selectivity of the representation, which again reveals the simulator's agency, then by the problem of clearly telling the mimetic from the diegetic, and thirdly, and most importantly, by the fact that in an interlingual translation the words we encounter are unmistakably those of the translating reporter.[26]

For Hermans, it is precisely to the extent that the translator is more than just a soundbox or mouth-piece animator that the translator's subject-position becomes discernible in translation. When translating translation theory and engaging with a text on a theoretical level in particular, the translator's perspective on the theory translated creates room for the expression of an attitude which works as a response to the theory expressed in the source text.

My reflexive translation of Bassnett's essay actualises this responsive aspect of translation as a process through which the translator explores her own reaction to a given text. In attempting to enact Bassnett's description of translation as an intimate dialogue between author and translator, I also construct my own approach to translation as critical response. Just as, according to Bassnett, 'translating Pizarnik *was* Bassnett writing',[27] so was translating Bassnett a pathway to articulating my own perspective on translation. In fact, many translation theories are formulated in response to prior texts. Lawrence Venuti's concept of foreignization, for instance, was partly inspired by Antoine Berman's approach in 'La traduction comme épreuve de l'étranger', which Venuti translated into English as 'Translation and the Trials of the Foreign'. Berman's own theory was developed in reaction to the theories of the German Romantics (including Friedrich Schleiermacher), as well as in response to Walter Benjamin's 'The Task of the Translator', a text with which Berman engages performatively in *L'Âge de la traduction*.

Jacques Derrida's 'Des Tours de Babel' provides another example of a translation theory developed in response to a prior text. As explained in the introduction to this monograph, in this essay Derrida undertakes a translation of Benjamin's 'The Task of the Translator' in order, ultimately, to present his own approach to translation – which both enacts and transgresses Benjamin's theory. Derrida's translation elaborates the idea that translating operates a 'conserving-and-negating lift',[28] thereby actualising Benjamin's view that translation functions as an organic extension of the original. However, Derrida also pushes the limits of Benjamin's text, for, by choosing to translate a French translation of it (instead of the German original), he also challenges Benjamin's idea that translating a text which is itself a translation is an impossible task. 'Translations', Benjamin claims, 'prove to be untranslatable not because meaning weighs on them heavily, but rather because it attaches to them all too fleetingly'.[29] With his intralingual translation of 'The Task of the Translator', Derrida responds to Benjamin's theory by extending it, and suggests that to respond to a text also implies going beyond it.

Similarly, in my practice, translating entails developing a critical stance. It involves reflecting and commenting on the text's key arguments while attempting to enact them. In my translation of 'Writing and Translating', the genre of the open letter itself epitomises this critical approach, which is further enhanced by the colouring of the letter and the different categories of speech the colours represent. The passages in red, for example, draw attention to the meta-textual aspect of my response to Bassnett's text. They signal my comments and highlight the fact that my letter is not a transparent, identical reproduction of Bassnett's essay, but an expression of my own perspective on the issues that she raises. Overall, the colour code functions as a self-reflexive commentary that seeks to explain visually the text's underlying structure, its internal design.

Response and responsibility

Portraying translation as an operation of response highlights the subjective dimension of the translator's relation to the source text. This does not mean, however, that the response is unreflective in relation to the writing it incarnates. Far from being removed from its source, the translator's response to a text is inevitably indebted to it. In very simple terms, the translation needs the original in order to come into being; it inevitably reflects an aspect of the work to which it responds. Derrida's essay 'What is a "Relevant" Translation?' provides a penetrating discussion of the indebtedness of translation to the source text. Having described the task of the translator as a 'duty' (or 'debt'), which is 'as inflexible as it is unpayable',[30] Derrida then literally inscribes the notion of indebtedness into his writing by deliberately inserting problems of translation for the future translators of his text. The use of the word *relevante*, for example – a multilingual term, borrowed from the English but marked by the meanings of the French verb 'relever' and noun 'relève' – epitomises this challenge, for, as Derrida explains, the term is not only '*in* translation' but it also serves 'to qualify translation and to indicate what a translation might be *obliged* to be, namely *relevant*'.[31]

Derrida's concept underlines the necessity yet impossibility for translation to constitute itself as a fully adequate response to the source text. This tension is actualised in Lawrence Venuti's own English translation of Derrida's text. As Venuti explains:

> Key terms like *relève*, which Derrida describes as untranslatable, have remained untranslated in most passages. But because *relève* is the object of a richly detailed interpretation, I have rendered it expansively in some instances, making explicit the range of meanings that it accumulates in Derrida's discussion.[32]

Venuti's decision to maintain and clarify the word *relève* exemplifies the double bind of relevance as concurrently an adequate response to, and an enhancement of, the source text – thus showing that enacting a previous utterance means both remaining at the mercy of the original and going beyond it. By often anticipating its own possible translations, Derrida's writing suggests that the response brought about during the translating process is already at play, as a possibility, in the source text. It implies that responding to a text is also, to a certain extent, to actualise its potentialities.

My theorisation of translation as a response to a previous utterance is itself conceived and elaborated as a possible interpretation of Bassnett's own account of translation in 'Writing and Translating'. Even though her essay explicitly formulates the idea of translation as dialogue, several other elements in her text point toward a view of translation as response. Throughout the essay Bassnett stresses the important role that translating authors such as Pizarnik and Pirandello played in the development of her own voice; she insists on the ideas of writing under influence, expressing herself in reaction to other texts and writing counter-poems. Her approach to translating recalls the experiential perspective of Clive Scott, who in *Translating Baudelaire* describes translation as a process of self-discovery:

> What if we read and translate in order to situate the ST in our own psycho-physiological response to it? I read Baudelaire in order to transpose him to my psychic, emotional and vocal range. This is not to confine the ST, but to be liberated by it, liberated not into Baudelaire so much perhaps as into territories of myself that Baudelaire makes available to me. (2000: 249)

From this point of view, translating is a self-expressive response through which the translator develops her own sense of self.

The translator responds to the source text on the basis of her own experience of it. In the words of Yves Bonnefoy, 'if the translation is not a crib, a mere technique, but an inquiry and an experiment, it can only inscribe itself – write itself – in the course of a life; it will draw upon that life in all its aspects, all its actions.'[33] Translating, from this perspective, is an operation of response which both calls upon and creates the translator's perception of herself, as though the 'self' of the translator were being constructed through translation. This self, Scott suggests, we might want to imagine as 'something unitary, something which has a particular style, something which has a certain vision of the text. But each translational act defines the translator in different ways.'[34]

In fact, each translation is also a translation of the self – the creation of a certain style, of a certain perception of oneself, of a certain vision of translation itself. The moment we acknowledge the subjective dimension of translational work, we become aware of various senses in which the translator is responsible to and for her work.[35]

Responsibility in translation lies in the translator's response to the source text, in the way she interprets it, represents it and expresses her own experience of it. As David Wills puts it in *Matchbook*, a collection of essays devoted to Derridean deconstruction, 'responsibility is precisely a gesture of response'.[36] The translator's responsibility resides in the articulation of her own perception of the source text, while making a claim of fidelity to that text. Responding, in this context, means both enacting and transforming the prior utterance; it implies saying something more than (or different from) the original. A response, in this approach, is not a folding back, or a return to the first utterance, but a displacement, a new act of communication. As Susan Petrilli suggests in *Translation, Translation*, to be adequate (I would say *relevant*) 'the translation-text must not simply repeat the [source text], but must establish a relation of answering comprehension to it'.[37] The responsible translator must *respond to* the original: she must render the source text, but she can only do so by interpreting it, reacting to it and transforming it.

As Petrilli points out, translation emphasises the responsive aspect of all writing (the fact that we write within a given context and respond to a certain tradition on the basis of our own history, expressing ourselves in response to other texts): 'To speak, to be a speaking subject, to be an author', she explains, 'is always to respond, and in fact all texts are a response.'[38] For Petrilli, the subject and the text can decide anything except the conditions that make them possible. 'This', she indicates, 'already emerges from the fact that every time the subject speaks, every time it produces a text, it is responding.'[39] Translation in this view is a response to a call, but as such it also formulates a call of its own:

> That to speak is to respond and that speaking can do nothing without presupposing that someone is listening, says clearly that this initiative does not belong to the subject, to the I, but, on the contrary, to the other: another with whom the subject is already communicating, to whom it must respond and answer to.[40]

Responsibility in translation is never just a movement of response – or rather, the response it articulates is also concurrently, and inevitably, an address.

A double sense of responsibility is thus at play in translation, for while responding to the source text the translator also addresses someone else: a reader, an audience. Even when literally responding to a text – as I do in my open letter to Bassnett – the response constitutes a new interpellation, an address which displaces the initial act of communication and its reception. My response to (and interpretation of) Bassnett's text does not end with my personal reading of it, nor does it simply return to the author. Although explicitly addressed to Bassnett, my open letter also calls upon other readers, implicitly asking to be seen and read by a wider audience. Response in translation is not circular; it does not go back to the first sender. Instead it establishes a new address that transforms the first utterance into a new act of communication. This is why a dialogic view of translation is questionable. By simultaneously responding to and addressing a call, translation shows that dialogue itself is not a reflexive operation whereby the message completes a full circle. For every utterance is to a certain extent part of a dialogue, a speaking with, an address to someone; and yet every act of communication is also threatened by the possibility that this address, this message, misses its destination.

In *The Postcard*: *From Socrates to Freud and Beyond*,[41] Derrida explains that the very structural condition of the act of sending a message is that it may not arrive. According to Derrida, as soon as we send a letter, we take the risk of it not arriving, for there is always a chance that the letter will get lost, that it will not reach its intended addressee. As Derrida makes clear, this does not imply that the letter will *never* arrive. Rather, it means that it '*may* always *not* arrive'.[42] For Derrida, there would be no letter without the possibility of it not arriving. This possibility is what defines its very structure as a letter, as *envoi*. Translating exacerbates this impossibility of securing delivery, and this is precisely what my letter to Bassnett aims to demonstrate, both metaphorically and literally – or '*letterally*' as David Wills playfully puts it in relation to Derrida's own performative approach in *The Postcard*.[43] From my perspective, response in translation is a deferred transmission, a displaced address which the sender can never fully control or direct.

Translating requires taking responsibility for one's personal response to a text – both with regard to the author of the original and to the reader of the target text. Translators are concurrently bound to the source text to which they must respond and exposed to an audience that they cannot entirely anticipate. As Walter Benjamin succinctly phrases it in 'The Task of the Translator', '[n]o poem is intended for the reader, no picture for the beholder, no symphony for the listener'[44] – or in Antoine Berman's

French version: 'Il n'est pas un poème qui soit fait pour celui qui le lit, pas un tableau pour celui qui le contemple, pas une symphonie pour ceux qui l'écoutent.'[45] According to Derrida, even when it is addressed to someone we know, the addressee of our text is not knowable, because the structure of the *envoi* makes its destination inescapably uncertain:

> J'écris non seulement parce que j'écris à quelqu'un que je connais ou que je suis supposé connaître, mais j'essaie d'instituer, par l'inscription d'une trace nouvelle [cf. l'acte d'écriture] qui doit être un évènement, le ou la destinataire, autrement dit l'autre. Ça peut être quelqu'un que je connais, mais ce quelqu'un que je connais ne sera le ou la destinataire de cette lettre qu'en la recevant, qu'en l'acceptant, qu'en la contresignant en quelque sorte. Donc ça veut dire que, au moment où je l'écris, l'autre n'existe, d'une certaine manière, pas encore.[46]

> I write not only because I write to someone I know or whom I am supposed to know, but I try to institute the addressee (i.e. the other) through the inscription of a new trace (i.e. the act of writing) which must be an event. It can be someone I know, but this someone I know will become the addressee of this letter only when they receive it, accept it and counter-sign it, so to speak. This means that at the moment of writing the letter, the other does not, to a certain extent, yet exist.[47]

For Derrida, the addressee of a letter does not exist until she receives it, accepts it, and counter-signs it. This means that when addressing a letter to someone, this someone is, ironically, not yet determined.

Just as it is impossible for a writer to predict every translatory response to her work, so the translator is unable to guarantee who the reader of her text will turn out to be. Paradoxically, at the very moment of addressing a text to a specific audience, the translator faces the impossibility of securing the specificity of this address. My open letter to Bassnett thematises and formalises this uncertainty, as my direct appeal is continuously threatened by the irruption of another, unknown reader. Further, because I did not send the letter to its primary addressee, its audience remains deliberately undecided, open and unknowable. Even if I decided to send the letter to the author, there is no guarantee that she would respond to it or even consider it. In fact, the very possibility of a lack of response signals that no address – even one which thematises its own displacement – can secure its own arrival. Destination cannot be controlled prior to reception, just as meaning cannot be decided before the act of reading. In my letter to Bassnett, the colour code seeks to provide guidance on how to read my French rendering of 'Writing and Translating'. It literally highlights and makes visible my response to Bassnett's theory. And yet it is up to the reader to decipher it, interpret it and respond to it. It is up to the reader to make my responsive translation *relevant*.

Conclusion: from dialogue to response

My examination of Susan Bassnett's approach to translation in this chapter suggests that, far from establishing 'some kind of dialogue' between author and translator, translating rather produces '*activations of the self*'.[48] My own practice highlights this idea by showing that, as a subjective and creative act of reading, translation involves both enacting the source text and responding to it – that is, expressing one's personal, sensory and intellectual perception of it. In the process of performing the other text, the translator also, and inevitably, presents her own interpretation of the original, positions herself in relation to it and develops her own understanding of what translating is about. Translation in this sense is metatextual. It does not only represent the source text, but also expresses the translator's attitude towards it. The process of translating creates a subject-position – a sense of self and a point of view – which gets inscribed in the translated text itself.

For Theo Hermans, translation studies needs a model which 'accounts for the way in which the translator's voice insinuates itself into the discourse and adjusts to the displacement which translation brings about'.[49] This model, according to Hermans, must view the translator as 'constantly co-producing the discourse, shadowing, mimicking [...], but occasionally – caught in the text's disparities and interstices; and paratextually – emerging into the open as a separate discursive voice.'[50] This is exactly what my performative translation of Bassnett's text strives to do by simultaneously reproducing her text and responding to it, concurrently confusing voices and distinguishing between them. In my letter, translation becomes a reply, a retort (*une réplique*). It presents an act of interpretation, similar to acting. Just as an actor's unique way of embodying and performing a script expresses her singularity and subjectivity, so does, in my practice, the translator's representation and re-enactment of the source text reflect her own vision of translation. In the process of performing a text, the translator creates a difference which functions as an embodied critical position.

Responsibility in translation resides in this difference. It lies in the translator's response to the source text, in this new act of communication which is not just a folding back, a reply, but also, synchronously and inevitably, a deferral, a new interpellation, a call. From this perspective, being responsible in translation is not just a matter of choosing between being faithful to the author of the original or serving the reader of the target culture, as Friedrich Schleiermacher's famous formula tends to suggest: 'Either the translator leaves the author in peace, as much as possible, and moves the reader towards him; or he leaves the reader in peace, as much as possible, and moves the author towards him.'[51] Instead, accountability in translation means answering to both author and reader, even while knowing that, as a heterogeneous address, this answer is itself subject to displacement and deferral.

A translator must account for her own impersonation of the source text. She must answer for the changes produced as a result of her subjective engagement with it. At the same time, the meaning of the text she creates is itself unstable and open, calling for further interpretation. Regardless of the amount of colouring and guidance provided, translation ultimately remains at the mercy of the reader, of this unknown and unknowable figure who always threatens to be other than the one I intend – a figure ingrained in her own subjectivity, historicity and experience. Responsibility resides in this deferred act of communication – in the displacement of the translator's response, in the uncertainty surrounding the reception of the call it formulates and in the indefinite deferral of this responsive call.

Notes

1   Derek Attridge, *Reading and Responsibility: Deconstruction's Traces* (Edinburgh: Edinburgh University Press, 2010), 135.
2   Susan Bassnett, 'Writing and Translating', in *The Translator as Writer*, ed. Susan Bassnett and Peter Bush (London: Continuum, 2006), 173–183.
3   Bassnett, 'Writing and Translating', 178.
4   Bassnett, 'Writing and Translating', 178.
5   Bassnett, 'Writing and Translating', 178–179.
6   Bassnett, 'Writing and Translating', 180.
7   Bassnett, 'Writing and Translating', 182.
8   Paschalis Nikolaou and Maria-Venetia Kyritsi, eds., *Translating Selves: Experiences and Identity between Languages and Literatures* (London & New York: Continuum, 2008), 7.
9   Jean Boase-Beier and Michael Holman, eds., *The Practices of Literary Translation: Constraints and Creativity* (Manchester: St. Jerome, 1999).
10 Eugenia Loffredo and Manuela Perteghella, eds, *Translating and Creativity: Perspectives on Creative Writing and Translation Studies* (London: Continuum, 2006).
11 Susan Bassnett and Peter Bush, eds, *The Translator as Writer* (London: Continuum, 2006).
12 Eugenia Loffredo and Manuela Perteghella, eds, *One Poem in Search of a Translator* (Oxford: Peter Lang, 2009).
13 Carol O'Sullivan, 'Multimodality as Challenge and Resource for Translation', *Journal of Specialised Translation* 20 (2011): 2–14.
14 Nikolaou and Kyritsi, *Translating Selves*, 7.
15 Nikolaou and Kyritsi, *Translating Selves*, 7.
16 Loffredo and Perteghella, *One Poem in Search of a Translator,* 19.
17 Clive Scott, *Literary Translation and the Rediscovery of Reading* (Cambridge: Cambridge University Press, 2012), 1.
18 Scott, *Literary Translation and the Rediscovery of Reading*, 2.
19 Scott, *Literary Translation and the Rediscovery of Reading*, 7.
20 Edoardo Crisafulli, 'The Quest for an Eclectic Methodology of Translation Description,' in *Crosscultural Transgressions: Research Models in Translation Studies II. Historical and Ideological Issues*, ed. Theo Hermans (Manchester: St Jerome, 2002), 36.
21 Douglas Robinson, *The Translator's Turn* (Baltimore and London: Johns Hopkins University Press, 1991), 71.
22 *Oxford English Dictionary* (Oxford: Oxford University Press, 2011).
23 Theo Hermans, 'The Translator's Voice in Translated Narrative', *Target* 8, no. 1 (1996): 23–48.
24 Hermans, 'The Translator's Voice in Translated Narrative', 24.
25 Basil Hatim and Ian Mason, *The Translator as Communicator* (London: Routledge, 1997), 147.
26 Theo Hermans, *The Conference of the Tongues* (Manchester: St Jerome, 2007), 74–75.
27 Bassnett, 'Writing and Translating', 178.
28 Jacques Derrida, *Margins of Philosophy*, trans. Alan Bass (Chicago: University of Chicago Press, 1978/1982), 23.
29 Walter Benjamin, 'The Task of the Translator', trans. Harry Zohn, in *The Translation Studies Reader*, ed. Lawrence Venuti (London & New York: Routledge, 1923/2004), 75.
30 Jacques Derrida, 'What Is a "Relevant" Translation?', trans. Lawrence Venuti, *Critical Inquiry* 27, no. 2 (1998/2001): 183.
31 Derrida, 'What Is a "Relevant" Translation?', 177.
32 Lawrence Venuti, 'Introduction', in Jacques Derrida, 'What Is a "Relevant" Translation?', trans. Lawrence Venuti, *Critical Inquiry* 27, no. 2 (2001): 173.
33 Yves Bonnefoy, 'Translating Poetry', trans. John Wilmer, in *Theories of Translation: An Anthology of Essays from Dryden to Derrida*, ed. Rainer Schulte and John Biguenet (Chicago & London: University of Chicago Press, 1992), 189.
34 Clive Scott, 'Translating the Art of Seeing in Apollinaire's "Les Fenêtres": the Self of the Translator, the Selves of Language and Readerly Subjectivity', in *Translating Selves: Experiences and Identity between Languages and Literatures*, ed. Paschalis Nikolaou and Maria-Venetia Kyritsi (London & New York: Continuum, 2008), 37.
35 Nikolaou and Kyritsi, *Translating Selves*, 10.
36 David Wills, *Matchbook* (Stanford: Stanford University Press, 2005), 7.

37 Susan Petrilli, 'Translation and Semiosis', in *Translation Translation*, ed. Susan Petrilli (Amsterdam: Rodopi, 2003), 24.
38 Susan Petrilli, 'The Intersemiotic Character of Translation', in *Translation Translation*, ed. Susan Petrilli (Amsterdam: Rodopi, 2003), 46.
39 Petrilli, 'The Intersemiotic Character of Translation', 46.
40 Petrilli, 'The Intersemiotic Character of Translation', 46.
41 Jacques Derrida, *The Postcard: From Socrates to Freud and Beyond*, trans. Alan Bass (Chicago & London: University of Chicago Press, 1979/1987).
42 Jacques Derrida, *Traces, archives, images et art* (Paris: INA, 2014), 74 (my translation).
43 Wills, *Matchbook*, 71.
44 Benjamin, 'The Task of the Translator', 75.
45 Antoine Berman, *La traduction et la lettre, ou L'auberge du lointain* (Paris: Seuil, 1999), 30.
46 Derrida, *Traces, archives, images et art*, 74.
47 Derrida, *Traces, archives, images et art*, 74 (my translation).
48 Nikolaou and Kyritsi, *Translating Selves*, 6.
49 Hermans, 'The Translator's Voice in Translated Narrative', 43.
50 Hermans, 'The Translator's Voice in Translated Narrative', 43.
51 Friedrich Schleiermacher, 'On the Different Methods of Translating', trans. Susan Bernofsky, in *The Translation Studies Reader*, ed. Lawrence Venuti (London & New York: Routledge, 1813/2004), 49.

Chapter 3
Human vs. Machine Translation
Henri Meschonnic's poetics of translating

> What bothers me about some of the people who identify with scientism is that their mechanical models often fall far short of the hypercomplexity of the machines, real or virtual, produced by humans and to which, for example, all the aporias or the 'impossibles' taken up by deconstruction bear witness, precisely there where it puts the most powerful formalizing machines to the test, in language; and it does this not in order to disqualify the 'machine' in general, quite the contrary, but in order to 'think' it differently (…).
>
> Jacques Derrida[1]

This chapter explores the hierarchy underlying Henri Meschonnic's poetics of translation, as developed throughout half a dozen of his texts, including *Éthique et politique du traduire*.[2] In this work, Meschonnic presents an overview of the translational issues he had been dealing with for decades as a poet, a translator and a critical thinker in rather lengthy theoretical works such as *Critique du rythme*[3] and *Poétique du traduire*.[4] Focusing more intensely on the question of ethics, Meschonnic's *Éthique et politique du traduire* emphasises the inseparability of theory and practice in translation, drawing partly on his own experience of writing poems, translating the Bible and composing essays about translation.

In this text, Meschonnic presents translation as an intrinsically reflexive practice, an activity which necessarily implies theoretical thinking. Thus, he explains:

> On peut donc considérer (…) que le problème majeur de la traduction est sa théorie du langage. Ce qui est bien, d'emblée, impliquer deux choses : l'inséparabilité entre ce que l'on appelle une théorie et ce qu'on appelle une pratique, c'est-à-dire qu'une pratique n'est pas une pratique si elle n'est pas réflexive ou

réfléchie, ce n'est qu'un ânonnement de recettes apprises, et si elle est cette réflexivité, cette pratique implique nécessairement une théorie d'ensemble du langage ; et réciproquement une théorie de la traduction qui ne serait pas la réflexion d'une pratique ne serait que de la linguistique de la langue appliquée sur du discours, c'est-à-dire de la non-pensée.[5]

We can therefore consider that the main problem of translation is its theory of language. From the outset, this implies two things: the inseparability of what is known as theory and what is called practice, that is to say that a practice is not a practice if it is not reflective or thoughtful, it is just a hesitant repetition of pre-existing codes [*un ânonnement de recettes apprises*]; but if it is reflective, such practice necessarily involves a comprehensive theory of language; and conversely, a translation theory that is not also a reflection on a particular practice would just be linguistics applied to discourse, that is to say non-thinking.[6]

For Meschonnic, there exists no practice of translation that is not also metatextual and reflective. Theory and practice cannot be separated in translation, according to Meschonnic, because, except when it is mechanical, the practice of translation always involves a thinking process, a form of decision-making, which manifests in return the translator's own perception of language and of translation.

The mechanical approach Meschonnic indirectly refers to in this passage is machine translation, a computerised translation practice which, according to Meschonnic, has contributed to the proliferation of non-reflective uses of language in translation. In this chapter, I address the question of reflexive decision-making in translation through comparative analysis of several automated and human translations of the above-quoted extract from Meschonnic's *Éthique et politique du traduire*. I examine Meschonnic's opposition of reflexive and unreflexive, doing so in light of Derrida's concept of undecidability – the idea that in order to come into being a decision must resist calculability. For Derrida, undecidability does not, as one might expect, refer to the inability to act or decide, but rather to the very 'condition of possibility of acting and deciding'.[7] We must be careful, Derrida stresses, not to confuse undecidability with indecision. The undecidable is not a pathos, but a structural condition. It is what remains unpredictable and exceeds the mechanical.[8]

Addressing the confusion surrounding Derrida's concept of undecidability, John Caputo explains:

Undecidability is taken, or mistaken, to mean a pathetic state of apathy, the inability to act, paralyzed by the play of signifiers that dance before our eyes, like a deer caught in a headlight. But rather than an inability to act, undecidability is the condition of possibility of acting and deciding. For whenever a decision is really a decision, whenever it is more than a programmable, deducible, calculable, computable result of a logarithm, that is because it has passed through the 'ordeal of undecidability.' One way to keep this straight is to see that the opposite of 'undecidability' is not 'decisiveness' but programmability, calculability, computerizability, or formalizability. Decision-making, judgment, on the other hand, positively *depends upon* undecidability, which gives us something to decide.[9]

For Derrida, every decision is structured by the experience of undecidability because a decision that doesn't go through the ordeal of the undecidable is not a decision: it is only the programmable application or unfolding of a calculable process.[10] A decision is a decision only if it exceeds the application of a rule or law.

In the following pages, I use Derrida's concept of undecidability to investigate the implications of a translation theory based on the binary oppositions human vs. machine, poetics vs. sign, reflexive vs. non-reflexive that underlie Meschonnic's approach in *Ethics and Politics of Translating*. Are such oppositions viable in practice? What do they mean concretely? And what are their consequences with regards to the development of machine translation? In answer to these questions, I explore the nature of reflexivity in translation through comparison of a series of human and machine translations of Meschonnic's comment about reflexive decision-making in translation. I interrogate the foundations of Meschonnic's definition of reflexivity in terms of an opposition to non-reflexivity, and suggest that a reflexive translation practice must go beyond the antinomy poetics vs. mechanics that guides Meschonnic's thought on translation.

Poetics vs. mechanics

Henri Meschonnic is a relatively unknown figure in the Anglophone world. A French poet, linguist and translator, he is the author of over a dozen texts about translation, only one of which has been translated into English thus far: *Ethics and Politics of Translating*. The main reason for this relative lack of recognition is to be found in Meschonnic's controversial positioning and deliberate isolation throughout his career, especially in opposing influential movements such as hermeneutics, structuralism and deconstruction. In France, Meschonnic is probably best known for his translations of the Old Testament. His key notions of rhythm and continuum (which rely on the use of appositions, alliterations, breaks and other devices aimed at recreating the flow of language) are directly related to his own experience of translating the Bible. For Meschonnic, translation is not just about rendering meaning, but also about reinventing the echo of words, the silences and pauses articulated in speech, the other ways in which meaning is created and conveyed. It is about expressing the physicality of language, its prosodic, consonantal and vocalic patterns.

The premise behind Meschonnic's approach is that the subject's relation to the world and to oneself is always mediated by language. Access to truth is never direct, as thoughts get created in and through language. Language is therefore always a creative activity for Meschonnic. It is an act of *poiesis* in the etymological sense (from the Greek 'to make'). Meschonnic's theory contrasts the creative process at play in poetic translation with non-reflective, mechanical uses of language. Machine translation, a 'translation which is performed wholly or partly by a computer,'[11] is the most obvious example of an unreflective translation practice, according to Meschonnic. In 'Traduire au XXIè siècle', Meschonnic firmly criticises representations of language that rely on the discontinuity signifier-signified of the linguistic sign, which, in his view, have been enforced by the development of automation in the second half of the twentieth century: 'The attempts at machine translation since the end of the Second World war', he explains, 'have contributed to developing a linguistics of translation [based on] the conceptualisation of language in the dualist terms of the sign.'[12] For Meschonnic, the discontinuity signifier-signified characteristic of machine translation constitutes a major obstacle to the advent of a practice based on the continuum of rhythm and poetics.

In Meschonnic's view, translating must go beyond the sign to perform not what the words say but what they do. For Meschonnic, language and life are interactive: 'Since any human relation has to take place through language, a linguistic relation takes on ethical and political dimensions, and since translation links together different linguistic systems, it deepens those dimensions.'[13] His approach is profoundly performative, and his aim, as Alexis Nouss notes in his preface to *Ethics and Politics of Translating*, is to destroy the binary conception of language and its binary organisation into sound and sense.[14] In seeking to do so, however, Meschonnic's theory establishes a new opposition between, on the one hand, automated translation – a mechanical and non-reflective activity, which relies on the 'repetition of pre-existing codes' ('un ânonnement de recettes apprises') – and, on the other hand, human translation – a creative and reflexive practice, which 'necessarily involves a comprehensive theory of language'.

Meschonnic's clear-cut distinction between mechanics and poetics in establishing the inseparability of theory and practice is contradictory and requires further investigation. For if there is no translation practice that is not also reflexive, machine translation should either not be considered a practice in the first place, or the idea that theory and practice cannot be separated only holds true for certain types of translation. In the next section, I put Meschonnic's comment about reflexive decision-making to the test of its own theory by presenting machine translation outputs of his text alongside human translations of it. Using once again the reflexive method deployed in the first two chapters of this book, I question the potency of a reflexive approach defined in opposition to non-reflexivity, mechanicity and discontinuity, while exploring the possibilities of a practice that strives to recognise uncertainty within mechanicity and offers to open the mechanical to the uncertain, regardless of whether it appears in human or in machine translation.

Translating Meschonnic reflexively: examples of human & machine translations

The translations below are based on the following excerpt:

> On peut donc considérer (…) que le problème majeur de la traduction est sa théorie du langage. Ce qui est bien, d'emblée, impliquer deux choses : l'inséparabilité entre ce que l'on appelle une théorie et ce qu'on appelle une pratique, c'est-à-dire qu'une pratique n'est pas une pratique si elle n'est pas réflexive ou réfléchie, ce n'est qu'un ânonnement de recettes apprises, et si elle est cette réflexivité, cette pratique implique nécessairement une théorie d'ensemble du langage ; et réciproquement une théorie de la traduction qui ne serait pas la réflexion d'une pratique ne serait que de la linguistique de la langue appliquée sur du discours, c'est-à-dire de la non-pensée.

Henri Meschonnic, *Éthique et politique du traduire* (Paris: Verdier, 2007), p. 43.

Human and Machine Translations

of

An excerpt from Henri Meschonnic's
Éthique et politique du traduire

We can therefore consider that the major problem of translation is his theory of language. That is, from the outset, involve two things: the inseparability of what is known as a theory and a practice called, that is to say that practice is not a practice if it is not reflective or thoughtful, it is learned that ânonnement of revenue and if it is this reflexivity, this practice necessarily involves a comprehensive theory of language, and conversely a theory of translation would not the reflection of a practice would only the language of the language applied to the discourse, that is to say the non-thinking.

(Google Translate,
1 September 2014)

We can therefore consider that the major problem of translation is his theory of language. That is, from the outset, involve two things: the inseparability of what is known as a theory and a practice called, that is to say that practice is not a practice if it is not reflective or thoughtful, it is learned that ânonnement of revenue and if it is this reflexivity, this practice necessarily involves a comprehensive theory of language, and conversely a theory of translation would not the reflection of a practice would only the language of the language applied to the discourse, that is to say the non-thinking.

(Babelfish,
1 September 2014)

It can therefore be assumed that the major problem of the translation is his theory of language. This is good, from the outset, involve two things: the inseparability between what is called a theory and what is called a practice, that is to say that a practice is not a practice if it is not reflexive or reflected, this is only a ânonnement of revenue learned, and if it is this reflexivity, this practice necessarily implies a theory of all of the language ; and conversely a theory of translation which would not be the reflection of a practice would be that of language of the language applied to the speech, that is to say the non-thinking.

(Dictionary.com,
1 September 2014)

We can therefore consider that the major problem of translation is his theory of language. What is good from the outset involve two things: the inseparability between what is called a theory and a practice called, that is to say that a practice is not practice if it is not reflexive or reflected, this is just droning of recipes learned and if this reflexivity, this practice necessarily imply a general theory of language; and conversely a theory of translation that is not the reflection of a practice would be only linguistic language applied to the speech, that is to say, non-thought.

(Google Translate,
20 January 2015)

We can therefore consider (…) that the main problem of translation is its theory of language. Which really implies two things: the inseparability of what we call theory and what we call practice, which is to say that a practice is not a practice if it is not reflexive or reflected, is but a babble of memorized recipes, and if it is reflexive, this practice necessarily implies an inclusive theory of language; and reciprocally, a theory of translation which would not be the reflection of a practice would merely be a linguistics of langue applied to discourse, that is to say a non-thought.

(Meschonnic 2007/2011: 61; trans. Pier-Pascale Boulanger)

We can therefore consider (…) that the main problem of translation is its theory of language. From the outset, this implies two things: the inseparability of what is known as theory and what is called practice, that is to say that a practice is not a practice if it is not reflective or thoughtful, it is just a hesitant repetition of pre-existing codes (un ânonnement de recettes apprises); but if it is reflective, such practice necessarily involves a comprehensive theory of language; and conversely, a translation theory that is not also a reflection on a particular practice would just be linguistics applied to discourse, that is to say non-thinking.

(Meschonnic 2007: 43; My translation)

The poetics of uncertainty

The limits of certainty

My exploration of Meschonnic's comment about the lack of reflexivity in automation starts with an analysis of its English translation by three online translation tools: Google Translate, Babelfish and Dictionary.com. Below is the result provided by Google Translate on 1 September 2014:

> We can therefore consider that the major problem of translation is **his (1)** theory of language. That is, from the outset, **involve (2)** two things: the inseparability of what is known as a theory and **a practice called (3)**, that is to say that practice is not a practice if it is not reflective or thoughtful, **it is learned that ânonnement (4) of revenue (5)** and if it is this reflexivity, this practice necessarily involves a comprehensive theory of language, and conversely a theory of translation would not **(5)** the reflection of a practice would only **(6)** the language of **the (7)** language applied to **the (8)** discourse, that is to say **the (9)** non-thinking.

As any fluent reader of English will notice immediately upon reading these lines, Google's translation presents several syntactical and lexical problems, which I will use as examples in my attempt to delineate the nature of reflexivity in translational decision-making processes. In (1), the masculine possessive determiner 'his' serves to translate the French word 'sa' in 'sa théorie du langage', instead of the neuter English possessive adjective 'its', which must be used alongside neuter nouns in English. In (2), the verb 'involve' is missing a grammatical subject. In (3), the subject and the complement are inverted ('ce que l'on appelle une pratique' becomes 'a practice called'). In (4), the tool fails to translate the term *ânonnement* into English and chooses to use the French term instead. In (5), the verb 'to be', which appears in the conditional mode in Meschonnic's French text, is omitted by the computer, which only manages to render the mode ('would'). Lastly, in (7), (8) and (9), the definite article 'the' is used incorrectly with English mass nouns such as 'language', 'discourse' and 'non-thinking'.

Each of these errors highlights in its own way the limits of machine translation as a mechanism based on pre-existing terminological correspondences. In the example given above, the machine proves unable to deal with lexical ambiguity (e.g. the polysemy of the term *recettes*), syntactic complexity (e.g. the use of neuter possessive pronouns) and idiomatic singularity (the occurrence of the word ânonnement). Google's mistakes suggest that the limits of a translating activity which is not 'reflective or thoughtful'[15] reside in its impossibility to deal with ambiguity, complexity and singularity.

Judging from the following example, moreover, Google's tool is not the only system to experience such limitations. Indeed, on the same day, Babelfish offered a translation of Meschonnic's comment which was exactly the same as Google's:

> We can therefore consider that the major problem of translation is **his (1)** theory of language. That is, from the outset, **involve (2)** two things: the inseparability of what is known as a theory and **a practice called (3)**, that is to say that practice is not a practice if it is not reflective or thoughtful, **it is learned that ânonnement (4) of revenue (5)** and if it is this reflexivity, this practice necessarily involves a comprehensive theory of language, and conversely a theory of translation would not **(5)** the reflection of a practice would only **(6)** the language of **the (7)** language applied to **the (8)** discourse, that is to say **the (9)** non-thinking.

In addition to highlighting their mechanicity, the perfect identity of the translations provided by Babelfish and Google Translate indicates the difficulty of finding a so-called 'mechanical' practice of translation which does not contain grammatical or lexical errors, even at the most basic level, for in both cases the results obtained are incongruous ('the non-thinking'), incoherent ('his theory of language') or entirely incomprehensible ('it is learned that ânonnement of revenue').

As has been widely acknowledged and discussed by translation scholars,[16] machine translation tends to produce poor-quality results, despite the wide variety of tools available. The following example, which is taken from Dictionary.com, provides additional support for the view that, in the main and for the moment, machine translation seems unable to produce intelligible and adequate texts, regardless of the tool employed:

> <u>It</u> **(1) can therefore** <u>be assumed</u> **(2)** that the major problem of **the (3)** translation is **his (4)** theory of language. This is **good (5)**, from the outset, **involve (6)** two things: the inseparability <u>between</u> what is called a theory and what is called a practice, that is to say that a practice is not a practice if it is not reflexive or <u>reflected</u>, this is only a **ânonnement of revenue** <u>learned</u> **(6)**, and if it is this reflexivity, this

practice necessarily implies a theory of all of **the (7)** language; and conversely a theory of translation which would not be the reflection of a practice would **(8)** be that of language of the **(8)** language applied to the <u>speech</u> **(9)**, that is to say **the (10)** non-thinking.

In this translation, words are underlined when the result given by Dictionary.com differs from the one proposed by Google Translate and Babelfish. We note, for instance, that the personal pronoun 'we' is replaced by 'it' in (1); that a passive voice is used where Google and Babelfish used an active structure in (2); and that 'discours' is translated as 'speech' rather than as 'discourse' in (9). Items in bold indicate grammatical and lexical errors which, like in the translations by Google and Babelfish, impede readability, as well as syntactical and terminological elements which modify the meaning of the source text.

For example, the active construction 'On peut donc considérer que' is replaced by the passive form 'It can therefore be assumed', the French adverb 'bien' is translated as the English adjective 'good', and 'recette' is translated as 'revenue' instead of 'recipe'. The translations provided by Dictionary.com in this passage are not wrong in themselves: the passive formulation 'It can therefore be assumed' is grammatically correct; the term *bien* may indeed be translated as 'good' in some cases; and the equivalent term for 'recette' in an economic context would certainly be 'revenue'. Instead, problems in comprehension arise because of the translation's contextual inadequacy to the source text, because of the system's incapacity to offer an English translation that matches the meaning and/or the construction of the source text, because of its inability to take into account the context in which the utterance takes place. As these examples suggest, reflexivity in translation does not only reside in producing an intelligible text in the target culture, it also relies on the faculty to interpret the source text in context. Thus, the major obstacle to machine translation appears to be the equivocality and context-dependency of language itself, the fact that there may exist several interpretations of any given text and that in any given language an idea may be expressed in multiple ways. From this point of view, reflexivity consists above all in the ability to deal with ambiguity.

According to Basil Hatim and Ian Mason, however, if the limits of automation raise problems of a linguistic order, they do not constitute genuine problems of translation. In their view, the challenges of automation are not translation challenges *per se*, because they are not the product of a genuine decision-making process. This is why, they claim, despite the significant development and improvement of translation tools in the past few decades, the main task of translators remains the same: to decide.[17] Hatim and Mason describe the reflexivity deployed during translation processes as follows:

1. Comprehension of source text:
   a. parsing of text (grammar and lexis)
   b. access to specialised knowledge
   c. access to intended meaning

2. Transfer of meaning:
   a. relaying lexical meaning
   b. relaying grammatical meaning
   c. relaying rhetorical meaning, including implied or inferable meaning, for potential readers.

3. Assessment of target text:
   a. readability
   b. conformity to generic and discoursal TL conventions
   c. judging adequacy of translation for specified purpose.[18]

Deliberately simplified though it is, this list of the faculties at play in a translating task provides a good illustration of the scope of translational decision-making, from the comprehension of the source text to the evaluation of the target text.

Unlike a machine, a human will seek to preclude the grammatical errors or semantic differences that arise during the translating process. For example, it would be very unlikely for a qualified translator to use definite articles with abstract nouns in English, or translate 'recette' as 'revenue' in the context of Meschonnic's comment. On the contrary, a human translation, like the one I propose below, will strive to prevent possible lexical and syntactic mistakes in order to ensure that the translated text is intelligible and that it represents the source text accurately:

> We can therefore consider that the main problem of translation is its theory of language. From the outset, this implies two things: the inseparability of what is known as theory and what is called practice, that is to say that a practice is not a practice if it is not reflective or thoughtful, it is just a hesitant repetition of pre-existing codes [un ânonnement de recettes apprises]; but if it is reflective, such practice necessarily involves a comprehensive theory of language;

and conversely, a translation theory that is not also a reflection on a particular practice would just be linguistics applied to discourse, that is to say non-thinking.[19]

The reflexivity at play in translation goes beyond the capacity to avoid or correct linguistic anomalies. It relies on decision-making – that is, on the aptitude to choose beyond existing propositions. This is demonstrated, for example, in the case of the expression 'ânonnement de recettes apprises', which finds no direct correspondence in English. Being unable to find, like Google Translate, Babelfish and Dictionary.com, an equivalent for the term *ânonnement* in the bilingual dictionaries I consulted,[20] I decided to offer an alternative translation – one which seemed to best represent the idea in English: 'a hesitant repetition of pre-existing codes'. In this framework, then, reflexivity in translation lies in the faculty to choose when no choices are available, the capacity to decide when faced by uncertainty.

Beyond certainty

Meschonnic's criticism of machine translation in *Ethics and Politics of Translating* is emblematic of a wider opposition in translation studies between literary translation and automation. Antoine Berman, for example, distinguishes *la traductologie* (the study of translation centred on linguistics, comparative literature and poetics) from *la traductique*, a new-born discipline which, in the wake of computer science and computer-integrated manufacturing, strives, according to him, to annex translational processes to systems of computation.[21] Even if, as Pier-Pascale Boulanger notes in her introduction to the English version of *Éthique et politique du traduire*, Meschonnic's theory seeks to override 'the traditional opposition that is made between poetry and ordinary language, verse and prose as well as writing and translation',[22] his description of machine translation as a non-reflexive practice corroborates the distinction poetics-mechanics at the centre of Berman's differentiation between *traductologie* and *traductique*.

In translation studies, the opposition human vs. machine is based on the idea that, since automation operates according to fixed rules and pre-established terminological correspondences, machine translation does not require decision-making. However, opposing automated and human translations in these terms does not take into account the fact that the equivalences that make machine translation possible are themselves the product of human decisions. There are currently three types of machine translation (or MT): rule-based MT, statistical MT and hybrid systems.[23] Rule-based MTs generate translation outputs on the basis of syntactic and semantic information retrieved from dictionaries and grammars. Statistical MTs, on the other hand, translate on the basis of statistical models whose parameters are derived from the analysis of bilingual text corpora. Hybrid systems, lastly, combine the properties of rule-based and statistical models.[24] In each case, the machine relies on human decision: with rule-based MT, lexical correspondences and syntactic rules are established by linguists, terminologists and computer scientists; in statistical MT, computation is based on existing human translations; and in hybrid models, the machine combines the linguists' expertise with real-life translation decisions.[25]

Human intervention is therefore omnipresent at each and every stage of machine translation, from selecting the source text and target language to post-editing the results provided by the computer. Furthermore, most automated translation systems deploy a decision-making process which is similar to human translation (selection of terms according to a complex combination of semantic, grammatical and contextual parameters). Not only this, statistical translation systems like Google also translate on the basis of existing human translations so they have, in that sense, the faculty to learn from real-life translational choices.[26] Thus, while in September 2014 Google Translate was unable to find an equivalent for the term *ânonnement*, and proposed to translate 'recipe' as 'revenue', a more recent search (in January 2015) showed that, in the meantime, the machine had 'learned' the signification of the word *ânonnement* ('droning') and that it was now capable of choosing a more relevant translation for the word *recette* ('recipe'):

> We can therefore consider that the major problem of translation is his theory of language. What is good from the outset involve two things: the inseparability between what is called a theory and a practice called, that is to say that a practice is not practice if it is not reflexive or reflected, this is just <u>droning of recipes</u> learned and if this reflexivity, this practice necessarily imply a general theory of language; and conversely a theory of translation that is not the reflection of a practice would be only linguistic language applied to the speech, that is to say, non-thought.

The result given by the machine is still clumsy ('droning of recipes'), but it confirms the tool's capacity to evolve and develop, while highlighting the important role that human translators play in this learning process, since they are the ones who provide the knowledge on which these automated models are based.[27] The fact that human input is so essential to machine translation, and that the interaction between humans and computation is so intricate, suggests that automated translation may not be as unreflective as it first seems – or rather, that what is unreflective and mechanical about it is not to be opposed to human translation, but understood as deriving from it.

Saying that translation is an intrinsically reflexive process presumes that human translation is always the result of a reflective decision-making process. However, as a linguistic operation, human translation itself can never fully escape codification. For it is precisely the codification of linguistic signs that makes translation possible. If, like Meschonnic, Derrida questions a one-dimensional distinction signifier/signified (by showing, for example, that each signified also occupies the position of a signifier),[28] contrary to Meschonnic, he also insists upon the necessity of maintaining this difference without which no practice of translation would be possible:

> nor is it a question of confusing at every level, and in all simplicity, the signifier and the signified. That this opposition or difference cannot be radical or absolute does not prevent it from functioning, and even from being indispensable within certain limits – very wide limits. For example, no translation would be possible without it.[29]

For Derrida, translation is inherent to the concept of sign itself, since in a relation of semiosis a sign always refers to another sign, which functions as its signifier, as its interpretant. The difference between signifier and signified is made possible, not because the signifier refers to a non-linguistic reality, but because 'language accrues, through fairly regulated repetition of signifiers in a general code, certain *instituted* meaning effects'.[30] What establishes the sign as code in Derrida's view is repeatability. It is precisely the codification and repeatability of which linguistic units are capable – their 'iterability', to use Derrida's terminology – that makes translation possible, for a sign or a mark that was not repeatable would not be a sign or a mark in the first place; it would not be an element in a language or a code. This goes for all marks, for marks as such, even if one could be found that had occurred only once. When it was uttered or written as a mark, it was constituted by the fact that it was repeatable, by its iterability.[31] Without the repeatability of linguistic signs in different contexts, translation, as a work of recontextualisation, would be impossible.

As David Bellos points out in *Is That a Fish in Your Ear*, a great deal of human translation relies on codification and repetition. Experienced professional translators who work in a familiar domain, for example, 'know without thinking that certain chunks of text have standard translations that he or she can slot in.'[32] At an even more basic level, Bellos explains, any translator knows that there are some regular transpositions between the two languages she is working with: the French personal pronoun *on*, for example, will almost always require the English sentence to be in the passive. Moreover, translators often develop their own automatisms as they gain more experience (mechanisms which they use to varying degrees depending on their familiarity with the source text, the time allocated to the translation task, etc.). In this respect, they behave like Google Translate, 'scanning their own memories in double-click time for the most probable solution to the issue at hand'.[33] Just like machine translation, human translators rely on the mechanicity of language, on the repeatability of the linguistic sign. And yet, because of its iterability, every sign also goes beyond the codification that makes it possible. The occurrence of a sign in a given context highlights its double status as a code which, because of its possible transposition to a different situation, exceeds the codification that produces it. 'There is *some* machine everywhere, and notably in language', Derrida explains. 'As soon as there is any calculation, calculability, and repetition, there is something of a machine.' However, 'in the machine there is an excess in relation to the machine itself: at once the effect of a machination and something that eludes machinelike calculation'.[34]

What exceeds calculation, for Derrida, is the undecidable – that domain which doesn't pertain to the ordeal of calculability, the event 'which in essence should remain unforeseeable and therefore not programmable'.[35] In translation, the undecidable can erupt anywhere, in human activity as well as in the machine. The treatment of the word *ânonnement* in translating Meschonnic's comment provides a good illustration of this. Its non-translation by Google Translate, for example, signals both the mechanicity of the computing system (its programmability) and the excess of the machine in relation to itself (the fact that not everything can be calculated, that the incalculable is everywhere, including in the machine). Moreover, the tool's capacity to translate a word whose meaning it did not know just a few months earlier shows that every new association of words, every linguistic combination (even one that takes place in or with the machine) is the result of a decision-making process, of something which at a given moment in time resisted mechanicity and programmability. In my translation of

Meschonnic's comment, the untranslatability of the term *ânonnement* (the fact that there exists no lexical unit corresponding to this word in the dictionaries examined) put me face to face with the incalculable, since I could not simply choose among pre-existing translations: I had to create my own translation, my own terminological correspondence. At once challenging and highlighting the codification at play in translation, the word *ânonnement* forced me to generate a new code, to associate 'ânonnement' with 'hesitant repetition'.

In fact, an English translation of Meschonnic's phrase already exists in Pier-Pascale Boulanger's version of *Éthique et politique du traduire*. In her English rendering of Meschonnic's comment, Boulanger translates 'ânonnement' as 'babble' ('a babble of memorized recipes') and, unlike me, she does not use the original French word in brackets to indicate the singularity of Meschonnic's expression. I decided not to follow her translation because 'babble' (defined as 'the confused sound of a group of people talking simultaneously' or 'the continuous murmuring sound of water flowing over stones in a stream')[36] does not convey the paradoxical combination of hesitation and iteration invoked by the term *ânonnement*, which is crucial to my critical reading of Meschonnic's comment. In my version, the word encapsulates the very uncertainty at play in translation – the fact that hesitation is intrinsic to iteration, that repetition itself contains an element of indecision, that regardless of whether it is human or automated, translating involves both mechanical reflexivity and critical reflexiveness, automatisms and creativity.

Towards more uncertainty

In translation, making a decision requires deciding beyond pre-existing options. It means developing new possibilities, creating alternative word associations, uncertainly and hesitantly. According to Derrida, without an experience of uncertainty, there would be no responsible decision. In his view, there is no ethical decision that does not pass through the trials of the 'perhaps', for a decision is responsible only if it exceeds calculability:

> The crucial experience of the *perhaps* imposed by the undecidable – that is to say, the condition of decision – is not a moment to be exceeded, forgotten, or suppressed. It continues to constitute the decision as such; it can never again be separated from it; it produces it *qua* decision *in and through* the undecidable; there is no other decision than this one (...) the instant of decision must remain heterogeneous to all knowledge as such, to all theoretical or

reportive determination, even if it may and must be preceded by all possible science and conscience. The latter are unable to determine the leap of decision without transforming it into the irresponsible application of a programme, hence without depriving it of what makes it a sovereign and free decision – in a word, of what makes it a decision, if there is one.[37]

From this perspective, a responsible translation is one that goes beyond the mechanicity of language, one that is turned towards the unknown. A responsible translation in this view does not merely require *taking* decisions as the French saying goes (choosing among available options) but *making* them (creating new, unprecedented correspondences). This is in fact exactly how Meschonnic himself defines translation. Translating for Meschonnic is an act of creation, a process of transformation, a poetic activity in the etymological sense of the word *poiesis*, 'to make'. However, while Meschonnic perceives creativity as a distinguishing feature of human reflexivity, I argue that it is a possibility integral to any linguistic activity, regardless of whether or not it involves automation.

Every translating act is potentially creative, whether it is literary or mechanical, operated by a human or a machine, since textual signification is always to a certain extent unstable, subject to uncertainty and open to the unknown. 'Even in technical translations, traditionally thought of as the least creative realm of professional translation', Douglas Robinson explains, 'the translator may well profit from a brainstorming technique involving divergent thinking and wild imagination – when faced by a truculent syntactic structure, for example'.[38] As Kathleen Davis further stresses, '[t]he meaning of any text is undecidable, since it is an effect of language and not something that can be extracted and reconstituted. Translators must therefore make decisions in this strong sense'.[39] In my translation, the untranslatability of the word *ânonnement* comes to symbolise the double bind of reflexivity in translation, as simultaneously invoking uncertainty and mechanicity, continuity and discontinuity, repetition and undecidability. The untranslatability of the term *ânonnement* (the fact that there were no English equivalents for this term in the dictionaries consulted) reminds us that even when words are translatable (when correspondences are already established between them in a given language pair), a decision remains to be *made*, since reusing a particular association of words, repeating it in a different context, can itself produce a new meaning, create something novel. In that respect, using automated translation is itself the expression of a decision, for which translators must be made responsible. The main question then is not how to distinguish the automated from the human, the machinelike from the poetic, the sign from rhythm, but how to open the mechanical to the uncertain, regardless of where it appears, in human or machine translation.

The machine is everywhere, in computer programmes as well as in human language; and yet all language, as codified as it may be, exceeds the programmability and calculability that makes its existence possible. All language is haunted by the possible irruption of the unknown. All linguistic decision is marked by the 'crucial experience of the *perhaps* imposed by the undecidable'.[40] This is why, according to Derrida, we must think the undecidable with the machine, not against it.[41] Exploring the unpredictable, the uncertain and the poetic within automation is exactly what Barbara Godard undertakes in her series of machine translations of Apollinaire's poem 'Les Fenêtres'. In *One Poem in Search of a Translator*, Godard uses machine translation tools such as Systran and Promt to explore the idea of the poem as a 'machine', where translation plays a critical role as 'developer' or 'multiplier', generating new poems.[42] Showing that automation works 'with the found materials of language as "ready-made" [...] to fashion new utterances', Godard's experiments draw attention to 'the process of continuous reframing of any translating project', and suggest that machine translation can itself be creative.[43] Staging the mechanicity of the poetic object as well as the machine's potential for creativity, Godard's translations highlight the doubly mechanistic and unpredictable character of automated translation.

Recognising the undecidable and the creative within the machine does not mean negating or rejecting mechanicity altogether. On the contrary, if the decision is that which must remain unforeseeable and non-programmable, in order to accede to the decision we must also 'take programming, the machine, repetition, and calculation into account'.[44] The stakes, from this point of view, are not to know whether translators should be advised to use machine translation or not, but to encourage a responsible practice of computer-assisted translation. Many machine translation tools available online today give the impression that human participation is superfluous.[45] Because they are simple to use, they tend to make users believe that translation can rely entirely on automation, that automation does not require human agency, that it is not traversed by ambiguity and uncertainty. However, ultimately it is the users of these tools who will be held responsible for the translation, since they are the ones who will decide what to do with the computer's results, in which context to reemploy them and/or how to transform them. If a responsible translation requires that we take into account the uncertainty at play in any translation task, how can we encourage a responsible usage of machine translation? How can we prompt users to question the results provided by the machine? And conversely, how can we cultivate uncertainty within the computer itself?

There are no definite answers to these questions. One possibility would be to have automated systems offer several translations of the same text, or to contextualise the use of its key words, or even to indicate the probability of their occurrence in different contexts. A machine that accounts for its own limits and acknowledges the element of uncertainty necessary to its responsible use would not only help professional translators to identify particularly complex translation problems (such as the translation of the word *ânonnement*), but also warn non-professional translators about possible errors and incongruences. Responsible usage of machine translation should also be a primary concern of translator training, according to Dorothy Kenney and Stephen Doherty. In their view, in an industry where professional translators rely increasingly on computer-assisted tools, educating translators who can demonstrate competencies in translation technology is essential.[46] Translators, they explain, must be able to evaluate the results given by the computing system and, when such evaluation is itself automated, be able to analyse the metrics and identify their limits. Furthermore, using online machine translation tools for professional purposes raises thorny ethical and legal questions, since in many cases translators must sign clauses of confidentiality which forbid them to upload originals into public platforms such as Google Translate. Training translators who are aware of these issues is therefore crucial for encouraging a responsible use of machine translation.

Conclusion: from poetics to undecidability

In this chapter, I have shown that in its attempt to undermine binary organisations of language into sound and sense, signifier and signified, continuum and discontinuum, Meschonnic's theory establishes another series of oppositions (human vs. machine, reflexive vs. non-reflexive, poetics vs. sign), which are in turn challenged, deconstructed and rethought in my practice by means of a performative translating approach that mirrors Meschonnic's own description of translation as an 'experimentation field of theories of language'.[47] The main and most urgent objective of Meschonnic's poetics of translating is to give (or give back) to translation its role as a tool for testing language theories and practices.[48] For Meschonnic, translating is an instrument of investigation, a laboratory of research – just as in my practice, I undertake reflexive translations of Meschonnic's comment in order to examine the limits of his critique of mechanicity. My experimentation with machine translation in this chapter both performs and enhances the performative and investigative aspects of Meschonnic's approach to translating, which, in *The Ethics and Politics of Translating*, he summarises as follows: 'The role of theory is to transform practices, the role of practices is to reveal theories.'[49]

Ultimately, my experimentation with Meschonnic's text suggests that a theory that opposes poetics and mechanics in translation is untenable in practice because programmability and reflexivity are both integral parts of human language, which the machine merely extends and reflects. Just like human translation, machine translation contains an element of uncertainty and ambiguity, an excess in relation to its own programmability, epitomised by the term *ânonnement*, the mark of hesitancy within repeatability. An automated translation will be considered responsible if it realises the full extent (and failure) of its own mechanicity – that is, if it accounts for the transgression of the code that it establishes, if it recognises the part of the undecidable at play in its own computability. In other words, a responsible practice of automated translation must account for its own limits as a linguistic operation, which remains inescapably unstable, open and uncertain; it requires that, through its operation, translators experience the impossible certainty of language itself. For if taking reflexivity out of the translation process means depriving translators of their faculty to decide when faced by the undecidable, a responsible practice of machine translation must conversely foster incalculability within the programmable, and recognise uncertainty within the certain.

The question of ethics in translation cannot be posited in terms of a pure opposition between a reflexive, thoughtful practice based on a performative view of language, on the one hand, and a machinelike activity relying on the duality of the linguistic sign, on the other. For performativity itself, as it is defined by Meschonnic (performing what the words do, their sensory effect, rather than what they say, their content), reproduces the binary division of the linguistic sign into form and content – a distinction which, I argue, language can never entirely escape, even (or perhaps even more so) when it attempts to overcome it. Today, machine translation is used across many domains, both professional and non-professional. And yet, not everyone is aware of the shortfalls and imperfections of the tools available. Inexperienced users are often oblivious to the fact that, behind the appearance of certainty, the results provided by the machine will necessarily require human decision-making, and that they (as users) are responsible for endorsing these results. Current machine-translation systems would certainly benefit from taking into consideration the elements of uncertainty at play in their mode of operation. Conversely, translation theory would surely profit from being more mindful of automation when thinking about translation, and of the undecidability at work in any translation task, regardless of whether or not it involves machine translation.

Notes

1   Jacques Derrida, *For What Tomorrow… A Dialogue*, trans. Jeff Fort (Stanford: Stanford University Press, 2001/2004), 48.
2   Henri Meschonnic, *Éthique et politique du traduire* (Paris: Verdier, 2007).
3   Henri Meschonnic, *Critique du rythme* (Paris: Verdier, 1982).
4   Henri Meschonnic, *Poétique du traduire* (Paris: Verdier, 1999).
5   Meschonnic, *Éthique et politique du traduire*, 43.
6   Meschonnic, *Éthique et politique du traduire*, 43 (my translation).
7   John D. Caputo, *Deconstruction in a Nutshell: A Conversation with Jacques Derrida* (New York: Fordham University Press, 1997), 137.
8   Jacques Derrida, 'Signature Event Context', in *Limited Inc.*, trans. Samuel Weber (Evanston: Northwestern University Press, 1972/1988), 122.
9   Caputo, *Deconstruction in a Nutshell*, 137.
10 Jacques Derrida, 'Force of Law: The "Mystical Foundation of Authority"', in *Deconstruction and the Possibility of Justice* (New York: Routledge, 1992), 24.
11 Marc Shuttleworth and Moira Cowie, *Dictionary of Translation Studies* (Manchester: St. Jerome, 1997), 99.
12 Henri Meschonnic, 'Traduire au XXIè siècle', *Quaderns: Revista de traducció* 15 (2008): 59 (my translation).
13 Alexis Nouss, 'Preface', in Henri Meschonnic, *Ethics and Politics of Translating* (Amsterdam and Philadelphia: John Benjamins, 2011), 8.
14 Nouss, 'Preface', 5.
15 Meschonnic, *Éthique et politique du traduire*, 43 (my translation).
16 For example:
    – Doug Arnold, 'Why Translation is Difficult for Computers', in *Computers and Translation: A Translator's Guide*, ed. Harold Somers (Amsterdam and Philadelphia: John Benjamins, 2003), 119–142.
    – John Hutchins, 'Multiple Uses of Machine Translation and Computerised Translation Tools', *International Symposium on Data and Sense Mining, Machine Translation and Controlled Languages–ISMTCL*, 2009.
    – Mikel L. Forcada, 'Machine Translation Today', in *Handbook of Translation Studies*, Volume 1, ed. Yves Gambier and Luc Van Doorslaer (Amsterdam and Philadelphia: John Benjamins, 2010), 215–223.
17 Basil Hatim and Ian Mason, *Discourse and the Translator* (London: Longman, 1990), 23.
18 Hatim and Mason, *Discourse and the Translator*, 21.
19 Meschonnic, *Éthique et politique du traduire*, 43.
20 – *Collins French Dictionary*, accessed 1 September 2014, http://www.collinsdictionary.com/dictionary/english-french.
    – *Oxford French Dictionary*, accessed 1 September 2014, http://www.oxforddictionaries.com/translate/french-english.
    – *Larousse Français-Anglais*, accessed 1 September 2014, http://www.larousse.fr/dictionnaires/anglais-francais.
21 Antoine Berman, *La traduction et la lettre, ou L'auberge du lointain* (Paris: Seuil, 1999), 17.
22 Pier-Pascale Boulanger, 'Introduction', in Henri Meschonnic, *Ethics and Politics of Translating* (Amsterdam and Philadelphia: John Benjamins, 2011), 14.
23 Dorothy Kenny and Stephen Doherty, 'Statistical Machine Translation in the Translation Curriculum: Overcoming Obstacles and Empowering Translators', *The Interpreter and Translator Trainer* 8, no. 2 (2014): 276.
24 Philipp Koehn, *Statistical Machine Translation* (Cambridge: Cambridge University Press, 2010), 314.
25 Forcada, 'Machine Translation Today', 220.
26 Kenny and Doherty, 'Statistical Machine Translation in the Translation Curriculum: Overcoming Obstacles and Empowering Translators', 278.
27 Andy Way and Mary Hearne, 'On the Role of Translations in State-of-the-Art Statistical Machine Translation', *Language and Linguistics Compass* 5, no. 5 (2011): 238.
28 To illustrate this point, Geoffrey Bennington gives the example of the dictionary: 'Look up the signified of an unknown signifier in the dictionary and you find more signifiers, never any signifieds' (Bennington and Derrida 1991/1999: 33).

29 Derrida, 'Signature Event Context', 19.
30 Kathleen Davis, *Deconstruction and Translation* (Oxford and New York: Routledge, 2014), 23.
31 Derrida, 'Signature Event Context', 7.
32 David Bellos, *Is That A Fish in your Ear?* (London: Penguin, 2011), 266.
33 Bellos, *Is That A Fish in your Ear?*, 266.
34 Derrida, *For What Tomorrow...* 49.
35 Derrida, *For What Tomorrow...* 49.
36 *Oxford English Dictionary* (Oxford: Oxford University Press, 2011).
37 Jacques Derrida, *Politics of Friendship*, trans. George Collins (London and New York: Verso, 1994/2005), 219.
38 Douglas Robinson, '22 Theses on Translation', *Journal of Translation Studies* 2 (1998): 100.
39 Davis, *Deconstruction and Translation*, 51.
40 Derrida, *Politics of Friendship*, 219.
41 Jacques Derrida, 'Above All, No Journalists!', trans. Samuel Weber, in *Religion and Media*, ed. Hent de Vries and Samuel Weber (Stanford: Stanford University Press, 2001), 87.
42 Barbara Godard, '"Windows" and "Fenêtres"', in *One Poem in Search of a Translator: Rewriting 'Les Fenêtres' by Apollinaire*, ed. Eugenia Loffredo and Manuela Perteghella (Oxford: Peter Lang, 2009), 207.
43 Godard, '"Windows" and "Fenêtres"', 208.
44 Derrida, *For What Tomorrow...* 49.
45 Kenny and Doherty, 'Statistical Machine Translation in the Translation Curriculum: Overcoming Obstacles and Empowering Translators', 288.
46 Kenny and Doherty, 'Statistical Machine Translation in the Translation Curriculum: Overcoming Obstacles and Empowering Translators', 276.
47 Meschonnic, *Ethics and Politics of Translating*, 49.
48 Meschonnic, *Ethics and Politics of Translating*, 120.
49 Meschonnic, *Ethics and Politics of Translating*, 64.

Chapter 4
Criticism and Self-Reflection
Antoine Berman's disciplinary reflexivity

The response to the question, 'Why is error, illusion, immanent to truth? Why does truth arise through mistakes?', is therefore quite simply: *because substance is already subject*. Substance is always already subjectivized: substantial Truth coincides with its very progression through 'subjective' illusions. At this point, another response to the question 'Why is error immanent to the truth?' emerges: *because there is no metalanguage*. The idea that one is able from the outset to account for error, to take it under consideration *as error*, and therefore to take one's distance from it, is precisely the supreme error of the existence of metalanguage, the illusion that, while taking part in illusion, one is somehow also able to observe the process from an 'objective' distance. By avoiding identifying oneself with error, we commit the supreme error and miss the truth, because the place of truth itself is only constituted through error.

Slavoj Žižek[1]

This chapter examines Antoine Berman's approach to reflexivity in translation. In Berman's theory, developed throughout half a dozen texts including *L'épreuve de l'étranger*,[2] 'La traduction comme épreuve de l'étranger'[3] and *Pour une critique des traductions*,[4] reflexivity in translation is conceived as a form of criticism. Himself a translator of literary texts (from German and Spanish into French), Berman perceives translation primarily as a critical activity. For him, translating is a process through which a literary work is analysed and judged. Reflexivity in this view refers to the translator's reflection and judgment on the original work, to the role of translation as a metatext, to its function as a text commenting another text. Through this act of criticism, the translated text makes visible hidden or latent aspects of the original, according to Berman, and as such it fulfils the ethical aim of translation, which, he argues, is to be 'an opening, a dialogue'.[5]

The type of reflexivity invoked by Berman's theory is *reflexive objectivation*, a critical revaluation of what members of a given field take for granted. This is why retranslation occupies such a central role in his theory. Retranslating is ethical for Berman because it not only involves reflecting upon a literary piece and thinking on the basis of that text, but also requires positioning oneself in relation to its previous translation(s) and glossing the choices involved through the prism of the translator's own decisions. In this respect, Berman's approach goes beyond establishing a purely analogical relation between translation and criticism. In Berman's view, like in the reflexive method deployed in this book, the critical nature of translational reflexivity is realised in the process of translating itself. However, while Berman's theory establishes a hierarchy between first translations and retranslations, the reflexive method adopted in my experimental translations of his work shows that any translating task involves positioning.

Berman's theorisation of translation as a form of criticism combines the various facets of reflexivity discussed so far in this monograph: the question of visibility (Lawrence Venuti), translation as a form of dialogue (Susan Bassnett), and metatextuality (Henri Meschonnic). Like each of these theorists, Berman insists on the need for increased self-awareness in translation. In the opening paragraph of *L'épreuve de l'étranger*, for example, he explains:

> The domain of translation has always been the site of a curious contradiction. On the one hand, translation is considered to be a purely intuitive practice – in part technical, in part literary – which, at bottom, does not require any specific theory or form of reflection. On the other hand, there has been – at least since Cicero, Horace, and Saint Jerome – an abundance of writings on translation of a religious, philosophical, literary, methodological or, more recently, scientific nature. Now, though numerous translators have written on their discipline, it is undeniable that until recently the bulk of these writings has come from non-translators. The definition of the 'problems' of translation has been undertaken by theologians, philosophers, linguists, or critics. This has had at least three consequences. First, translation has remained an underground, hidden activity because it did not express itself independently. Second, translation as such has largely remained 'unthought', because those who dealt with it tended to assimilate it to something else: (sub-)literature, (sub-)criticism, 'applied linguistics'. Finally, the analyses produced almost exclusively by non-translators, whatever their qualities may be, inevitably contain numerous 'blind spots' and irrelevancies.[6]

For Berman, a reflexive study of translation is essential to an ethical translation practice. Reflection on translation has become, he argues, '*an internal necessity* of translation itself'.[7] This reflexivity in response to the discipline, and at its heart, acquires a psychoanalytic dimension in his theory, as we shall see, and becomes the very condition for overcoming the ethnocentric violence at play in translation.

In the following pages, I explore the scope and significance of Berman's claim about the ethical necessity for reflexivity through an analysis of his main theoretical works, an inspection of their English translations, and a discussion of my own experience of back-translating these texts into French. Can reflexivity guarantee ethics in translation? If so, what would such reflexivity need to entail? And to what extent could it be systematised? My inquiry into reflexivity in this chapter draws a parallel between the productive criticism proposed by Berman and the reflexive method engaged in translating Berman. I start by providing a brief summary of Berman's thought on translation, before presenting my critical translations of excerpts from English versions of his works, *The Experience of The Foreign*, 'Translation and the Trials of the Foreign'[8] and *Toward a Translation Criticism*.[9] I then offer an analysis of my back-translations, suggesting that in Berman's theory reflexivity is in fact inseparable from self-reflexivity.

Reflexive criticism

Antoine Berman's approach to reflexivity in translation is rooted in the belief that it is no longer possible to practise translation without reflecting on it.[10] For him, the proliferation of theoretical texts on translation in the twentieth century indicates the will and need for translation to become an autonomous, reflective practice. Reflexivity, in Berman's view, is not so much a matter of visibility, in the sense championed by Lawrence Venuti, but rather an operation of reflection and self-reflection. As Françoise Massardier-Kenney puts it in the introduction to her translation of *Pour une critique des traductions,* 'the premise of *Toward a Translation Criticism* is that translation has reached a stage at which it aspires to be more than a practice'.[11] It is ready 'to reflect on the translation experience itself, to think about translation in a way that combines theoretical considerations with the experience of translation'.[12]

Based on an analytical criticism of translations – which bears a close resemblance to the critical work at play in translation research in general, and in the reflexive method in particular – the new form of commentary

Berman advocates would give access, he claims, both 'to the language of the original – to the way in which poetry and thought are deployed – and to the actual *work* of translation [...] that becomes commentary of the original (of its letter) and analysis of its translation (of the way in which the letter of the original was transmitted)'.[13] Insisting upon the need to bring closer together the discourse on translation and the work of translation itself, Berman's approach suggests that translation ethics are not realisable without a reflexive analysis of practical translations.

Reflecting on the act of translating is crucial for Berman. Translation needs to be thought reflexively through an interpretative reading of texts because criticism and translation are structurally related: 'Whether he feeds on critical works or not to translate such-and-such book, the translator acts like a critic at all levels.'[14] Like criticism, translation is a form of reading, a way of commenting on the original work which reveals its hidden side (*son versant caché*). In Berman's view, one 'has never really analysed a text before translating it'.[15] When translation is a retranslation, it further becomes a criticism of previous translations: it functions both as a *developer*, in the photographic sense of making the image visible (highlighting the historicity of translations), and as an evaluative analysis (showing that previous versions are either deficient or obsolete) – two aspects which, according to Berman, lie at the heart of the duality of any critical act.

Translation constitutes an analytical operation, in the psychoanalytic sense, for Berman. In *L'épreuve de l'étranger*, Berman opposes the impulse (or drive) of translation, 'that species of narcissism by which every society wants to be a pure and unadulterated whole', with the ethical aim of translation, its essence, which is to be 'an opening, a dialogue, a cross-breeding, a decentering'.[16] By extending the original and revealing its hidden potential, criticism would contribute, according to Berman, to realising translation's essence as opening, and thus fulfil its ethical purpose. Since translation is itself perceived as a critical activity by Berman, '[t]he criticism of a translation is thus that of a text that itself results from a work of a critical nature'.[17] As criticism of criticism, translation criticism would effect the ethical aim of translation by allowing it to gain access to its own being as opening, as dialogue and as *mise en rapport*.[18] According to Berman, the meta-critical process at play in translation criticism enables a form of reflexivity that questions existing assumptions about translation and accomplishes its ethical nature.

Framing my own reflexive approach as a response to Berman's call for productive criticism, in the following pages I undertake back-translations of selected passages from some of Berman's most influential writings to inquire into his characterisation of translation as opening and dialogue. The sample translations I present in the next section, which are taken from *The Experience of the Foreign*, 'Translation and the Trials of the Foreign' and *Toward a Translation Criticism*, exemplify the challenges of an ethics of translation based on self-awareness, as defined by Berman in these works. Far from fostering an opening to the other, I suggest, Berman's theorisation of reflexivity rather instigates a return to oneself. My translations question the possibility of an ethics of translation based on reflexivity, where reflexive thinking is understood as increased self-knowledge or heightened self-awareness. In exploring the contradictions of Berman's theory, these retranslations also highlight the limits of the reflexive method itself, as a possible application of Berman's concept of productive criticism.

Back-translating Berman into French: example of a productive retranslation

The following critical translations/commentaries are based on excerpts from:

Antoine Berman, *The Experience of the Foreign*, translated by *Stefan Heyvaert*, © 1992, reproduced by permission of SUNY Press.

Antoine Berman, 'Translation and the Trials of the Foreign', in *The Translation Studies Reader*, edited and translated by Lawrence Venuti (London and New York: Routledge, 2004).

Antoine Berman, *Toward a Translation Criticism*, translated by Françoise Massardier-Kenney (Kent: Kent State University Press, 2009).

L'expérience de l'Autre
ou le jugement de l'étranger :
vers une critique des traductions

Les extraits ci-dessous sont tirés des traductions en langue anglaise de plusieurs textes d'Antoine Berman: la traduction de L'épreuve de l'étranger *(1984) par Stefan Heyvaert intitulée* The Experience of the Foreign *(1992), une traduction de l'essai « La traduction comme épreuve de l'étranger » (1985) par Lawrence Venuti qu'il intitule « Translation and the*

Trials of the Foreign » (2000) et la traduction par Françoise Massardier-Kenney de Pour une critique des traductions *(1995), qu'elle traduit par* Toward a Translation Criticism *(2009).*

Ces fragments ont été sélectionnés sur la base de leur pertinence pour l'étude du concept de réflexivité dans la théorie de la traduction chez Berman. Ils ont été retraduits en français en s'inspirant des principes développés par Berman lui-même dans ses écrits, à savoir la traduction littérale, l'analytique traductologique et la critique productive des traductions.

Les concepts centraux de l'œuvre de Berman sont traduits ici sur plusieurs niveaux. Tout d'abord, ces traductions sont conçues comme une mise en pratique directe de la théorie bermanienne et des questionnements qu'elle soulève. La réflexivité y est donc avant tout abordée comme mise en application des principes de littéralité, d'analytique et de critique des traductions. D'autre part, ces extraits sont des retraductions vers le français de textes anglais eux-mêmes traduits à partir du français. Ils déploient par-là un mouvement circulaire réflexif qui consiste à replier les textes de Berman sur eux-mêmes. En tant que traductions de traductions, ces versions fonctionnent comme des doubles des textes originaux, dont ils visent à manifester d'« autres versants ». Il s'agit enfin de penser la notion de réflexivité par-delà la singularité des langues en question, c'est-à-dire au niveau de la réflexivité du langage au sens large, à travers des traductions commentées qui miroitent l'approche analytique proposée par Berman.

Cette démarche se veut plurielle, à commencer par le titre choisi qui reflète non seulement la multiplicité des textes sources mais aussi la variété des interprétations possibles.

Dans les pages qui suivent, les voix de Berman, de ses traducteurs et de ses commentateurs sont délibérément assemblées de façon polyphonique.

A.   L'expérience de l'Autre

Les extraits qui suivent apparaissent dans le préambule de Berman à L'épreuve de l'étranger.

*Ils ont été traduits à partir de la traduction de Stefan Heyvaert (*The Experience of the Foreign*), dont une partie de mon titre (*L'expérience de l'Autre*) s'inspire. La formulation de Heyvaert, reprise dans ma traduction, met en lumière une ambivalence cruciale dans l'œuvre de Berman : la* question du point de vue. En effet, de quelle expérience parle-t-on lorsque l'on dit l'expérience de l'étranger ? De mon expérience de l'Autre et de son altérité ? Ou bien de l'expérience éprouvée par un autre, cet autre pour qui l'Autre, c'est moi ? La question reste ouverte. Les réponses sont multiples.

Dans la traduction qui suit, les mots du texte de Berman et de Heyvaert ont été ajoutés entre parenthèses pour signaler non seulement les différences principales entre l'original, sa traduction et/ou ma propre version, mais aussi pour souligner leurs ressemblances, en particulier lorsque cette similitude peut sembler inattendue.

Par ailleurs, les notes de bas de page ont été insérées afin de clarifier certains aspects de l'œuvre de Berman, mettre en lumière les principaux choix de Heyvaert ou expliquer mes propres décisions en réaction à ces deux textes.

La traduction manifeste

Ainsi s'ouvre L'épreuve de l'étranger.

Le titre dans le texte original de Berman est « La traduction au manifeste ». Il évoque l'idée d'un mouvement à travers l'article contracté « au », qui suggère le passage d'une pratique concrète de la traduction à l'élaboration d'une théorie de cette activité. « Un manifeste » désigne un « exposé théorique » présentant les fondements conceptuels d'un mouvement ou d'une activité. Une autre reformulation possible du titre d'origine serait : « Vers une théorisation de l'acte traductif ». Car c'est bien de cela dont il s'agit dans cette introduction pour Berman : souligner la nécessité d'une réflexion sur l'acte du traduire qui aille au-delà de ses expériences singulières.

En anglais, Stefan Heyvaert choisit de traduire ce titre par : « The manifestation of translation ». « Manifestation » en anglais fait référence à « un évènement, une action, ou un objet qui montre de manière concrète quelque chose d'abstrait ou théorique » (OED 2011; ma traduction). Autrement dit, « the manifestation of translation » serait l'acte par lequel certains aspects de la traduction, considérés comme abstraits, théoriques ou dissimulés, deviendraient visibles, concrets, manifestes. La traduction de Heyvaert dénote une interprétation psychanalytique du titre original de Berman : manifestation comme symptôme, comme expression d'autres aspects du texte, comme réflexion de ses versants refoulés.

Les choix de ces titres ne sont pas anodins. Ils reflètent la démarche singulière propre à chacun des deux auteurs dans le cadre de leur projet respectif.

Dans ce texte, Berman part de traductions réelles (celles des Romantiques allemands) en vue d'élaborer une théorie de la traduction comme épreuve de l'étranger. Heyvaert, quant à lui, prend pour point de départ la pensée de Berman, qu'il cherche, par l'acte de traduction, à communiquer dans un contexte anglophone. Ainsi, le projet de Berman s'inscrit dans une démarche théorisante de la traduction en tant que produit, texte, œuvre culturelle – tandis que l'approche de Heyvaert est celle d'un traducteur qui, en s'efforçant de reconstruire le discours de Berman dans une autre langue, dévoile en même temps sa propre expérience de la traduction comme processus analytique.

Mon choix « la traduction manifeste » se situe dans ce va-et-vient entre la démarche théorisante de Berman (La traduction au manifeste ») et l'approche analytique de Heyvaert (« La manifestation de la traduction »). Dans « la traduction manifeste », la traduction rend visible, manifeste, comme chez Heyvaert, mais elle le fait de manière active : elle devient agent de l'action de manifester. L'accent est mis sur le processus de mise en lumière lui-même (la traduction comme acte de manifester), plutôt que sur le résultat (la traduction comme symptôme d'autre chose). L'absence de complément d'objet souligne par ailleurs la multiplicité des objets possibles (que manifeste-t-elle ?), tandis que la formulation nominative de Heyvaert (« the manifestation ») n'autorise pas cette pluralité.

« La traduction manifeste » est très proche du titre original de Berman (« La traduction au manifeste »). Cependant, l'idée de mouvement du pratique vers le théorique qu'évoque ce dernier disparaît avec l'effacement du « au ». De ce fait, la temporalité du devenir (sous-entendue dans la formulation « [de] la traduction [jusqu'] au manifeste ») est remplacée par celle de la simultanéité (le présent de l'indicatif). Ce synchronisme c'est celui de la théorie et de la pratique, leur inséparabilité. Le passage du pratique vers le théorique que Berman cherche à théoriser dans L'épreuve de l'étranger, fait ainsi place, dans ma traduction, à un processus de concomitance : pratique et théorie sont indissociables. La traduction manifeste. La pratique théorise.

Dans ce sens, la traduction manifeste également en termes de « résistance » : elle résiste à la reproduction aussi bien de l'original que de sa traduction. Elle va au-delà de l'original de Berman puisqu'elle remplace le devenir par la simultanéité. Et elle conteste la version de Heyvaert car la traduction y est comprise comme réflexion plutôt que comme révélateur de l'original. Dans « la traduction manifeste », les symptômes ne préexistent pas à l'acte du traduire, ils sont créés à travers le processus traductif lui-même. Ma *traduction manifeste certains aspects du texte original bermanien et de la traduction de Heyvaert, non pas en rendant visibles leurs versants cachés, mais en choisissant d'en actualiser certains aspects.*

Le domaine de la traduction a toujours été le site d'étranges [*curious*, curieuses][1] contradictions. D'un côté, la traduction est considérée comme une pratique purement intuitive – en partie technique, en partie littéraire – qui, au fond, ne requiert pas une théorie ou une réflexion particulières. De l'autre, il existe – au moins depuis Cicéron, Horace et Saint Jérôme – une abondance de textes [*writings*, écrits] qui traitent de la traduction d'un point vue religieux, philosophique, littéraire, méthodologique et, enfin, scientifique. Or, bien que de nombreux traducteurs commentent leur activité [*discipline*, métier], jusqu'à récemment la majorité de ces écrits provenait de non-traducteurs. La définition [*definition*, définition] des « problèmes » de la traduction est ainsi l'œuvre des théologiens, des philosophes, des linguistes et des critiques. Ceci a au moins trois conséquences. D'abord, la traduction est restée une activité souterraine, cachée, car elle ne s'exprimait pas de manière autonome [*did not express itself independently*, ne s'énonçait pas elle-même]. Par ailleurs, la traduction en tant que telle demeure largement « impensée » (*unthought*, « impensée comme telle ») car ceux qui s'y intéressent jusqu'à présent ont tendance à l'assimiler à autre chose : à de la (sous-)littérature, à de la (sous-)critique, à de la « linguistique appliquée ». Enfin, les analyses produites quasi-exclusivement [*exclusively*, fatalement] par des non-traducteurs, indépendamment de leurs qualités, contiennent inévitablement des « angles morts » et des éléments inadéquats [*irrelevant*, non pertinents].

Notre siècle a connu un changement progressif et la constitution d'un vaste corpus de textes de traducteurs.[2] De plus, la réflexion sur la traduction est devenue une *nécessité interne* de la traduction même, comme cela avait été en partie le cas dans l'Allemagne classique et romantique. Cette réflexion ne prend pas exactement la forme [*form*, visage] d'une « théorie », telle qu'on la trouve dans *Sous l'invocation de saint Jérôme* par Valery Larbaud. Mais elle indique en tout cas la volonté qu'a la traduction de devenir une

---

[1] Dans le texte de départ comme dans la traduction, Berman et Heyvaert utilisent respectivement les mots « curieux » et « curious » pour qualifier les contradictions qui sous-tendent la pratique de la traduction. J'ai choisi pour ma part d'employer le terme « étranges » qui fait écho et rappelle le concept d'« étranger », central à la traductologie bermanienne.

[2] Dans le texte original de Berman, le terme « corpus » est mis en italiques. Cette emphase disparaît dans la traduction de Heyvaert.

pratique autonome, capable de se définir et de se situer soi-même, et par conséquent de se communiquer, de se partager et de s'enseigner.[3]

Une condition ancillaire

Notre préoccupation est de savoir ce que la traduction signifie dans le contexte culturel actuel. Cette question s'accompagne d'un problème d'une intensité presque douloureuse. Je fais référence ici à quelque chose qu'on ne peut pas ne pas mentionner – la condition obscure, refoulée, interdite [*reprieved*, réprouvée] et *ancillaire* de la traduction, qui se répercute [*reflects upon*, répercute] sur la condition du traducteur de sorte qu'il est impossible de nos jours de faire de cette pratique une discipline autonome.

La condition de la traduction est non seulement ancillaire ; elle est, aux yeux du public et aux yeux des traducteurs eux-mêmes, suspecte [*suspect*, suspecte]. Après tant de réussites, de chefs-d'œuvre, de soi-disant impossibilités vaincues, comment l'adage italien *traduttore tradittore* peut-il encore servir de [*still remain in place*, encore fonctionner comme] jugement dernier sur la traduction? Pourtant il est vrai que dans ce domaine, la fidélité et la trahison font constamment l'objet de débats [*are at issue*, il est sans cesse question de...]. « Traduire, écrivait Franz Rosenzweig, c'est servir deux maîtres » : ainsi va la métaphore ancillaire. Il s'agit de servir l'œuvre, l'auteur, la langue étrangère (premier maître), mais aussi le public et sa propre langue (second maître). Ceci constitue ce qu'on peut appeler le drame du traducteur. (...)

Le temps est venu de méditer ce refoulement [*repression*, statut refoulé] de la traduction et les « résistances » qui le sous-tendent. Le problème peut se formuler ainsi[4] : toute culture résiste à la traduction, même si elle en a fondamentalement besoin [*even if it has an essential need for it*,

---

[3] La structure passive employée dans la traduction anglaise n'est pas présente dans l'original. Elle reflète la lecture psychanalytique de Heyvaert : la traduction est personnifiée, elle possède une volonté, un désir, un pouvoir, mais elle devient passive, comme si « ça » parlait à travers elle. Cette passivité va toutefois à l'encontre de l'autonomisation que Berman cherche à attribuer à la traduction dans ce texte, à savoir « la volonté dont fait preuve la traduction de devenir une pratique autonome, capable de se définir et de se situer soi-même, et par conséquent de se communiquer, de se partager et s'enseigner. » L'emploi de pronoms et de verbes réflexifs n'y est pas anodin : il s'agit d'amorcer une autonomisation de la traduction par la réflexivité.

[4] Ici l'emploi du réflexif impersonnel « se formuler », qui s'éloigne de la traduction de Heyvaert (« We may formulate »), vise à rendre compte de la dimension psychanalytique de la question, puisqu'il s'agit d'exprimer le refoulé, de dire ce qui ne peut être dit, d'énoncer ce qui ne veut pas être énoncé. Le texte de Berman se situe entre la version de Heyvaert et la mienne ; il s'appuie sur une formule impersonnelle mais n'emploie pas le réflexif (« Ce que l'on pourrait formuler ainsi »).

même si elle a besoin essentiellement de celle-ci]. La *visée* [*aim*, visée][5] même de la traduction – ouvrir à travers l'écriture un certain rapport à l'Autre, pour féconder ce qui est Propre [*what is one's Own* ; le Propre] par la médiation de ce qui est Étranger [*what is Foreign* ; l'Étranger][6] – s'oppose à la structure ethnocentrique de toute culture[7], cette espèce de narcissisme qui pousse chaque société à vouloir être un Tout pur et non mélangé. La traduction porte une trace de la violence du métissage.[8] Herder en était bien conscient [*well aware of*, l'a bien senti] lorsqu'il comparait une langue qui n'a pas encore traduit, ou une langue qui n'a jamais été traduite, à une jeune vierge.[9] Peu importe qu'une langue et une culture vierges soient en réalité aussi fictives qu'une race pure. Nous avons affaire ici à des traits inconscients [*wishes*, souhaits]. Chaque culture se veut [*wants*, voudrait être] auto-suffisante et utilise cette auto-suffisance imaginaire pour briller sur les autres et s'approprier leur patrimoine. La culture romaine antique, la culture française classique et la culture nord-américaine moderne en sont des exemples frappants.

[5] J'ai choisi de traduire « aim » par « visée » (plutôt que par « but » ou « objectif ») car « visée » se rapproche plus de l'idée de quête, d'idéal, élaborée par Berman. Notons par ailleurs l'absence d'italiques dans le texte anglais pour « aim ». L'emphase originale de Berman, effacée en anglais, est rétablie dans ma version.

[6] L'approche de Heyvaert diffère de celle de Berman. Dans la version de Heyvaert (« what is Foreign/one's Own »), l'Etranger et le Propre sont définis dans leur rapport au sujet, et non pas dans l'absolu. Berman, quant à lui, emploie une formulation plus abstraite : il parle « du » Propre et « de l' » Etranger. Chez Berman ce sont « le Propre » et « l'Etranger » universels. En ce qui me concerne, j'ai décidé de suivre la version de Heyvaert pour souligner la contingence de ces deux catégories, qui ne peuvent exister que du point de vue d'un sujet historique. Car si l'on admet que la visée de la traduction est d'ouvrir un certain rapport à l'Autre, la question est aussi de savoir comment définir le « Propre », par rapport à qui et par rapport à quoi.

[7] Heyvaert emploie à nouveau une forme passive (« is opposed »), là où Berman utilise une tournure active (« heurte de front »). Pour ma part, j'ai opté pour un réflexif (« s'oppose ») pour mettre en scène l'autonomisation réflexive recherchée par Berman.

[8] Dans ma version la traduction devient le sujet grammatical de la phrase : c'est elle qui porte la « trace de violence du métissage », contrairement aux formulations passives de l'original (« il y a ») et de la traduction américaine (« there is »). Par ailleurs, mon emploi du mot « trace » est inspiré de la formulation de Heyvaert (« a tinge of violence »), qui est plus spécifique que celle de Berman (« quelque chose de la violence ») et évoque l'image d'une cicatrice – symbole de l'impossibilité d'une culture à être « un Tour pur et non mélangé ».

[9] Remarquons ici une différence majeure entre Berman et Heyvaert. Dans ce passage, Berman fait référence à une analogie de Herder, comparant « une langue qui n'a pas encore traduit », c'est-à-dire une langue qui n'a jamais entrepris une activité traduisante, à une jeune vierge. Cette idée de culture ou langue « vierge » que Berman qualifie aussitôt de « fictive » est difficile à cerner et conduit à un contresens chez Heyvaert qui la traduit par son contraire : « une langue qui n'a jamais été traduite ». Ainsi, la « langue qui n'a pas encore traduit » se transforme en « langue qui n'a jamais été traduite ». Cette inversion est intéressante car elle reflète non seulement l'ambiguïté de ce concept purement imaginaire de langue qui n'a jamais traduit, mais aussi parce qu'elle met en lumière la question de point de vue qui sous-tend les oppositions binaires propre/étranger, soi/autre, langue traduisante/langue traduite qui régissent la théorie bermanienne. En inversant la dynamique proposée par Berman, la traduction de Heyvaert révèle, sans doute involontairement, à la fois le parti pris de Berman et son propre positionnement. Dans ma version, j'ai choisi de conserver les deux pôles proposés par Berman et Heyvaert afin de rendre compte de cette pluralité de points de vue.

Pourtant la traduction occupe une position ambiguë. D'une part elle se soumet à cette injonction appropriatrice et réductrice, elle se constitue comme l'un de ses agents. Ce qui produit des traductions ethnocentriques, ou ce que l'on appelle de « mauvaises » traductions. Mais d'autre part, la *visée éthique* du traduire est par nature contraire à cette injonction [emphase originale][10] : l'essence de la traduction est d'être une ouverture, un dialogue, un croisement [*cross-breeding*, métissage][11], un décentrement. La traduction est « une mise en rapport », ou elle n'est *rien* [emphase originale].[12]

Cette contradiction entre la visée réductrice de la culture et la visée éthique du traduire se retrouve à tous les niveaux – au niveau des théories et des méthodes de traduction (comme, par exemple, dans l'opposition perpétuelle [*perennial*, sempiternelle] entre les défenseurs de la « lettre » et

[10] J'ai retranscrit la tournure passive de l'anglais de Heyvaert, plutôt que la version active de Berman, car l'emploi du verbe d'état « être » préfigure l'idée d'essence développée plus en détail dans la phrase suivante. Mon objectif est de mettre en avant ce qui constitue, me semble-t-il, une limite majeure de la pensée bermanienne dans ce texte : son besoin de définir l'essence du traduire, sa visée « pure ». Je considère qu'il s'agit d'une limite car l'essence d'une chose est par définition ce qui, en elle, ne peut changer ou se transformer. Or la traduction, en tant que pratique, ne peut être définie de façon permanente ni abstraite, c'est-à-dire par-delà ou en-dehors des actes de transformation singuliers et contingents qui l'incarnent.

[11] En traduisant « métissage » par « cross-breeding », Heyvaert opte pour une interprétation à connotation biologique, qui renvoie à l'idée d'instinct, plutôt qu'à celle de dépassement des pulsions. J'ai décidé de garder cette notion de « croisement » suggérée par Heyvaert pour deux raisons : d'une part, car le terme soulève une contradiction majeure dans la théorie bermanienne entre le croisement comme ouverture (la visée éthique de la traduction), et le croisement dans sa manifestation animale (l'instinct éthnocentrique de toute culture); et d'autre part, car « croisement » ajoute une dimension spatiale, présente dans « cross » de « cross-breeding », qui renvoie à l'étymologie latine de la traduction, *translatio* (« carried across », « crossing »).

[12] Heyvaert traduit « une mise en rapport » littéralement par « a putting in touch with », suivant ainsi la méthode littérale bermanienne, inspirée de Schleiermacher, qui préconise un rétablissement de la lettre de l'original. Toutefois sa formulation est maladroite en anglais et souligne indirectement à mon sens les limites du littéralisme recommandé par Berman. Car qu'est-ce que la lettre ? Qu'est-ce traduire à la lettre ? Celle-ci se trouve d'ailleurs le plus souvent être un mot (un mot-à-mot). Et c'est là bien là tout son problème : la lettre ne veut rien dire en elle-même. Ou, pour le dire autrement, en termes derridiens, elle ne peut signifier que par *différance*. Ce n'est que dans le contexte de sa mise en rapport aux autres graphèmes, et à leur espacement, que la lettre peut créer du sens – de même que la signification d'un mot isolé, hors contexte, reste flottante, multiple, ambiguë. Le littéralisme c'est l'illusion du hors contexte. Or la lettre agit toujours dans un contexte, même lorsque ce contexte se donne pour but d'en faire abstraction. C'est pour cela que les traductions littérales paraissent souvent étranges ou déconcertantes. Ce ne sont pas les mots « a » « putting » « in » « touch » « with » en eux-mêmes qui sont incongrus, mais leur assemblage, leur inadéquation dans la langue anglaise. En ce sens, une traduction littérale est tout aussi déformante qu'une traduction dite « non-littérale », qui privilégierait le sens. D'ailleurs, et c'est là un paradoxe majeur, l'idée de littéralisme ne peut fonctionner que si la lettre permet de conserver non seulement la forme du texte source mais aussi son sens, c'est-à-dire la singularité de son mode de signification. Or cette conservation opère forcément un déplacement. Dans ma version, j'ai conservé l'expression originale de Berman (« mise en rapport ») car c'est la seule à pouvoir véritablement reproduire la lettre de Berman – c'est-à-dire réactualiser littéralement toutes les lettres de l'expression employée par Berman (« m », « i », « s », « e », « e », « n », « r », « a », « p », « p », « o », « r », « t »). Mais j'ai ajouté des guillemets pour signaler le fait qu'il s'agit d'un concept emprunté à l'auteur, d'une citation, d'une recontextualisation, d'une nouvelle mise en rapport, qui opère forcément un déplacement de la lettre, une nouvelle adresse, une nouvelle « mise en rapport ».

ceux de « l'esprit » [*spirit*, sens], ainsi qu'au niveau de la pratique traduisante [*translating practice*, pratique traduisante][13] et de l'être psychique du traducteur. Ici, pour que la traduction puisse accéder [*gain access*, accéder] à son être propre, une *éthique* et une *analytique* de la traduction sont requises.[14]

Ethique de la traduction

Au niveau théorique, l'éthique de la traduction consiste à faire ressortir, affirmer et défendre la visée pure de la traduction en tant que telle. Elle consiste à définir ce qu'est la fidélité. La traduction ne peut pas seulement se définir[15] en termes de communication, ou de transmission de messages, ou de *rewording* élargi.[16] Elle ne peut pas non plus se concevoir[17] comme une activité purement esthétique ou littéraire,[18] même lorsqu'elle est intimement liée à la pratique littéraire dans un espace culturel donné. Traduire [*translation*, traduire][19] c'est bien sûr écrire et transmettre. Mais cette écriture et cette transmission ne prennent leur vrai sens qu'à partir de la visée éthique qui les régit. En ce sens, la traduction est plus proche de la science que de l'art, pour ceux qui considèrent que l'art est éthiquement irresponsable.[20]

[13] Berman s'intéresse clairement ici au processus traductif plutôt qu'au produit « traduction », comme l'indique l'expression « pratique traduisante ».

[14] Notez de nouveau le choix de la structure passive de Heyvaert (« are required »), là où Berman a recours à une tournure active (« la traduction… exige une *éthique* et une *analytique* »).

[15] J'ai choisi encore une fois d'employer un verbe réflexif (« se définir ») au lieu de conserver la tournure passive de Heyvaert (« cannot be defined »), qui reproduit mimétiquement celle de Berman (« ne peut être traduite »). Par ce choix, je souhaite souligner réflexivement le problème central que Berman aborde dans ce passage, à savoir comment définir la fidélité en traduction : s'agit-il de coller à la lettre de l'original (comme Heyvaert le conçoit et le matérialise ici en conservant la structure passive de Berman) ou bien de la réinterpréter en lui donnant une autre forme (comme j'ai décidé de le faire, en préférant actualiser formellement l'autonomisation de la traduction à travers l'utilisation d'un verbe réflexif) ?

[16] Dans l'original « rewording » est écrit en italiques, en référence à la première catégorie de traductions identifiée par Roman Jakobson dans « Aspects linguistiques de la traduction » (1963). L'italique et la référence sont maintenus dans la traduction de Heyvaert. En revanche, l'aspect multilingue y disparaît.

[17] Ici, l'utilisation de verbes réflexifs est filée, répétée, pour maintenir une continuité avec la phrase précédente, comme c'est le cas dans l'original (voir note 15).

[18] L'original et la traduction de Heyvaert utilisent tous deux une barre oblique entre « esthétique » et « littéraire » (respectivement « littéraire/esthétique » et « literary/esthetical »), donnant ainsi l'impression que les deux termes sont interchangeables. Par souci de clarté, j'ai décidé de remplacer la barre oblique par la conjonction de coordination « ou » qui rend à chacun de ces termes leur particularité et marque leur différence.

[19] Tandis qu'ici Berman fait clairement référence à l'activité de « traduire » (« translating »), Heyvaert utilise quant à lui le mot « traduction », qui peut aussi bien désigner le produit que le processus.

[20] En choisissant la formulation « for those who », Heyvaert ne s'inclut pas parmi ceux qui considèrent que l'art est éthiquement irresponsable, et suggère ainsi qu'il s'oppose à ce point de vue. Le positionnement de Berman est plus ambigu car il se veut moins partial, plus objectif, comme l'illustre l'emploi du pronom impersonnel « on » et le modérateur « du moins » » : « si l'on pose du moins l'irresponsabilité éthique de l'art » (Berman 1984: 17).

Définir plus précisément cette visée éthique, et libérer par-là la traduction de son ghetto idéologique, voilà l'une des tâches d'une théorie de la traduction.

Mais cette éthique positive suppose à son tour deux choses. D'abord une *éthique négative* [emphase originale], c'est-à-dire une théorie des valeurs idéologiques et littéraires qui ont tendance à dévier [*turn away*, à détourner][21] la traduction de sa visée pure [*pure aim*, pure visée].[22] La théorie de la traduction non ethnocentrique est aussi une théorie de la traduction ethnocentrique, c'est-à-dire de la *mauvaise traduction* [emphase originale]. J'appelle mauvaise traduction la traduction qui, généralement sous couvert de transmissibilité, opère une négation systématique de l'étrangeté [*strangeness*, étrangeté] de l'œuvre étrangère.

Analytique de la traduction

Par ailleurs cette éthique négative devra [*must*, devrait][23] être complétée par une *analytique de la traduction et du traduire* [emphase originale].[24] La résistance culturelle produit une systématique de déformations[25]

---

[21] J'ai choisi le terme « dévier » plutôt que « détourner » pour renforcer la connotation négative suggérée par la traduction anglaise et rendre compte du contexte sociologique dans lequel s'inscrit l'emploi de ce mot dans la phrase originale, à savoir « les valeurs idéologiques et littéraires ». La déviance fait en effet référence à la position de quelqu'un qui conteste, transgresse ou se met à l'écart des normes en vigueur dans un système social donné. Ce choix souligne une contradiction fondamentale. En principe, dévier c'est transgresser, or chez Berman dévier devient presque une norme – puisqu'en établissant l'ouverture vers l'Autre comme essence ou visée pure de la traduction, sa théorie systématise le refus de l'ethnocentrisme, ce qui a pour effet de le normaliser. En établissant ce qu'est ou doit être une bonne traduction, cette visée de la traduction devient un modèle à suivre, une norme prescriptive, un impératif catégorique.

[22] J'ai choisi de dévier et de l'original et de la version anglaise, en remplaçant « pure visée » par « visée pure », car cette formule inversée imite la structure de l'expression « visée éthique » à laquelle elle fait écho. Ce parallélisme soulève plusieurs questions. En quoi cette visée est-elle pure ? Pourquoi la pureté de cette visée serait-elle nécessairement éthique ? Comment différencier une visée pure d'une visée impure ?

[23] Noter la force du modal prescriptif « must » de Heyvaert, par opposition au conditionnel de Berman « devrait ». J'ai choisi quant à moi d'employer le futur qui renvoie au concept de *visée*, à l'idéal de quelque chose à venir (voir note 5).

[24] Ce qui est intéressant dans la formulation de Berman, qui est imitée par Heyvaert et que j'ai également conservée, c'est la distinction entre la traduction comme produit et le traduire comme activité. D'emblée Berman esquisse l'idée d'une analytique qui se préoccupe non seulement du texte traduit, mais qui fait partie intégrante de l'acte du traduire – idée que Berman développe plus en détail dans *Pour une critique des traductions*.

[25] L'emploi du pluriel chez Heyvaert, là où Berman utilise le singulier, montre que le premier conçoit la déformation à l'œuvre dans la traduction comme une opération multiple, pouvant prendre plusieurs formes, tandis que le second la considère dans son unicité, ne faisant pas de distinction entre les différentes sortes de déformation.

[*deformations*, déformation] qui s'opèrent[26] aux niveaux linguistique et littéraire et qui conditionnent le traducteur, qu'il le veuille ou non, qu'il le sache ou non. La dialectique réversible de la fidélité et de la trahison est présente chez le traducteur, même dans sa position ambiguë d'écrivant[27] : le pur traducteur est celui qui a besoin d'écrire à partir d'une œuvre étrangère, d'une langue étrangère et d'un auteur étranger.[28] Détour notable. Sur le plan psychique, le traducteur est ambivalent. Il veut forcer des deux côtés : forcer sa langue à se lester d'étrangeté[29] et forcer l'autre langue à se dé-porter (*trans-port*, se déporter) dans sa langue maternelle.[30] Il se présente comme un [*presents himself*, se veut] écrivain, mais n'est que ré-écrivain. Il est auteur – mais jamais L'Auteur. Son œuvre de traducteur est une œuvre, mais elle n'est jamais L'Œuvre. Ce réseau d'ambivalences tend à déformer la visée pure de la traduction et à se greffer sur le système idéologique de déformations [*ideological deformation*, système idéologique déformant][31] évoqué plus haut. À le renforcer.

Pour que la visée pure de la traduction soit autre chose qu'un vœu pieux ou un « impératif catégorique », on se doit d'ajouter à l'éthique de la traduction

---

[26] Dans cette phrase, l'emploi du verbe réflexif « s'opérer », là où Berman et Heyvaert utilisent la forme simple « opérer », vise à souligner la contradiction qui sous-tend le processus traductif en tant qu'activité réflexive. Il s'agit de la coexistence d'un agent actif qui décide des changements (une opération de transformation qui a conscience d'elle-même) et d'une certaine dépossession dans cette action (comme si les changements s'opéraient aussi malgré soi). Cette interprétation du texte bermanien est d'ailleurs confirmée par le reste de la phrase : « déformations (…) qui conditionnent le traducteur, qu'il le veuille ou non, qu'il le sache ou non ».

[27] Noter que Heyvaert efface complètement la notion d'« ambiguïté » dans sa traduction anglaise : dans sa version la « position ambiguë d'écrivant » devient « his position as a writer » (une « position d'écrivain »). De plus, la traduction de Heyvaert gomme la distinction que Berman établit entre les positions d'« écrivain » et d'« écrivant » – concepts empruntés à Barthes pour désigner respectivement l'activité de celui qui « ne cesse de provoquer (…) une interrogation au monde » et l'action de celui qui « considère que sa parole met fin à une ambiguïté du monde, institue une explication irréversible. » (Barthes 1964 : 154-156).

[28] Noter la répétition de l'adjectif *foreign* (« étrangère ») chez Heyvaert, tandis que chez Berman l'épithète n'apparaît qu'une seule fois à la fin de la phrase pour qualifier les trois substantifs qui le précédent. Le choix de Heyvaert est sans doute motivé par le propos de Berman lui-même dans ce texte, et en particulier son insistance sur le rapport à l'œuvre et à la langue étrangères, qu'il ne cesse d'opposer à la culture et à la langue maternelles. Heyvaert ne fait donc que reproduire le binarisme propre/étranger qui sous-tend l'œuvre de Berman, même si paradoxalement dans ce cas précis sa traduction s'éloigne de la lettre bermanienne. J'ai décidé de conserver la répétition de Heyvaert pour rendre compte de la volonté excessive de Berman de définir le processus traductif en termes d'opposition propre/étranger, comme s'il était possible de démarquer définitivement ces catégories.

[29] Noter le choix de Heyvaert de rendre « étrangeté » par « strangeness » (subjectif, psychanalytique), plutôt que par « foreignness » (social, culturel).

[30] Voir Berman 1984 : 18.

[31] Heyvaert omet le mot « système », inverse « idéologie déformante » et « déformation idéologique », et ne conserve pas la forme plurielle employée plus haut (voir note 21). J'ai décidé quant à moi de rester fidèle à mes choix antérieurs, c'est-à-dire de souligner l'idée de système et l'idée de pluralité.

une analytique.[32] Le traducteur doit « se mettre en analyse », repérer les systèmes de déformation[33] qui menacent sa pratique et opèrent de façon inconsciente au niveau de ses choix linguistiques et littéraires – systèmes qui dépendent simultanément des registres de la langue [*language*, langue], de l'idéologie, de la littérature et du psychisme [*make-up*, psychisme] du traducteur. On peut presque parler de *psychanalyse de la traduction* comme Bachelard parlait d'une *psychanalyse de l'esprit scientifique* : elle implique la même ascèse, la même opération scrutatrice sur soi. Cette analytique peut se vérifier [*be verified*, se vérifier], s'effectuer [*be carried out*, s'effectuer] par des analyses globales et restreintes. Dans un roman, par exemple, on peut étudier le système de traduction employé. Dans le cas d'une traduction ethnocentrique, ce système tend à détruire le système de l'original. Tout traducteur peut observer en lui-même [*within himself*, sur lui-même] la réalité redoutable de ce système inconscient. Par sa nature, ce travail analytique [*this analytic*, ce travail analytique], comme tout travail d'analyse, doit être pluriel. Ainsi on s'acheminerait vers une pratique ouverte, et non plus solitaire, du traduire. Et vers l'institution d'une *critique des traductions* [*criticism of translation*, critique des traductions][34] parallèle et complémentaire à la critique des textes. De plus, à cette analytique de la pratique traduisante devrait s'ajouter une analyse textuelle[35] effectuée dans l'horizon de la traduction [*carried out in the background of translation*, effectuée dans l'horizon de la traduction][36] : tout texte à traduire présente une systématicité propre, que le mouvement de la traduction rencontre,

---

[32] Heyvaert choisit une formulation inversée qui l'oblige non seulement à répéter le mot « traduction » là où Berman ne l'emploie qu'une seule fois, mais aussi à clore sa phrase (et donc à mettre l'accent) sur la question « éthique » plutôt que sur celle d'« analytique » : « an analytic of translation should be added to the ethics of translation » (Heyvaert 1992: 6).

[33] Ici Heyvaert décide de coller à l'expression de Berman « systems of deformation » (« systèmes de déformation »), contrairement aux occurrences précédentes (voir notes 21 et 25).

[34] Notons l'emploi du singulier dans la traduction de « critique des traductions » par Heyvaert, repris également par Massardier-Kenney dans sa traduction de l'ouvrage de Berman du même titre, *Pour une critique des traductions*. En anglais, le singulier suggère une critique de l'activité traductive en général (c'est-à-dire une théorie du traduire), tandis que Berman parle d'une critique des traductions au pluriel, c'est-à-dire dans leurs manifestations multiples, qu'il met sur un plan parallèle aux critiques d'autres textes.

[35] Il y a encore une fois chez Heyvaert inversion des éléments de la phrase présentés dans l'original de Berman : l'analyse textuelle est antéposée de sorte que l'emphase de Berman est atténuée.

[36] C'est en réponse à cet appel de Berman en faveur d'une analyse textuelle en arrière-plan de la traduction que la présente retraduction de son œuvre propose de faire sa propre analyse, en même temps que celle des textes qu'elle incarne, à travers ces notes de bas de pages, ainsi que par le biais de commentaires explicatifs et l'insertion de fragments de l'original entre parenthèses. C'est en effet une pratique analytique elle-même engagée dans l'acte du traduire que Berman semble esquisser ici, à travers la formulation « dans l'horizon de la traduction », que j'ai choisi de conserver.

affronte et révèle.[37] En ce sens, Pound pouvait dire que la traduction est une forme *sui generis* de critique, dans la mesure où elle rend manifeste les structures cachées d'un texte. Ce-système-de-l'œuvre est à la fois ce qui offre le plus de résistance à la traduction et ce qui la permet et lui donne un sens.

B. Le jugement de l'étranger

Le texte qui suit est extrait d'un article de Berman paru en 1985, intitulé « La traduction comme épreuve de l'étranger ». Il a été traduit ici à partir de sa traduction en langue anglaise par Lawrence Venuti, publiée sous le titre « Translation and the Trials of the Foreign » (2000).

Contrairement à Heyvaert, Venuti choisit de traduire « épreuve » non pas par « expérience », mais par « trial ». Ce mot a deux acceptions en anglais : au sens large, il renvoie à un test, un essai ou un examen visant à déterminer la qualité d'un objet d'étude ; d'autre part, il désigne une affaire de justice portée devant un tribunal. Qu'il s'agisse d'une appréciation qualitative ou d'un dossier juridique, le terme implique un acte de jugement.

En traduisant « épreuve » par « trial », Venuti met l'accent sur un aspect particulier de la traductologie bermanienne. Chez Venuti, il ne s'agit plus de faire l'expérience personnelle et subjective de l'Autre, comme c'était le cas chez Heyvaert, mais plutôt d'établir l'étrangeté comme critère de jugement. Car pour Venuti la traduction doit avant tout être l'expression du point de vue de l'étranger, de son étrangeté, de sa différence. A travers la traduction de ce mot pivot dans la théorie bermanienne, ce sont des interprétations très différentes qu'esquissent chacun des traducteurs : Heyvaert se centrant principalement sur l'expérience subjective du traducteur dans la culture d'accueil, tandis qu'en faisant de l'étrangeté un gage de qualité, Venuti cherche surtout à défendre la spécificité de la culture source.[38]

---

[37] Heyvaert ne garde pas l'idée de « mouvement » dans sa traduction, dont il omet le terme. Par ailleurs, il substitue une voix passive (« Every text to be translated presents its own systematicity, encountered, confronted, and revealed by the translation ») à la structure active de Berman, que ma version rétablit, en vue (encore une fois) d'actualiser formellement l'autonomisation de la traduction revendiquée par Berman.

[38] Ces deux positions sont bien sûr plus complexes qu'il n'y paraît. La lecture psychanalytique de Heyvaert évoque l'étrangeté non pas dans sa manifestation culturelle (l'étranger comme celui qui est hors de la culture nationale), mais comme faisant partie intégrante de l'identité (le sujet comme étranger à lui-même). L'expérience de l'étrangeté, qui chez Heyvaert régit aussi le rapport du sujet à lui-même, va au-delà de l'opposition culture d'accueil/culture source, telle qu'elle est articulée par Berman. D'autre part, en établissant l'étrangeté comme critère principal de la bonne traduction, Venuti choisit effectivement le point de vue de l'étranger, celui du texte source. Or cette position est en soi ambiguë puisqu'elle n'est concevable que dans la perspective de la culture d'accueil, sans laquelle l'étranger ne serait ni défini ni même perceptible.

Avec le terme « trial », Venuti se concentre sur l'aspect critique de l'acte traductif et souligne que, pour Berman, traduire c'est juger. C'est interpréter l'original, analyser et apprécier ses caractéristiques propres. C'est aussi évaluer les choix opérés dans les traductions précédentes, lorsque celles-ci existent. C'est enfin juger ses propres choix, faire l'auto-critique de ses propres décisions de traducteur.

Cette traduction d'une traduction du texte de Berman interroge la conception de l'acte traductif comme jugement. Comment différencier une bonne traduction d'une mauvaise ? L'étrangeté est-elle toujours adéquate ? Comment adopter une position de juge ? Et comment définir la position de juge en traduction ?

Dans les pages qui suivent, ces questions sont abordées, et représentées formellement, à travers une mise en page en colonnes qui témoigne d'une démarche performative critique. Les colonnes évoquent les sections verticales d'un dictionnaire ou d'un journal. Elles visent à reproduire visuellement la fonction à la fois explicative et normative des dictionnaires, en tant qu'ouvrages de référence proposant des traductions jugées bonnes ou adéquates. Comme dans un dictionnaire, chacune des trois colonnes démarquées dans ma traduction explique le concept dont il est question : respectivement l'analytique négative, l'analytique positive et la critique des traductions. Or comme elles fournissent les variantes d'une même explication, ces colonnes établissent aussi des équivalences entre elles, c'est-à-dire entre le texte de Berman, la traduction de Venuti et ma traduction de la version de Venuti. L'explication s'opère donc à la fois de façon monolingue, au sein de chacune des trois colonnes en question, et de manière interlinguistique, dans le passage d'une colonne à l'autre.

Dans le domaine journalistique, les colonnes renvoient souvent par métonymie à une tribune critique, une rubrique de journal dans laquelle une personnalité exprime publiquement ses opinions sur un sujet d'actualité. Une tribune est habituellement l'œuvre d'une personnalité externe à la rédaction. Elle exprime une voix distincte de celle du journal. Elle énonce, pour ainsi dire, le jugement d'un « étranger ». Au-delà de sa fonction comparatiste, la mise en page exploite donc la dimension journalistique des colonnes pour souligner la composition tripartite de cette traduction, à la fois compte-rendu, analyse et critique.

Chez Berman, l'acte traductif est lui-même un acte de jugement, une tribune dans laquelle le traducteur exprime son interprétation de l'œuvre originale *et sa position par rapport aux traductions précédentes lorsqu'elles existent. Pour lui, la retraduction est un acte critique à part entière : « Toute traduction est défaillante, c'est-à-dire entropique, quels que soient ses principes. (…) La retraduction surgit de la nécessité non certes de supprimer, mais au moins de réduire la défaillance originelle » (Berman 1990 : 5). Cette retraduction réflexive des concepts d'analyse négative, positive et critique préconisés par Berman propose d'explorer formellement et conceptuellement le potentiel évaluatif, analytique et critique de l'acte traductif conçu comme jugement.*

Analytique (négative)

Mon analyse de la traduction de Venuti repose sur le critère d'évaluation négative énoncé par Berman dans ce passage, c'est-à-dire le système de déformation textuelle qui opère dans toute traduction et qui l'empêche d'être « l'épreuve de l'étranger ». Il s'agit d'identifier et de signaler les déformations qui, dans le texte de Venuti, effacent la particularité du texte source. Or juger les changements opérés selon les critères proposés par Berman est plus complexe qu'il n'y paraît. Doit-on considérer la traduction d'« épreuve » par « trial » comme une déformation de la spécificité du texte d'origine ou bien comme l'actualisation de sa singularité ? Qu'en est-il du remplacement d'« épreuve » par « jugement » dans ma traduction ? Et comment établir la particularité du texte source en premier lieu ?

Le choix de « trial » par Venuti reproduit en partie la polysémie de l'original « épreuve » mais il la déplace, puisqu'il en accentue le caractère évaluatif (« trial »). Ma traduction amplifie cet aspect en proposant de traduire « trial » par « jugement ». A chaque étape traductive le mot semble ainsi acquérir un sens de plus en plus spécifique, de moins en moins ambigu. Les traductions d'« épreuve » par « trial » et « jugement » seraient en ce sens des exemples de clarification et d'appauvrissement qualitatif – deux des douze tendances déformantes décrites par Berman dans ce texte. Or, dans les deux cas, si la traduction déforme la singularité du mot « épreuve », elle actualise en même temps son utilisation particulière dans ce contexte, en incarnant l'aspect évaluatif de l'approche traductive et analytique bermanienne.

L'instance la plus marquante de « déformation textuelle » dans la traduction de Venuti se trouve, me semble-t-il, dans la substantivation de l'adjectif « analytic ». Dans « the analytic of translation », l'épithète anglais est utilisé comme un substantif par mimétisme avec l'expression française « analytique de la traduction », employée par Berman. Or le nom « analytique » n'a pas d'équivalent grammatical en anglais. La traduction de Venuti reproduit donc la spécificité du texte source mais il introduit une distorsion grammaticale qui n'existe pas dans le texte original : il déforme en conservant. La traduction de Venuti montre indirectement que la déformation est inévitable en traduction, qu'elle fait partie (comme l'indique Berman lui-même dans ce passage) de tout processus traductif – d'où mon choix de la traduire par « déformation de la traduction » et de la signaler visuellement par une déformation de la police.

(Ma traduction)	(Venuti 2004: 278)	(Berman 1985: 279)
Je propose d'analyser brièvement le système de déformation textuelle qui opère dans toute traduction et qui l'empêche d'être « le jugement de l'étranger ». J'appellerai cet examen analytique la *déformation* de la traduction. Analytique dans les deux sens du terme – analyse détaillée du système déformant, et donc analyse dans le sens cartésien, mais aussi dans le sens psychanalytique, puisque le système est largement inconscient, comme ensemble de tendances ou forces qui conduisent la traduction à dévier de sa visée pure. L'analytique de la traduction est ainsi conçue pour découvrir ces forces et montrer où elles sont pratiquées dans le texte (…).	I propose to examine briefly the system of textual deformation that operates in every translation and prevents it from being a "trial of the foreign." I shall call this examination the analytic of translation. Analytic in two senses of the term – detailed analysis of the deforming system, and therefore an analysis in the Cartesian sense, but also in the psychoanalytic sense, insofar as the system is largely unconscious, present as a series of tendencies or forces that cause translation to deviate from its essential aim. The analytic of translation is consequently designed to discover these forces and to show where in the text they are practiced (…).	Je propose d'examiner ici brièvement le système de déformation des textes qui opère dans toute traduction, et qui l'empêche d'être une « épreuve de l'étranger ». Cet examen, je l'appellerai l'analytique de la traduction. Il s'agit d'une analytique au double sens du terme : d'une analyse, partie par partie, de ce système de déformation, donc d'une analyse au sens cartésien. Mais aussi au sens psychanalytique, dans la mesure où ce système de déformation largement inconscient, se présente comme une série de tendances, de forces déviant la traduction de sa pure visée. L'analytique de la traduction se propose par conséquent de mettre à jour ces forces et de montrer les points sur lesquels elles s'exercent (…).

Analytique (positive)

L'analytique positive décrite par Berman est une analytique négative renversée : il s'agit cette fois d'identifier et d'analyser les opérations qui limitent, et non pas favorisent, les déformations traductives. Il s'agit en d'autres termes de reconnaître les stratégies qui conservent la particularité du texte source au lieu de les effacer. Or, comme suggéré précédemment, définir la particularité du texte source est une tâche difficile et inévitablement subjective, qui se révèle d'autant plus complexe lorsque le texte source est lui-même une traduction d'un texte théorique sur la traduction, comme c'est le cas ici. Car il faudrait pouvoir non seulement caractériser la singularité de l'original mais aussi évaluer la qualité de sa traduction. Selon quels critères dois-je juger la traduction de Venuti ? Selon les principes énoncés par Berman ou selon l'interprétation qu'en offre son traducteur ? Et comment, dans les deux cas, faire abstraction de mon propre positionnement face à ces deux textes ?

Qu'elle soit positive ou négative, une analytique qui détermine la qualité d'une traduction exclusivement sur la base du maintien de l'étrangeté du texte source est problématique car inévitablement relative. Le système d'analyse préconisé par Berman devient obsolète si je l'applique à ma traduction, puisque le rapport propre/étranger de la première traduction s'y trouve remis en cause. Dans ce redoublement de l'acte traductif, le texte de Venuti devient à son tour étranger. En tant que traduction qui est elle-même traduite, son texte occupe ainsi une position double : il est à la fois le « propre » et l'« étranger » d'un autre texte ; il est en même temps texte cible de l'original de Berman et texte source de ma traduction. Ma traduction n'est en ce sens ni propre, ni étrangère. Elle est à la fois propre et étrangère : elle est double, elle est un autre double du texte de Berman.

Dans ma traduction, l'analytique devient elle-même déformation – littéralement (le mot « déformation » remplace le terme « analytique »), formellement (le texte est décomposé sous forme de colonnes) et théoriquement (l'acte analytique déconstruit la théorie bermanienne). Ma traduction cherche par-là, d'une part, à reproduire la déformation à l'œuvre dans la substantivation du mot « analytic » par Venuti, et d'autre part, à souligner la nature déformante de toute analytique de la traduction. L'analytique préconisée par Berman semble ignorer qu'en proposant de révéler les déformations traduisantes, elle contribue en même temps à les créer.

Les douze tendances déformantes identifiées par Berman dans ce texte ne sont négatives que parce qu'elles sont perçues et présentées comme telles (cf. vulgarisation, appauvrissement qualitatif, appauvrissement quantitatif, destruction des rythmes, etc.). La terminologie évaluative employée par Berman pour décrire ces tendances établit un cadre analytique binaire et prescriptif selon lequel l'altération du texte source est appréhendé en termes péjoratifs et la résistance au changement de façon positive. Or la traduction est par définition dé-formante dans la mesure où elle dé-(fait) le texte source pour le (re)-former. La question n'est donc pas de savoir si les choix effectués sont bons ou mauvais selon qu'ils limitent ou non les déformations, mais d'analyser ce que disent et font ces transformations.

En traduisant « critique des traductions » par « critique of translations » au lieu de « translation criticism », par exemple, Venuti choisit de reproduire le terme français « critique » à la lettre, au lieu de lui substituer son homologue anglais « criticism ». Ce choix n'est ni bon ni mauvais en soi, puisque les deux termes sont acceptables en anglais. Ce qu'il montre, en revanche, c'est l'effort de Venuti de coller à la lettre de l'original et la priorité qu'il donne à l'exigence de littéralité revendiquée par Berman. Dans sa traduction de Pour une critique des traductions, Massardier-Kenney préfère quant à elle traduire critique par « criticism » qui, explique-t-elle, est la traduction du sens général du terme tel qu'il est employé dans la tradition romantique allemande à laquelle Berman s'affilie. Ici, chaque traduction opère une déformation, non pas au sens péjoratif du terme mais dans la mesure où elle engage un choix face à la pluralité des traductions possibles.

Dans ce projet traductif, et contrairement à Berman, l'analytique n'est pas conçue comme une analyse évaluative des déformations opérées au cours de l'acte traductif, mais comme une activité elle-même déformante, traduisante. Ainsi l'analyse voile en même temps qu'elle dévoile. En donnant une autre forme aux textes qu'elle incarne, elle les révèle autant qu'elle les dissimule. Elle en accentue certains aspects, et par-là en tempère d'autres. En soulignant le choix de « critique » par Venuti, par exemple, ma traduction met de côté ses autres décisions, comme celle d'accentuer « negative » par l'italique ou de remplacer « analytique positive » par « counterpart ». Mon approche de la traduction comme acte analytique et de l'analyse comme acte traductif substitue ainsi à la critique binaire de Berman (successivement négative puis positive) une analytique productive, dans laquelle les déformations traductives ne sont pas perçues en termes défavorables mais représentées visuellement, incarnées formellement, dans un but critique.

Dans ma traduction, la critique devient criticisme au sens kantien, c'est-à-dire une forme d'examen qui vise à dépasser l'opposition traditionnelle entre empirisme et rationalisme. Dans la théorie kantienne de la connaissance, le criticisme stipule que si l'être humain ne peut pas connaître la vérité des choses en soi (noumènes), il peut expliquer ce qu'elles sont pour soi – ce qu'elles représentent pour lui (phénomènes). De même, ici, le criticisme désigne une pratique d'investigation des phénomènes traductifs qui refuse de s'instituer en juge, préférant au contraire incarner son propre positionnement et contribuer tangiblement aux déformations qu'elle décrit. Mon approche répond ainsi indirectement à l'appel de Berman en faveur d'une critique qui ne soit « ni simplement descriptive, ni simplement normative ».

(Ma traduction)	(Venuti 2004: 278)	(Berman 1985 : 279)
Cette analytique négative devrait être accompagnée d'une contrepartie positive, une analyse des opérations qui ont toujours limité la déformation, bien que de manière intuitive et non-systématique. Ces opérations constituent une sorte de contre-système destiné à neutraliser, ou atténuer, les tendances négatives. Cette analytique rendra possible en retour <u>un criticisme</u> – une critique des traductions qui ne soit ni simplement descriptive, ni simplement normative.	This negative analytic should be extended by a positive counterpart, an analysis of operations which have always limited the deformation, although in an intuitive and unsystematic way. These operations constitute a sort of counter-system destined to neutralize, or attenuate, the negative tendencies. The negative and positive analytics will in turn enable a <u>critique of translations</u> that is neither simply descriptive nor simply normative.	Cette analytique, négative, devrait être prolongée par une analytique positive, soit une analyse des opérations qui, de tout temps, mais d'une manière intuitive et asystématique qui a limité leur portée–ont constitué une sorte de contre-système destiné à neutraliser, ou à atténuer, ces tendances négatives. Analytique négative et analytique positive devraient à leur tour permettre une <u>critique des traductions</u> qui ne soit ni simplement descriptive, ni simplement normative.

Critique des traductions

Pour Berman, l'analytique positive et l'analytique négative sont le point de départ de ce qu'il appelle la critique des traductions, c'est-à-dire une approche critique productive qui ne soit « ni simplement descriptive ni simplement normative ». Cette démarche, que Berman développe plus en détail dans Pour une critique des traductions, *s'apparente étrangement à la méthode réflexive adoptée ici qui, elle, ne vise non pas à émettre un jugement évaluatif sur la qualité des traductions existantes ni à justifier ses propres choix en fonction d'un critère normatif, mais à explorer les manifestations, la portée et les limites de la critique des traductions proposée par Berman. Il ne s'agit donc pas de dire si les choix traductifs (en l'occurrence ici de Venuti) sont bons ou mauvais mais d'examiner ce qu'ils peuvent provoquer en moi : leurs effets potentiels et ma position par rapport à eux. Dans une telle démarche, le jugement n'est plus une évaluation des déformations, mais une analyse déformante. Ainsi, on se fait juge non pas dans le sens d'une impartialité présumée, mais plutôt dans un sens à la fois analytique (une critique des causes et des effets possibles d'une traduction dans un contexte donné) et performatif (une analytique productive reposant sur une proposition de choix alternatifs). Dans une telle démarche la traduction présente non pas un jugement de valeur absolue sur les traductions précédentes, mais son propre jugement, à la fois partiel et subjectif, contingent et relatif, indéfiniment ouvert à l'ajout potentiel d'une autre traduction, d'une autre colonne, d'une autre critique – la possibilité de cet autre jugement ajournant continuellement l'acte du jugement dernier.*

Dans l'extrait qui suit, l'acte traductif devient lui-même un acte analytique, une tribune dans laquelle je mets en analyse les textes de Venuti et de Berman, non pas en en dévoilant les aspects cachés pour les en libérer, mais en énonçant mon rapport à eux. Ce que j'exprime dans cette colonne, c'est l'inanité d'une analyse visant à révéler ou à étouffer les forces déformatrices à l'œuvre dans une traduction. Prenant pour point de départ l'argument de Berman selon lequel seule une « mise en analyse » de la pratique traductive permet de neutraliser l'inconscient, ma traduction amplifie le questionnement esquissé par la formulation hypothétique de Venuti « if the unconscious is to be neutralized » en substituant à l'analyse prétendument neutralisante de Berman une analytique transformatrice, qui voile en découvrant et dévoile en recouvrant. Cette ambivalence est représentée visuellement par un surlignage en gris, qui couvre autant qu'il signale.

(Ma traduction)	(Venuti 2004: 278)	(Berman 1985: 279)
Berman souligne ici un point essentiel : les déformations traductives sont non seulement inévitables mais aussi ce qui pousse inconsciemment les traducteurs à traduire. Il faudrait donc d'après lui examiner ces forces inconscientes pour s'en libérer. Or en devenir conscient ne suffit pas. Pour les neutraliser, Berman suggère, il faut mettre en analyse la pratique elle-même. C'est précisément ce que j'essaie de faire dans cette colonne : mettre la traduction en « analyse ». Mais pas dans l'espoir d'en « révéler » les aspects cachés ou d'en « neutraliser » les forces inconscientes. Ici, l'analyse est un acte lui-même transformateur, qui ne peut révéler qu'en dissimulant.	The negative analytic is primarily concerned with ethnocentric, annexationist translations and hypertextual translations (pastiche, imitation, adaptation, free rewriting), where the play of deforming forces is freely exercised. Every translator is inescapably exposed to this play of forces, even if he (or she) is animated by another aim. More: these unconscious forces form part of the translator's being, determining the desire to translate. It is illusory to think that the translator can be freed merely by becoming aware of them. The translator's practice must submit to analysis if the unconscious is to be neutralized.	L'analytique négative concerne au premier chef les traductions ethnocentriques, annexionnistes, et les traductions hyper-textuelles (pastiche, imitation, adaptation, recréation libre) où le jeu des forces déformantes s'exerce librement. Mais en réalité, tout traducteur est exposé à ce jeu de forces, même s'il est animé d'une autre visée. Plus: ces forces inconscientes font partie de son être de traducteur, déterminent son désir de traduire. Il est illusoire de penser qu'il peut s'en délivrer en en prenant simplement conscience. Seule une « mise en analyse » de son activité permet de les neutraliser.

C. Vers une critique des traductions

Ce troisième et dernier volet consacré à l'œuvre d'Antoine Berman aborde la traduction de Pour une critique des traductions (1995) *par Françoise Massardier-Kenney, ouvrage publié en anglais sous le titre :* Toward a Translation Criticism (2009).

Ce choix signale de front une lecture spécifique du texte bermanien. « Toward » évoque effectivement une idée de mouvement, de direction, comme si cette critique n'était jamais entièrement réalisable ou complète, mais toujours en devenir, tournée vers (« toward ») et productrice d'autre chose. J'ai décidé de reproduire cet effet dans ma version du titre (« Vers une critique des traductions ») car dans ma démarche, les actes critique et traductif ne sont pas une finalité, un objectif à atteindre ou un désir à réaliser, mais un processus d'investigation, de réflexion et de création, indéfiniment ouvert.

*Par ailleurs, Massardier-Kenney substitue au pluriel de l'original (*Pour une critique des traductions*) le singulier de « translation criticism », dans lequel le substantif « translation » est antéposé à « criticism » et fonctionne comme un adjectif. Cette décision suggère que la critique en question a pour objet le concept de traduction au sens large et théorique, plutôt que les traductions réelles dans leurs manifestations concrètes et multiples. Ce choix diffère de celui de Venuti qui, dans « Translation and the Trials of the Foreign » (2000), décide de maintenir le pluriel en traduisant cette même expression par « a critique of translations ». Dans ma traduction, j'ai choisi de conserver le pluriel de la formule bermanienne pour souligner l'aspect tangible de cette démarche critique, telle qu'elle est développée par Berman et mise en pratique ici à travers cette (non-)traduction réflexive d'extraits de* Toward a Translation Criticism.

« Ce qui est important à noter, c'est que critique et traduction sont structurellement parentes. Qu'il se nourrisse de livres critiques ou non pour traduire tel livre étranger, le traducteur agit en critique à tous les niveaux. Lorsque la traduction est re-traduction, elle est implicitement ou non critique des traductions précédentes, et cela en deux sens : elle « révèle » au sens photographique, comme ce qu'elles sont (les traductions d'une certaine époque, d'un certain état de la littérature, de la langue, de la culture, etc.), mais son existence peut aussi attester que ces traductions étaient soit déficientes, soit caduques : on a de nouveau la dualité d'un acte critique. » (Berman 1995 : 40)

"What is important to note is that criticism and translation are structurally related. Whether he feeds on critical works or not to translate such-and-such book, the translator acts like a critic at all levels. When translation is a retranslation, it is, implicitly or not, a 'criticism' of previous translations in two senses: it is a *developer*, in the photographic sense of the term of making the image visible; it makes translations visible as what they are (i.e., translations belonging to a specific time, a specific state of literature, language, culture, etc.), but its existence can only attest that these translations are either deficient or obsolete. Here again we encounter the duality of the critical act." (Massardier-Kenney 2009: 26)

Extrait et traduction choisis et assemblés par Silvia Kadiu.

« Car ce sont ces œuvres qui appellent et autorisent quelque chose comme la critique, parce qu'elles en ont *besoin*. Elles ont besoin de la critique pour *se* communiquer, pour *se* manifester, pour *s'*accomplir et *se* perpétuer. Elles ont besoin du miroir de la critique. » (Berman 1995 : 39)

"For it is these works that call for and authorize something like criticism because they *need* it. They need criticism to communicate *themselves*, to manifest *themselves*, to accomplish *themselves* and perpetuate *themselves*. They need the mirror of criticism." (Massardier-Kenney 2009: 26)

Extrait et traduction choisis et assemblés par Silvia Kadiu.

« Il n'y a pas de traducteur sans position traductive. Mais il y a autant de positions traductives que de traducteurs. Ces positions peuvent être *reconstituées* à partir de traductions elles-mêmes, qui les disent implicitement, et à partir des diverses énonciations que le traducteur a faites sur ses traductions, le traduire ou tous autres 'thèmes' ». (Berman 1995 : 75)

"There is no translator without a translating position. But there are as many translating positions as there are translators. These positions can be reconstituted from the translation themselves, which express them implicitly, and from the various statements that the translator has made about his translations, about translating, or about any other themes." (Massardier-Kenney 2009: 59)

Extrait et traduction choisis et assemblés par Silvia Kadiu.

« Or la notion même de sujet (...) suppose tout à la fois celle d'*individuation* (tout sujet est ce sujet-ci, unique), celle de *réflexion* (tout sujet est un soi, un être qui se rapporte à 'soi-même') et celle de *liberté* (tout sujet est responsable). (...) Tout traducteur entretient un rapport spécifique avec sa propre activité, c'est-à-dire une certaine « conception » ou « perception » du traduire, de son sens, de ses finalités, de ses formes et de ses modes. » (Berman 1995 : 60-74)

"However, the very notion of subject (...) supposes both the notion of *individuation* (every subject is this subject right here; it is unique), of *reflection* (every subject is a 'oneself' [*soi*], a being that relates to 'oneself' [*soi-même*]), and of *freedom* (every subject is responsible). (...) Every translator has a specific relationship to his own activity, a certain conception or perception of translation, of its meaning, its purpose, its forms and modes." (Massardier-Kenney 2009: 45-58)

Extrait et traduction choisis et assemblés par Silvia Kadiu.

« Pour que le mouvement de l'analyse soit à la fois transparent, riche et ouvert sur la pluralité des « questions » que pose la dimension traductive, on peut suggérer trois 'procédures' qui font, par ailleurs, de l'analyse un véritable *travail d'écriture*. La première est la clarté d'expression (...). La deuxième est la *réflexivité* incessante du discours qui « desserre » le face-à-face original/traduction(s) et s'accomplit avant tout sous la forme de la digressivité. Que l'analyse, dans le parcours du ponctuel, soit réflexive, signifie d'abord qu'elle n'en reste pas à un collé-collé des textes confrontés (au double sens de *se* coller à *eux* et de *les* coller entre eux), mais qu'elle s'en éloigne perpétuellement pour les éclairer à la bonne distance, se retourner sur son propre discours et ses propres affirmations, etc. » (Berman 1995 : 89-90)

"In order for the movement of the analysis to be transparent, rich, and open to the plurality of questions posed by the translating dimension, let me suggest three procedures that make the analysis an authentic labor of writing. The first is clarity of expression (...). The second procedure is the unceasing *reflexivity* of the discourse that 'loosens' the encounter between original and translation and is realized foremost in the form of *digressivity*. To say that the analysis, when moving through specific examples, is reflexive means that it goes further than sticking the texts side by side (in the sense of sticking close *to them* and sticking *them* together), and also that it always moves away from them to shed light at the proper distance, to look back on its own discourse and statements." (Massardier-Kenney 2009: 72)

Extrait et traduction choisis et assemblés par Silvia Kadiu.

« La comparution d'autres traductions dans l'analyse d'une traduction a également valeur *pédagogique*. Les 'solutions' apportées par chaque traducteur à la traduction d'une œuvre (qui sont fonction de leurs projets respectifs) sont si variées, si inattendues, qu'elles nous introduisent, lors de l'analyse, et pour ainsi dire sans autre commentaire, à une double dimension *plurielle* : celle de la traduction, qui est toujours *les* traductions, celle de l'œuvre, qui existe elle aussi sur le mode de la pluralité (infinie). » (Berman 1995 : 85)

"The appearance of other translations in the analysis of a translation also has a pedagogical value. The 'solutions' brought by each translator to the translation of a work (which depend on their respective projects) are so varied, so unexpected, that they introduce us, during the analysis, and almost without any other comment, to a dual *plural* dimension: that of translation, which is always that of translations in the plural, and that of the work itself, which also exists in the mode of an infinite plurality." (Massardier-Kenney 2009: 68)

Extrait et traduction choisis et assemblés par Silvia Kadiu.

« Toutes les analyses et types d'analyses évoqués jusqu'à présent se caractérisent par leur hétérogénéité, *leur absence de forme et de méthodologie propres. Par forme d'une analyse de traduction,* j'entends une structure *sui generis,* adaptée à son objet (la comparaison d'un original et de sa traduction, ou de ses traductions), forme suffisamment *individuée* pour se distinguer d'autres genres d'analyses. J'entends par là aussi *une forme qui se réfléchit elle-même, thématise sa spécificité et, ainsi, produit sa méthodologie ; une forme qui non seulement produit sa méthodologie, mais cherche à fonder celle-ci sur une théorie explicite de la langue, du texte et de la traduction.* » (Berman 1995 : 45)

"All the analyses and types of analyses described up to now are characterized by their heterogeneity and their lack of autonomous form and methodology. By *form of translation analysis,* I mean a discursive structure *sui generis,* adapted to its subject (the comparison between an original and its translation[s]), a form sufficiently *individuated* to be distinguished from other types of analysis. I also mean a form that is self-reflecting, that thematizes its specificity and, thus, produces its methodology; a form that not only produces its methodology but attempts to found it upon an explicit theory of language, of the text, and of translation." (Massardier-Kenney 2009: 32)

Extrait et traduction choisis et assemblés par Silvia Kadiu.

« Dans ce cas, l'analyse doit se faire critique positive, « productive », au sens ou Friedrich Schlegel parlait d'« une critique qui ne serait pas tant le commentaire d'une littérature déjà existante, achevée et fanée, que l'organe d'une littérature encore à achever, à former et même à commencer. Un organon de la littérature, donc une critique qui serait elle-même productive, au moins indirectement. » (Berman 1995 : 96)

"the analysis must become a positive criticism, a 'productive' criticism in the sense Friedrich Schlegel spoke of 'a criticism that would not be so much the commentary of an already existing, finished and withered literature, as the organon of a literature still to be achieved, to be formed, and even to be begun. An organon of literature, therefore a criticism that would not only explain and conserve, but that would be productive itself, at least indirectly (*Kritische Schriften* 424-5, qtd in Berman, *The Experience of the Foreign* I 123)." (Massardier-Kenney 2009: 78)

Extrait et traduction choisis et assemblés par Silvia Kadiu.

Je souhaite clore cette (non-)traduction du texte de Berman par une réflexion explicative que j'espère à la fois critique et productive.

Le premier objectif de cette (non-)traduction de Pour une critique des traductions, *qui met des textes en rapport silencieusement plutôt qu'en les reformulant, est de représenter de manière concrète l'idée centrale de la traductologie bermanienne, selon laquelle la traduction fonctionne comme un commentaire du texte original. Cette pensée y est exprimée typographiquement par l'insertion des traductions existantes de Massardier-Kenney, non pas dans une colonne parallèle au texte original ou de façon interlinéaire à la manière des éditions bilingues, mais sous la forme de remarques ou commentaires (comments). La version en langue anglaise de Massardier-Kenney vient ainsi véritablement commenter le texte original de Berman. Si elle donne à voir formellement la dimension commentative de l'acte traductif dans son rapport au texte source, cette (non-) traduction montre aussi que la traduction n'est pas un miroir de l'original, comme le voudrait Berman, mais plutôt une réflexion d'elle-même. En d'autres termes, la traduction, telle qu'elle est représentée dans cette (non-) traduction, commente le texte original mais ne le réfléchit pas ; ou plutôt, si elle révèle, ou réfléchit, quelque chose c'est avant tout elle-même, c'est-à-dire ses propres choix et son positionnement par rapport au texte de départ.*

Commentaires qui sont redoublés d'un commentaire soulignant la provenance, la sélection et l'agencement des extraits (cf. « Extrait et traduction choisis et assemblés par Silvia Kadiu »).

C'est effectivement ainsi qu'il faut comprendre l'effet typographique réfléchissant employé ci-dessus. Celui-ci est appliqué aussi bien au texte de Berman qu'à sa traduction par Massardier-Kenney afin de montrer que, si les choix opérés dans l'acte traductif fonctionnent comme un commentaire du texte qu'il incarne, traduction et œuvre originale ne sont pas tant le miroir l'une de d'autre que leur propre reflet.

Comme toute traduction, cet agencement est lui aussi le résultat d'un certain nombre de décisions. Il s'agit tout d'abord de la sélection de certains passages (une dizaine dans un livre de 250 pages) ; il est question aussi du choix des titres (qui apparaissent bel et bien dans le texte de Berman mais à des endroits différents) ; il s'agit enfin de fragmenter le texte original et d'en réorganiser les éléments choisis. Or cet agencement n'est pas une traduction à proprement parler, car je n'y retraduis pas moi-même le texte de Berman ; je ne propose pas d'alternatives aux solutions de Massardier-Kenney ; je ne substitue pas au texte de Berman une autre version française inspirée de la traduction anglaise. Je me contente de citer les passages de l'original qui me paraissent les plus pertinents, et de les mettre en rapport avec la traduction qu'en propose Massardier-Kenney. Est-ce qu'un tel travail de réagencement peut être considéré comme une traduction, c'est-à-dire comme un acte performatif par lequel un texte commente et incarne à la fois un autre texte?

Bien que ne proposant pas d'alternatives traductives à proprement parler, cette (non-)traduction commente et incarne les deux versions qui la précèdent en mettant en scène leur relation, telle que le texte d'origine la théorise. Tout comme la traduction, la non-traduction fonctionne elle aussi ici comme un méta-texte et une représentation—méta-texte dans la mesure où le refus de traduire peut lui-même signifier quelque chose (que la traduction existante est satisfaisante ou que l'original ne nécessite/mérite pas d'être traduit, par exemple) ; et représentation puisqu'elle se propose de donner forme à la thèse centrale de l'original. Non-traduction inachevée donc, car l'absence d'alternatives dans ce cas constitue en soi une alternative. Elle est traduction car elle fait, elle produit, elle crée autre chose, même si cette création « n'est qu' » un collage de citations.

Ma (non-)traduction n'est donc pas une non-traduction. La non-traduction consisterait à ne pas traduire du tout. Ce serait refuser de produire quelque chose. Ce serait renoncer à créer. Or ma (non-)traduction fabrique quelque chose, quelque chose de différent—à travers l'absence même de traduction. Elle intervient (elle vient entre le texte de Berman et la traduction de Massardier-Kenney qu'elle met en rapport et par rapport auxquels elle se positionne) pour montrer que la partialité de l'acte traductif opère déjà au niveau de la sélection des textes à traduire. En soulignant sa propre partialité et son positionnement face aux textes qu'elle actualise, cette (non-)traduction met en scène ma propre interprétation de la théorie bermanienne. Tout comme l'approche digressive adoptée dans ma traduction de Heyvaert et mon analytique déformante de la traduction de Venuti, cette (non-)traduction porte la réflexivité au-delà de l'horizon bermanien. Qu'elle soit expérience de l'Autre, jugement de l'étranger ou criticisme, l'épreuve du traduire traversée ici déconstruit l'opposition entre réflexivité et auto-réflexivité, et suggère que la seule expérience éthique que l'on puisse faire dans l'acte du traduire est celle de notre propre partialité.

Translation as self-reflection

Productive criticism

Berman's project of a productive criticism stems from his observation that existing analyses of translation lack an autonomous form and distinct methodology.[19] His purpose is to develop a method that is specific to translation and that can bring to light its capacity for self-reflection.[20] In *Toward a Translation Criticism*, he describes the analytical practice that he advocates in the following terms:

> I mean a discursive structure *sui generis*, adapted to its subject (the comparison between an original and its translation[s]), a form sufficiently individuated to be distinguished from other types of analysis. I also mean a form that is self-reflecting, that thematizes its specificity and, thus, produces its methodology; a form that does not only produce its methodology but attempts to found it upon an explicit theory of language, of the text, and of translation.[21]

The reflexive approach deployed in this monograph responds very closely to the analytical methodology called for by Berman. Using translation as a tool for critical reflection, the reflexive method is a discursive structure adapted to its subject (theories calling for greater reflexivity in translation); it is sufficiently individuated to be distinguished from other types of analysis (since it comments by reflexive enactment rather than by analysis alone); and it is a self-reflecting form that thematises its specificity and produces its own methodology (which varies according to the theory it proposes to enact). At once an analysis and an extension, an enactment and a commentary, a practice and a theory, the reflexive approach discussed and developed in this book exemplifies Berman's idea of productive criticism, 'a criticism that would not only explain and conserve, but that would be productive itself'.[22]

The reflexive method is a form of theory-in-the-making. It produces theories through the act of translating itself. As seen in previous chapters, performing a theory reflexively also involves going beyond its contexts and confines, responding to it, commenting on it. Through the reflexive lens, the translating act becomes the locus of a metatext that develops by enactment its own translation theory. The reflexive method echoes Berman's description of translation criticism as an inquiry which 'attempts to realize itself as a productive, life-giving, critical act'.[23] In both approaches, works *need* the mirror of criticism 'to communicate *themselves*, to manifest *themselves*, to accomplish *themselves* and perpetuate *themselves*'.[24] If, as Berman argues, criticism is essential to fulfilling the ethical purpose of translation (as opening, dialogue and *mise en rapport*), then to what extent does the reflexive method, as a possible form of productive criticism, accomplish such an ethical aim? This question is central to my inquiry in this chapter. In the previous section, I presented back-translations of three texts by Berman, following Berman's own claim that, as criticism of previous translations, retranslating is an ethical act which 'makes translations visible as what they are (i.e. translations belonging to a specific time, a specific state of literature, language, culture, etc.)'.[25] Retranslations are ethical in Berman's view because they highlight their own historicity as critical reflections of prior texts. In response, my back-translations of Berman's texts show that translating is a contingent, reflective and critical act, regardless of whether it is a retranslation or not.

Back-translating Berman's work into French does certainly function as a commentary on its previous translations – namely Stefan Heyvaert's *The Experience of the Foreign*, Lawrence Venuti's 'Translation and the Trials of the Foreign' and Françoise Massardier-Kenney's *Toward a Translation Criticism*. My decision to conserve both interpretations of the term épreuve as 'experience' (Heyvaert) and as 'trials' (Venuti) in my back-translation of the title (*L'expérience de l'Autre ou le jugement de l'étranger*) enacts Berman's idea of translation as an extension of the source text (as revealing its other sides), signalling overall the multiple meanings and possible interpretations of the word épreuve. As such, my translation also indirectly highlights the partiality of the readings underlying the prior translations, each of which focuses on a specific interpretation of Berman's theory: Heyvaert's choice of 'experience' expresses a psychoanalytic reading, whereas Venuti's 'trials' emphasises the cultural issues at stake. And yet, my refusal to choose between these two interpretations, and my choice to keep them both in my translation, is just as partial as Heyvaert's and Venuti's decisions. Like the two other translations, my choice focuses on and emphasises a specific aspect of Berman's theory: his idea that translation should function as a developer and multiplier of the original.[26] In maintaining both interpretations of the term épreuve in the title, and furthermore adding a subtitle in reference to a third work, my back-translation expands Berman's theory by actualising its various possible readings, and ultimately suggests that translating is always an interpretative act, regardless of whether it is a first, second or third translation.

The reflexive approach adopted in my translation of Berman's texts, then, is no less partial than non-reflexive translation methods. Translating reflexively does not so much consist in applying a theory back on itself, as enacting one's own understanding of a theory or concept when translating it into another form – starting with the selection of concept(s) to be investigated and performed. In the case of my reflexive translations of Berman, for example, I decided to focus on the concepts of analytics of translation, productive criticism and retranslation, precisely because of their resonance with the reflexive method. In fact, the selection of concepts to be enacted and performed forms a crucial part of the interpretative and critical work at play in a reflexive approach to translating translation theory, which my compilation of back-translated fragments of Berman's work aims to represent. Choosing to assemble extracts from various texts, instead of following the linear structure of a specific work, seeks to highlight the interventionist nature of translating as a process of decision-making. It also raises the question of the limits of any thinker's theory, and therefore of how to best translate it. Where does a concept like productive criticism begin and end? Should the translator translate the theorist's whole body of work? Should she also take into account the theorist's own practice as a translator? And what if this theory differs from his practice, as in Berman's case?[27] More generally, to what extent should a translator draw on any other knowledge she has of the work of a theorist and of its context to translate it into another form or idiom?

In the introduction to her translation of *Pour une critique des traductions*, Massardier-Kenney makes clear that her approach to translating Berman's book into English was deliberately performative – that is, informed by Berman's own translation theory. 'The principles I used to translate Berman's text', she explains, 'were those proposed by Berman in the text itself.'[28] Even though it is seemingly similar to my own approach, however, Massardier-Kenney's performative practice differs in that it does not thematise its own partiality. For identifying and interpreting the principles proposed by Berman in the text itself is not straightforward. While opting 'for clarity and directness' following 'Berman's own avoidance of jargon and technical terms', Massardier-Kenney also acknowledges 'the presence of this tension between [Berman's] lucid prose and some terms that may seem jargony'.[29] Her translation strives 'to preserve his fluid, direct, clear style' while at the same time trying to 'keep some specialized terms when [...] their precision of expression seem[s] integral to Berman's thought'.[30] Here, 'Berman's thought' is in fact inseparable from Massardier-Kenney's own reading of it, for her translation of Berman's theory also gives an indication of her own view of translation, based on her interpretation of Berman's hermeneutic approach. '[E]very translation is at the same time an interpretation', Massardier-Kenney stresses in her introduction, quoting Gadamer,[31] to explain Berman's concept of translation criticism, thus echoing Berman's own claim that '[t]here is no translator without a translating position'.[32] Like any translation, reflexive translations are the product of a decision-making process, which reflects in return the translator's own perception of the source text. The relation to this prior text, or to the 'Other', as Berman calls it, is therefore never just a movement of opening in translation, but is also ineluctably a return to oneself. As such, reflexivity in translation is in fact inseparable from self-reflexivity.

Self-reflexivity

It is indeed as a means towards increased self-knowledge and self-awareness, rather than as a simple opening towards the Other, that Berman's ethics of translation based on reflexivity must be understood. In Berman's theory, critical reflexivity – the pre-condition for the actualisation of an ethical approach to translation – does not so much give access to the foreign, as he claims, but rather reinforces a sense of selfhood. Despite its call for a 'reflection on the properly ethical aim of the translating act' which would involve receiving the 'foreign as foreign',[33] Berman's theory at best enables 'self-recognition'.[34] For Berman, an ethical approach to translating involves transforming the translating language by accentuating the foreignness of the foreign work; and yet, Berman admits, the foreign text becomes intelligible only through 'mirroring' and 'reflection', when the reader recognises himself or herself in the translation.[35] As Barbara Godard further explains in 'L'Éthique du traduire: Antoine Berman et le "virage éthique" en traduction':

> Berman, en somme, ne s'intéresse pas à l'Autre en tant qu'Autre dans toute sa discontinuité historique, ni à l'Autre en tant que radicalement Autre et hétérogène comme Levinas, mais à l'Autre du Même, l'Autre absorbé par le Même dans son devenir ou *Bildung*, ce mouvement circulaire du 'passage par l'étranger pour accéder au propre' qu'il avait lui-même tant critiqué.[36]

> Berman, in other words, is neither interested in the Other as Other, in its historic discontinuity, nor in the Other as radically Other, like Levinas, but in the Other of the Same, the Other incorporated in

the Same, in its becoming or *Bildung*, in this circular movement of 'passing through the foreign to reach the self' which he had so much criticised.[37]

For Godard, Berman is less concerned with the 'Other as radically Other' than with the 'Other as Same', in a circular movement which consists of 'passing through the foreign in order to reach the self'.[38] Ultimately then, I argue that in Berman's theory, a reflexive, analytical approach to translation is considered ethical not because it establishes a relation to the Other but because it reveals one's own positioning in relation to this Other.

My reading of Berman's theory suggests that an ethical translation for him is not a translation that makes readers aware that they are reading a translation, but one that makes translators aware of their own positioning in relation to the source text and culture. In putting self-reflexive criticism at the centre of an ethics of translation, Berman's approach echoes Pierre Bourdieu's emphasis on self-reflexivity as crucial 'to keep[ing] closer watch over the factors capable of biasing research'.[39] For Berman,

> [e]very translator has a specific relationship to his own activity, a certain conception or perception of translation, of its meaning, its purpose, its forms and modes. Conception and perception are not purely personal, since the translator is indeed marked by a whole historical, social, literary, and ideological discourse on translation (and on the writing of literature). The translating position is, so to speak, the compromise between the way in which the translator (...) perceives the task of translation, and the way in which he has internalized the surrounding discourse on translation (the norms).[40]

In Berman's theory, a self-reflexive study of translation is essential for fulfilling translation's ethical aspiration towards self-knowledge. This is why, in Berman's view, the ethics of translating must be complemented by an analytic of translation in the psychoanalytic sense. According to Berman, the translator has to 'subject himself to analysis' to 'localise the systems of deformation that threaten his practice and operate unconsciously on the level of his linguistic and literary choices'.[41] One could almost call this, he stresses, a *'psychoanalysis of translation'*.[42]

Berman's analytics of translation are rooted in the Benjaminian conception of translation as a potentiation of the original. 'Every text to be translated', Berman explains, 'presents its own systematicity, encountered, confronted, and revealed by the translation'.[43] As 'a *sui generis* form of criticism [that] lays bare the hidden structures of a text',[44] translation calls for an analytical approach which would bring to light the system of deformation that prevents it from fulfilling its ethical aim, which is 'to open up in writing a certain relation with the Other, to fertilize what is one's Own through the mediation of the Other'.[45] Berman's analytics are primarily negative: they consist of identifying a bad translation, one 'which, generally under the guise of transmissibility, carries out a system of negation of the strangeness of the foreign work'.[46] Berman does stress the need for a positive counterpart, but he does not explicitly formulate what it would entail. In fact, the only operation that combines the negative and positive analytics which, according to Berman, can form the groundwork for a critique of translations that is 'neither simply descriptive nor simply normative', is retranslation.[47] Retranslation constitutes the best form of analytics for Berman, one which at once allows a criticism of prior translations and offers the possibility for better alternatives to existing translations. Reflection must be the task of analysis, he argues: 'to criticize in all fairness the translator's choices, (...) to open the horizon for other choices, other solutions'.[48] In his view, it is only through a succession of retranslations that the work can actually reach 'its whole and utter "revelation"'.[49] In fact, in Berman's theory retranslating represents an analytical process in the psychoanalytic sense of uncovering a hidden or repressed truth, of making the unconscious conscious. Through its analysis of prior translations, he perceives that retranslation would liberate translation from its deforming drive, and allow it to uncover latent aspects of the original.

In the same way as the principal aim of psychoanalysis is to unleash unconscious thoughts, retranslating for Berman should seek to give rise to the voice of the Other, to the foreignness of the original suppressed in prior translations. It is all the more important to 'liberat[e] the violence repressed in the [foreign] work [by] accentuating its strangeness' since, for Berman, history abounds with examples of ethnocentric translations:

> A superficial glance at the history of translation suffices to show that, in the literary domain, everything transpires as if [ethnocentric] translation came to usurp and conceal [literal translation]. As if it were suddenly driven to the margins of exception and heresy. As if translation, far from being the trials of the Foreign, were rather its negation, its acclimation, its 'naturalization.' As if its most individual essence were radically repressed.[50]

Hence the necessity for reflection on the properly ethical aim of the translating act.[51] The repressed status of translation, the negation of its essence as access to the foreign, creates the need for an analytic of translation 'that shows how (and why) the aim has, from time immemorial (although not always), been skewed (...) and assimilated to something other than itself'.[52] It is in this sense that, for Berman, retranslating exemplifies an ethical practice of translation:

> The 'solutions' brought by each translator to the translation of a work (which depend on their respective projects) are so varied, so unexpected, that they introduce us, during the analysis, and almost without any other comment, to a dual *plural* dimension: that of translation, which is always that of translation*s* in the plural, and that of the work itself, which also exists in the mode of an infinite plurality. Through the work of analysis, the reader is thus freed from any naiveté or dogmatism.[53]

Retranslating always involves a level of critical reflexivity, according to Berman. It is the heightened expression of the reflexive essence of all translation.

And yet, ironically, in Berman's analytics the reflexive essence of translation as opening to the Other can only be realised as self-recognition and a return to oneself. My own experience of back-translating Berman has shown me that reflexivity in his theory, like in the reflexive method adopted to translate it, is indeed inseparable from self-reflexivity. While retranslating Berman reflexively and attempting to enact his analytics of translation performatively, I experienced much uncertainty concerning the concepts of own/foreign, self/Other, ethnocentric/estranging. Who was the 'Other' in my retranslation of Berman's work: Berman's original text or its respective readings by Heyvaert, Venuti or Massardier-Kenney? How can one pinpoint the foreignness of a text if translation is essentially a hermeneutic act, an interpretation, an endeavour to understand the Other? And, assuming that such otherness can be identified, how must one translate it into another form: by sticking to the letter of the original (as Heyvaert often does, choosing to reproduce the passive tone and grammatical structure of Berman's text) or by giving it another form (as I have done in many places, preferring, for example, to actualise the empowerment of translation called for by Berman through the use of reflexive verbs)? What I encountered in the process of back-translating Berman was the ineffectiveness of striving to free translation from its 'ethnocentric' impulse, and the irrelevance of such a term revealed in the process of back-translation. I experienced the futility of attempting to translate Berman's work without interpreting it; the impossibility of stepping outside my own understanding of, and critical stance towards, his texts. I found myself limited by Berman's 'system of deformations', unable to judge the translations by Heyvaert, Venuti and Massardier-Kenney according to Berman's analytics – that is, without also deforming (and giving another form to) the theoretical aspects enacted.[54] What I developed and expressed while back-translating Berman's texts was in fact my own relation to, view of, and position towards Berman's translation theory and its prior translations.

The recurring references to psychoanalysis in Berman's translation theory are not arbitrary. Berman's circular approach, which views translating as the construction of one's identity by the means of a speculative encounter with the Other, directly echoes Lacan's concept of 'mirror stage'. In Lacan's critical reinterpretation of the work of Freud, the 'mirror stage' refers to the process through which an external image of the body (reflected in a mirror, or represented to the infant through the figure of another person) produces a psychic response that gives rise to the mental representation of an 'I': the infant identifies with the image, which serves as the basis for her emerging perception of selfhood.[55] Berman's theorisation of translation in *L'épreuve de l'étranger* follows a similar structure, since for him translation is the operation through which a culture becomes aware of its own identity: 'The formulation and the development of a national culture of its own can and must proceed by way of translation, that is, by an intensive and deliberate relation to the foreign.'[56] For Berman, the ethical aim of translation as critical reflexivity is a mode of self-discovery: it is a detour via the Other which heightens self-awareness. However, contrary to Berman's theory, in Lacan's account self-recognition can never be fully achieved, or completed. For, in seeing her behaviour reflected in the mirror or in the imitative gestures of the other person, the subject is also confronted with the unreality of her own identity (the fact that her sense of selfhood is an illusory, fictional construction). This specular moment, which is not just an epoch in the history of the individual but an operation of identification in which 'the battle of the human subject is permanently being waged',[57] establishes self-formation as a substantially alienating experience. In fact, a psychoanalytic approach to translation, and to research on translation, would indicate that if reflexivity can bring about increased self-knowledge, as Berman argues, it also requires recognising the illusory, partial and incomplete nature of such knowledge.

Berman's theory states that analytical reflexivity, productive criticism and theoretical reflection on the experience of translating are necessary for an ethical translation practice – that is, for a better understanding of the ethical purpose of translating, and therefore for a potential liberation from its ethnocentric inclination. At the same time, however, Berman also acknowledges that becoming aware of the ethnocentric forces at play may not be enough to achieve the ethical aim of translation:

> The negative analytic is primarily concerned with ethnocentric, annexationist translations and hypertextual translations (pastiche, imitation, adaptation, free rewriting), where the play of deforming forces is freely exercised. Every translator is inescapably exposed to this play of forces, even if he (or she) is animated by another aim. More: these unconscious forces form part of the translator's being, determining the desire to translate. It is illusory to think that the translator can be freed merely by becoming aware of them. The translator's practice must submit to analysis if the unconscious is to be neutralized. It is by yielding to the 'controls' (in the psychoanalytic sense) that translators can hope to free themselves from the system of deformation that burdens their practice.[58]

For Berman, being conscious of 'the play of deforming forces' derailing translation from its ethical purpose is insufficient. To overcome ethnocentric impulses and neutralise unconscious forces, it is the practice itself that must submit to self-analysis. Only a self-reflexive study of translation is able to bring about such liberation, in Berman's view. Hence his demand that translation should become its very own criticism, that it should move beyond its manifestation as practice to endorse its critical role as theory. 'To say that the analysis, when moving through specific examples, is reflexive,' he explains, 'means that [...] it always moves away from them to shed light at the proper distance, to look back on its own discourse and statements'.[59] For Berman, a self-reflexive study of translation is essential for fulfilling translation's ethical aspiration towards self-knowledge.

Berman's call for disciplinary reflexivity bears a close resemblance to Pierre Bourdieu's notion of reflexive knowledge in the field of sociology. In *Science of Science and Reflexivity*, Bourdieu advocates a self-reflexive approach whereby researchers would systematically 'apply to their own practice the objectivating techniques that they apply to [their object of study]' in order to limit the effects of historical, social and cultural determinisms onto the knowledge acquired, and provide for a higher degree of freedom with respect to the social constraints that bear on the researcher.[60] However, while seeking to develop a 'reflexivity reflex' in the social sciences, and personally engaging in self-analysis, Bourdieu also highlights the limits of reflexivity, showing that, ultimately, there is no neutral or outside standpoint from which the researcher can conduct her research.[61] Researchers can never fully transcend their position because they cannot become aware of all the conditions that govern their choices and their positioning, even when such positioning seeks to overcome its own partiality through increased self-awareness. Self-knowledge is an impossible task, an unrealisable fantasy, as Judith Butler explains in *Giving an Account of Oneself*,[62] not only because the subject and circumstances involved in the quest for self-knowledge are constantly changing, but also and perhaps more importantly because the unconscious is itself continuously evolving. Awareness, or the visibility, of hidden conditions is not necessarily liberating, because the very process of becoming aware of something or making something visible makes one unaware of or renders invisible something else. In other words, if reflexive approaches do bring about some form of self-knowledge, such knowledge remains both partial and resistant to measurement.

Even when a researcher is not intentionally manipulative, her approach to and interest in reflexive translation strategies may themselves be influenced by factors of which she is unaware, or which are part of a mode of thinking of which she is unconsciously unwilling to divest herself. There is no solution to the limits of reflexivity – to the fact that I can never become aware of all the conditions that determine my decisions as a translator or as a researcher – nor even to the problem of delimiting the limits of reflexivity (for saying that there is no solution to the limits of reflexivity may itself be symptomatic not just of a partial but of a motivated stance). Acknowledging the limits of reflexivity does not mean negating the possibility of ethics, however. In fact, according to Judith Butler, experiencing one's self-opacity requires that we establish another form of ethics, one that is not based on the idea of a transparent, self-sufficient subject, but which rather accounts for its inability to establish fully the grounds for its own emergence. Recognising our incapacity ever to reach full awareness or self-knowledge is in itself ethical, for Butler, in that it creates a space for a generous and compassionate attitude towards others, with whom we share such an incapacity.[63] Hence, 'we must recognize that ethics requires us to risk ourselves precisely at moments of unknowingness'.[64] Perhaps the greatest benefit of the reflexive method adopted in my experimental translation of Berman's theory, then, is its ability to make us experience the limits of self-reflexivity itself – since in attempting to translate a text reflexively we encounter the impossibility of enacting fully our understanding of the source text, and are forced into a tangible experience of our own foreignness to ourselves.

The reflexive method presents a psychoanalytic approach to translating that displaces the concepts of 'Self' (*Propre*) and 'Other' (Étranger). As Monique Schneider explains:

> Dans l'itinéraire freudien, l'étranger a (…) changé de place; il n'est plus rencontré comme porteur de cette menace qu'il s'agirait, soit de rejeter au dehors, soit de laisser circuler; il fait soudain corps avec l'investigateur lui-même. Ce n'est plus l'autre que Freud rencontre comme étranger, c'est lui-même qui se retrouve placé, du moins tel qu'il se voit dans le regard de l'autre, en position d'étranger.

[65]In the Freudian itinerary, the foreign has (…) changed places; it is no longer perceived as bearing a threat which the subject would have to either repel, or allow to circulate; it suddenly becomes one with the investigator himself. It is no longer the other that Freud encounters as foreign, but himself which gets relocated, at least in the way he sees himself in the eye of the other, into the position of foreigner.[66]

From a psychoanalytic and clinical perspective, alterity does not refer to an external entity that the subject encounters and then needs to accept or reject; it rather designates the specular operation of reflection through which we experience our own foreignness to ourselves. In psychoanalytic theory this operation is primarily linguistic, since the relation Subject–Other takes place in language.[67] Self-opacity itself is a symptom of our obscure relation to language – of the fact that the language we learn and speak is never entirely ours. We learn and speak a language that precedes us, even though we act *as though* it belonged to us, *as though* it was ours. Our identification with language can therefore never be fully complete: 'one shall never inhabit the language of the other', Derrida reminds us, 'when it is the only language that one speaks'.[68] Putting us face to face with the impossibility of encountering the Other fully, with our incapacity to experience the Other other than as an otherness within our own selves, the reflexive method confronts us with our shared condition as linguistic beings whose relation to ourselves – to our intentions, to our hopes, to our ideas – is never transparent. Mediated by the 'only one language' that I speak and which 'is not mine',[69] my understanding of the world, of others and of myself appears, through the reflexive lens, in all its obscurity, partiality and indeterminacy.

The reflexive method adopted in my back-translation of Berman's works highlights its own incapacity to realise itself completely, making me experience the impossibility of performing Berman's theory other than as a partial positioning towards it. The reflexive method occasions a redefinition of ethics and reflexivity in translation. It shows that reflexivity can only be achieved partially and negatively – that is, by acknowledging its own impossibility. Reflexivity in this sense does not consist of striving to secure visibility, awareness or self-knowledge; it involves recognising that anyone's task as a translator, or as a researcher on translation, is inescapably incomplete, indefinite and fragmentary. And it is precisely in its capacity to make us experience the limits of reflexivity that the reflexive method is at its most pertinent. If as Berman argues, 'the properly *ethical* aim of the translating act' is to 'receiv[e] the foreign as foreign',[70] then admitting one's own limitations as a translator or as a translation scholar constitutes the first step towards developing an ethical practice of translation. For, as Judith Butler suggests, following Levinas, receiving the Other as Other means accepting that its otherness will fatally remain Other, unknowable. In this context, ethics resides in the putting into question of the ego, the knowing subject, self-consciousness.[71]

A deconstructionist, psychoanalytic approach to translation entails questioning the very assumption that reflexivity secures ethics. It means recognising the element of uncertainty at play in any translating task, admitting that translation and research on translation always incurs a risk: the risk of unknowingness. Unknowingness – or undecidability – opens up the possibility of ethical decision-making, according to Derrida, for 'it is in the undecidable moment (when […] one does not know what to decide), that any proper decision can occur'.[72] In Derrida's philosophy, undecidability is at once the reason why a decision can never be absolutely rational, objective and predictable, and the very condition for responsible decision-making:

> A decision in this sense is never simply an attempt to make the 'right' (and therefore already decided) choice from predetermined or 'presented' options. It necessarily entails responsibility because it 'can only come into being in a space that exceeds the calculable program that would destroy all responsibility by transforming it into a programmable effect of determinate causes. (Derrida 1988: 116).

Only when faced with an impossible decision – one for which a pre-existing 'right' choice is not 'presented' – do we decide.[73]

It is because a decision remains heterogeneous to the calculations, knowledge and consciousness that nonetheless condition it that it can be considered ethical. Drawing from Levinas's philosophy of alterity, as developed notably in *Humanism of the Other*, Derrida's concept of undecidability suggests that ethics may only be experienced interrogatively as unknowingness and self-opacity. 'Could it not be argued', Derrida asks, that 'decision and responsibility are always *of the other*? They always come back or come down to the other, from the other, even if it is the other in me?'[74] Responsible decision-making is haunted by alterity and the impossibility of an encounter with it. It is a moment of madness, which establishes every human decision as both accountable to the person making it and the expression of her own self-opacity.

This does not mean that one should make blind decisions, however. On the contrary: 'One must know as much as possible, one must deliberate, reflect, let things mature', Derrida affirms. But, 'however careful one is in the theoretical preparation of the decision, the instant of the decision, if there is to be a decision, must be heterogeneous to this accumulation of knowledge. Otherwise, there is no responsibility'.[75] Derrida does not reject or deny calculation altogether. In fact, there has to be some calculation, he claims. 'Still, calculation is calculation', he continues. 'And if I speak so often of the incalculable and the undecidable it's not out of simple predilection for play in order to neutralize decision: on the contrary, I believe there is no responsibility, no ethico-political decision that must not pass through the proofs of the incalculable or the undecidable'.[76] In a deconstructionist approach to translation generally, like in the reflexive method in particular, responsible decision-making takes place as critical interrogation, wherein being critical does not mean selecting from pre-existing options or judging according to transmitted rules, but deciding in the strong sense – that is, by taking a risk. The act of decision-making by which the translator becomes responsible for her translation, and which makes her decision ethical, is not entirely knowable or understandable at the moment of decision-making. For an ethical translation cannot be programmed or predicted; it can only be assumed, and invented, in the act of translating itself.

Conclusion: from reflexivity to risk-taking

Berman's theorisation of translation as reflexive criticism establishes a hermeneutic approach to reflexivity in translation, doubled by disciplinary self-reflexivity. For Berman, translating is essentially a reflexive activity that is not possible without an interpretative reading of texts, without the elaboration of a rational system of choices.[77] A reflexive study of translation is therefore crucial for realising the interpretative essence of translation as opening to the foreign – for Berman, the ultimate ethical aim of any translation act. As a form of productive criticism, which analyses the translation process through the activity of (re)translating, the reflexive approach adopted in my back-translations of Berman's works exemplifies the theoretical reflexivity he champions, its limitations as well as its ambition. It shows that his understanding of translational reflexivity does not so much give access to the foreign, as he claims, but rather yields a return to oneself that is itself never fully complete. In this relation, my reflexive approach also highlights its own limits as a method that can only be realised negatively as self-reflexivity.

The purpose of Berman's ethics of translation is to provide increased self-knowledge and self-awareness. In contrast, a deconstructionist approach to translating shows that if reflexivity can bring about increased self-knowledge, this is the knowledge of partiality and self-opacity. Like the operations of language, translation and research on translation are a never-ending process of deferral, which, however reflexive they might be, remain fatally incomplete, partial and open. 'Even if one knows everything', as Derrida suggests, 'the decision, if there is one, must advance toward a future that is not known, that cannot be anticipated'.[78] 'If one anticipates the future by predetermining the instant of decision', he continues, 'then one closes it off, just as one closes it off if there is no anticipation, no knowledge "prior" to the decision. At a given moment, there must be an excess or heterogeneity regarding what one knows for a decision to *take place*, to constitute an *event*.[79] And this is why, according to Butler, ethics requires us to risk ourselves precisely at moments of unknowingness.

My translation of Berman's texts is conceived as an experiment in the risks of unknowing. It proposes to theorise, by enactment, the limits of an ethics of translation based on reflexivity. As such, it presents in turn a critical practice that gives priority to responsibility over knowledge – or, in Levinasian terms, an approach to translation ethics wherein '[e]thical testimony is a *revelation* that is *not a knowledge*'.[80] From this perspective, translating reflexively involves encountering the elusiveness and incompleteness of any experience of alterity – that of language, of others, of oneself. In a reflexive translation, the Other is not a foreign culture, or a national identity, but our universal linguistic estrangement: the fact that, as Lacan suggests, there is no metalanguage,[81] no space outside language from which I can neutrally observe and describe language.[82]

Far from negating the possibility of an ethics of translation, to acknowledge the limits of reflexivity is in fact to foster an ethical attitude that accounts for the subject's incapacity to comprehend the range of the conditions informing her decisions and their consequences. Experiencing the limits of self-reflexivity as a shared human condition enables an ethics of translation based on uncertainty and vigilance. Training translators who understand the limits of reflexivity is essential in developing an ethical approach to translation that recognises its shortcomings and values humility. Moreover, putting translators face to face with their own self-opacity serves to make them experience, albeit negatively, the value of self-reflexive decision-making, on the condition it is embraced in its incompleteness and in its imperfect realisation. For, crucially, acknowledging in oneself the limits of self-reflexivity does not mean abandoning reflexivity altogether. Being critical about the ability of reflexivity to realise its purpose is itself a form of reflexive thinking – one that invites translators and researchers to welcome continual self-interrogation, humility and compassion.

In this respect, the reflexive method engaged in these back-translations of Berman's work proves a useful critical tool, wherein translating is itself perceived as an act of self-interrogation (recognition of one's own limits), an experience of humility (uncertainty towards one's own decisions) and an opening to the Other (risking ourselves at moments of unknowingness). In the reflexive method, analysis is a productive activity wherein decision-making, and hence risk-taking, takes place in the singularity, and incalculability, of each translation event. Responsibility is experienced as an enactment of one's own understanding and response to a text, and yet this responsibility can only be apprehended as becoming, evolving, being open to that which cannot be predicted, to unforeseeable encounters with unknown readers. In this framework, translation ethics are no longer understood as the experience or the trials of the foreign, but as the proofs of the incalculable through which one becomes responsible – proofs which, like a tentative impression of a page, invoke the transitory state of something still to come. Translating reflexively means pushing a text beyond itself, beyond its own boundaries, and in the process abandoning ourselves to the Other, calling for the Other to take us beyond ourselves.

Notes

1   Slavoj Žižek, *Interrogating the Real* (London and New York: Bloomsbury Revelations, 2005), 22.
2   Antoine Berman, *L'épreuve de l'étranger* (Paris: Gallimard, 1984).
3   Antoine Berman, 'La traduction comme épreuve de l'étranger', *Texte*, no. 4 (1985): 67–81.
4   Antoine Berman, *Pour une critique des traductions* (Paris: Gallimard, 1995).
5   Antoine Berman, *The Experience of the Foreign*, trans. Stefan Heyvaert (New York: SUNY Press, 1992), 4.
6   Berman, *The Experience of the Foreign*, 1.
7   Berman, *The Experience of the Foreign*, 1.
8   Antoine Berman, 'Translation and the Trials of the Foreign', in *The Translation Studies Reader*, ed. Lawrence Venuti (London and New York: Routledge, 2004).
9   Antoine Berman, *Toward a Translation Criticism*, trans. Françoise Massardier-Kenney (Kent: Kent State University Press, 2009).
10 Berman, *The Experience of the Foreign*, 1.
11 Françoise Massardier-Kenney, 'Introduction' to *Toward a Translation Criticism*, trans. Françoise Massardier-Kenney (Kent: Kent State University Press, 2009), vii
12 Massardier-Kenney, 'Introduction', vii.
13 Berman, *Toward a Translation Criticism*, 14.
14 Berman, *Toward a Translation Criticism*, 28.
15 Berman, *Toward a Translation Criticism*, 60.
16 Berman, *Toward a Translation Criticism*, 4.
17 Berman, *Toward a Translation Criticism*, 29.
18 Berman, *The Experience of the Foreign*, 20.
19 Berman, *Toward a Translation Criticism*, 32.
20 Massardier-Kenney, 'Introduction', viii.
21 Berman, *Toward a Translation Criticism*, 32.
22 Berman, *The Experience of the Foreign*, 123.
23 Berman, *Toward a Translation Criticism*, 79.
24 Berman, *Toward a Translation Criticism*, 26.
25 Berman, *Toward a Translation Criticism*, 67.
26 Berman, *Toward a Translation Criticism*, 28.
27 See Marc Charron, 'Berman, étranger à lui-même?' *TTR: traduction, terminologie, rédaction*, 14, no. 2 (2001): 97–121.
28 Massardier-Kenney, 'Introduction', xi.
29 Massardier-Kenney, 'Introduction', xi–xiii.
30 Massardier-Kenney, 'Introduction', xiii.
31 Hans-Georg Gadamer, *Truth and Method*, trans. Joel Weinsheimer and Donald G. Marshall (New York: Continuum, 1991), 384.
32 Berman, *Toward a Translation Criticism*, 59.
33 Berman, 'Translation and the Trials of the Foreign', 276.
34 Berman, 'Translation and the Trials of the Foreign', 278.
35 Berman, *The Experience of the Foreign*, 65.
36 Barbara Godard, 'L'Éthique du traduire: Antoine Berman et le virage "éthique" en traduction', *TTR: traduction, terminologie, rédaction* 14, no. 2 (2001): 64.
37 Godard, 'L'Éthique du traduire: Antoine Berman et le virage "éthique" en traduction', 64 (my translation).
38 Godard, 'L'Éthique du traduire: Antoine Berman et le virage "éthique" en traduction', 64 (my translation).
39 Pierre Bourdieu, *Science of Science and Reflexivity*, trans. Richard Nice (Cambridge: Polity Press, 2001/2004), 89.
40 Berman, *Toward a Translation Criticism*, 58.
41 Berman, *The Experience of the Foreign*, 6.
42 Berman, *The Experience of the Foreign*, 6.
43 Berman, *The Experience of the Foreign*, 7.
44 Berman, *The Experience of the Foreign*, 7.
45 Berman, *The Experience of the Foreign*, 4.

46 Berman, *The Experience of the Foreign*, 5.

47 Berman, 'Translation and the Trials of the Foreign', 278.

48 Berman, *Toward a Translation Criticism*, 73.

49 Berman, *Toward a Translation Criticism*, 57.

50 Berman, 'Translation and the Trials of the Foreign', 277.

51 Berman, 'Translation and the Trials of the Foreign', 277.

52 Berman, 'Translation and the Trials of the Foreign', 278.

53 Berman, *Toward a Translation Criticism*, 69.

54 This indecision behind how to apply Berman's binary analytics to my own retranslation is represented in grey in my version. The use of the grey colour aims to express my reluctance to judge translations purely in terms of errors or mistakes. In my approach, the analytical work at play in translating is not a judgment of wrongdoing but an analysis of effects, a reflection on the possible interpretations that a specific choice of words may generate. Interestingly, Berman's own application of the analytics is ambivalent. While in *Pour une critique des traductions*, Berman negatively criticises almost all existing French translations of Donne's poem 'Going to Bed', in *L'Âge de la traduction*, he dismisses the mistakes ('défaillances') of de Gandillac's translation of Benjamin's 'The Task of the Translator' into French as unimportant and decides to use them as a means of reflecting on Benjamin's language – 'réfléchir sur la langue de Benjamin' (Berman, *L'Âge de la traduction*, 78).

55 Jacques Lacan, 'The Mirror Stage', in *Écrits: A Selection*, trans. Alan Sheridan (London: Routledge/Tavistock, 1949/1977), 1–6.

56 Berman, *The Experience of the Foreign*, 32.

57 Malcolm Bowie, *Lacan* (Cambridge: Harvard University Press, 1991), 21.

58 Berman, 'Translation and the Trials of the Foreign', 278.

59 Berman, *Toward a Translation Criticism*, 72.

60 Bourdieu, *Science of Science and Reflexivity*, 89–90.

61 Bourdieu, *Science of Science and Reflexivity*, 107–114.

62 Judith Butler, *Giving an Account of Oneself* (New York: Fordham University Press), 2005.

63 Butler, *Giving an Account of Oneself*, 20.

64 Butler, *Giving an Account of Oneself*, 136.

65 Monique Schneider, 'À l'origine de la psychanalyse, l'étranger ', *Filigrane* 1, no. 5 (1996): 10.

66 Schneider, 'À l'origine de la psychanalyse, l'étranger', 10 (my translation).

67 See Bowie, *Lacan*, 81–85.

68 Jacques Derrida, *Monolingualism of the Other; or, The Prosthesis of Origin*, trans. Patrick Mensah (Stanford: Stanford University Press, 1996/1998), 57.

69 Derrida, *Monolingualism of the Other*, 27.

70 Berman, 'Translation and the Trials of the Foreign', 277.

71 Simon Critchley, *The Ethics of Deconstruction: Derrida and Levinas* (Edinburgh: Edinburgh University Press, 1992), 4.

72 Nicole Anderson, *Derrida: Ethics under Erasure* (London and New York: Continuum, 2012), 108.

73 Kathleen Davis, *Deconstruction and Translation* (Oxford and New York: Routledge, 2014), 51.

74 Jacques Derrida, *Adieu to Emmanuel Levinas*, trans. Pascale-Anne Brault and Michael Naas (Stanford: Stanford University Press, 1997/1999), 23.

75 Jacques Derrida, 'Nietzsche and the Machine,' *Journal of Nietzsche Studies* 7, no. 7 (1994), 37.

76 Jacques Derrida, '"Eating Well", or the Calculation of the Subject: An Interview with Jacques Derrida', in *Who Comes After the Subject?*, ed. Eduardo Cadava, Peter Connor and Jean-Luc Nancy (New York and London: Routledge, 1991), 108.

77 Berman, *The Experience of the Foreign*, 301.

78 Jacques Derrida, *Negotiations: Interventions and Interviews, 1971-2001*, ed. Elizabeth Rottenberg (Stanford: Stanford University Press, 2002), 231–232.

79 Derrida, *Negotiations: Interventions and Interviews, 1971-2001*, 231–232.

80 Emmanuel Levinas, *Ethics and Infinity: Conversations with Philippe Nemo*, trans. Richard A. Cohen (Pittsburgh: Duquesne University Press, 1982/1985), 108.

81 Jacques Lacan, *Écrits*, trans. Bruce Fink (New York: W. W. Norton, 1966/2007), 688.

82 As Juan-David Nasio further explains in *Five Lessons on the Psychoanalytic Theory of Jacques Lacan*: 'The statement that there is no metalanguage means that there is no meta-language or object-language. In effect, from the moment when a language attempts to externalize itself and speak of an object-language, it fails. It can never entirely complete itself and close itself on

itself. The metalanguage cannot escape the weakness which opens any language to the outside: and this is why it fails to envelop and contain a supposed object-language. (...) 'There is no metalanguage' means that there is no purportedly external and closed language that refers to the unconscious, without the unconscious breaking that language. Any language is exposed to the affects of the unconscious. There is no speech that is not affected by the unconscious. (...) 'There is no metalanguage' means: there is no way to speak of the unconscious with words that mean something without that speech itself being affected by the unconscious.' (Juan-David Nasio, *Five Lessons on the Psychoanalytic Theory of Jacques Lacan*, trans. David Pettigrew and François Raffoul (Albany: SUNY Press, 1992/1998), 68.)

Conclusion
Towards self-critical engagement in translation

> The possibilization of the impossible must remain at one and the same time as undecidable – and therefore as decisive – as the future itself. Without the opening of an absolutely undetermined possible, without the radical abeyance and suspense marking a *perhaps*, there would never be either event or decision. Certainly. But nothing takes place and nothing is ever decided without suspending the *perhaps* while keeping its living possibility in living memory. If no decision (ethical, juridical, political) is possible without interrupting determination by engaging oneself in the *perhaps*, on the other hand, the same decision must interrupt the very thing that is its condition of possibility: the *perhaps* itself.
>
> Jacques Derrida[1]

(Self-)reflexivity

This book has given insight into translation theories that call for greater reflexivity in translation, and sought to map the various aspects of reflexivity brought into focus in each case. It has shown that whether relying on the visibility of a text's translation status (Venuti), dialogic creativity (Bassnett), reflective decision-making (Meschonnic) or self-awareness (Berman), the reflexive approach championed in each case is conceived in opposition to non-reflexivity: transparency, fidelity, mechanicity and repression. My experimental approach in this book has revealed that in practice the distinction between reflexivity and non-reflexivity is more unstable, ambiguous and fuzzy than these theories tend to suggest, since in translation visibility *produces* invisibility; the translator's response *constitutes* a new address; mechanicity *is criss-crossed* by indeterminacy, and self-knowledge *includes* awareness of self-opacity.

I began this book by asking whether reflexivity could be systematised so as to foster an ethical practice of translation. In response, I have argued that reflexivity, as described by Venuti, Bassnett, Meschonnic and Berman, cannot bring about and secure the empowerment of translation that they seek. Each of their theories strives to establish a reflexive approach that would enable translators to welcome the Other as Other, whether through foreignization, intimate dialogue, creative poetics or retranslation. However, instead of instigating an ethical opening towards the Other, the radically different, the unknown, these reflexive systems end up operating a circular return to the Self, whether through self-reference, self-discovery, self-reflection or self-knowledge. My exploration in this volume has indicated that in these views reflexivity is inseparable from self-reflexivity, even though it is not recognised or theorised as such.

The reflexive method has highlighted the difficulty, and yet the necessity, of distinguishing clearly the reflexive from the self-reflexive in translation. The reflexive act of folding a theory back on itself through translation reflects something about the translator herself, her interpretation of the texts translated and her view of translation, her *self-reflexivity*. Moreover reflexivity, attending to the theories of others, I have suggested, not only invokes self-reflexivity, enacting my own perception of their texts, but also manifests as an experience of the limits of that self-reflexivity itself: the impossibility to encompass or control the factors driving my own decisions as a translator. Instead of calling for greater reflexivity in translation, the reflexive method as I have developed it here acknowledges both the intricate imbrication of reflexivity and self-reflexivity in translation, and the necessity to maintain their difference.

This work has redefined reflexivity in translation in terms of an impossible self-reflexivity. Throughout the practical as well as the discursive components of this book, reflexivity has been theorised as an experience of uncertainty, indeterminacy and undecidability. Unlike translation theories that advocate greater transparency, the reflexive method as I have investigated it suggests that reflexivity can only be apprehended negatively, at moments of hesitancy, ambiguity and self-opacity. The main difference between the reflexive method *practised* here, as opposed to translation theories that *call for* reflexivity, is that my practice reveals the limitations of the empowering value that such theories attribute to reflexivity itself. Instead of asserting that reflexivity can make up for the lack of neutrality in translation, my reflexive method shows that no amount of highlighting, pointing or self-awareness can secure an ethical practice of translation.

The reflexive approach advanced and practised in this book does not claim to conquer bias. Rather, it suggests that no practice of translation or research on translation can provide an antidote to the limits of self-reflexivity, or enable translators to overcome partiality. Furthermore, it emphasises the futility of such an ambition, and self-critically examines its own powerlessness to fulfil the fantasy of a stable, systematic approach to translation ethics. As I have tried to demonstrate throughout this volume, the reflexive method offers more than a reflexive approach: it is a critical and self-critical translation practice, which invites translators, translation scholars and trainers to welcome continual examination, and to interrogate self-interrogation itself.

In investigating the particular form of reflexivity involved in the translation of translation theory, this book has challenged on multiple levels translation theories that identify reflexivity with ethics. Going beyond the opposition reflexive vs. non-reflexive, by redefining reflexivity in relation to self-reflexivity, it has sought to develop an experimental translation practice which is at once critical and self-critical, rather than simply reflexive. Furthermore, the reflexive method engaged throughout this volume has introduced practical examples of a deconstructionist approach to translation, as well as playful tools for engaging with theory in the classroom. In the rest of this conclusion, I would like to draw this work to an end by further demonstrating what I believe to be the greatest contribution of the reflexive method to translation studies, both as a working deconstructionist practice of translation and as a creative translation pedagogy.

A deconstructionist approach

The reflexive method inspired by Jacques Derrida's approach in 'Des Tours de Babel' proves a uniquely productive tool for exploring the applicability of theories calling for greater reflexivity in translation. Playing particular theoretical approaches off against each other by translating them in line with their own guiding principles provides a way of engaging with theory which is at once practical and critical, experimental and analytical. Each of the experiments in translation I have presented here uses the process of translating to question current approaches to reflexivity in translation, while proposing a tentative alternative. My ~~foreignizing~~ translation of Venuti's *The Translator's Invisibility* theorises reflexivity not as an attempt to secure, through foreignization, the visibility of a translation's status as translation, but rather as an attempt to take into account the potential failure of that performative gesture. Similarly, my open letter to Susan Bassnett extends her description of translation as an intimate dialogue between author and translator, and presents reflexivity in translation as a responsive enactment of a prior utterance. Furthermore, in my experimentation with machine translation, the word *ânonnement*, which in Meschonnic's account signifies the lack of reflection characteristic of automated translation, comes to symbolise the hesitation underlying any decision-making process in translation, whether or not it is carried out with the help of computation. Lastly, my analytical back-translations of Antoine Berman's works question the possibility of an ethical translation practice based on self-awareness, and strive to redefine reflexivity in translation as an experience of uncertainty and incalculability.

Using translation to take these texts beyond the theoretical aporias within them, my reflexive method is framed within a deconstructionist approach that views translation as 'a conserving-and-negating lift',[2] a work of recontextualising which both suppresses the original and extends it, erases it and goes beyond it. The reflexive method is a form of deconstructive writing which, as Derrida suggests,

> must inevitably partition itself along two sides of a limit and continue (up to a certain point) to respect the rules of that which it deconstructs or of which it exposes the deconstructibility. Hence, it always makes this dual gesture, apparently contradictory, which consists in accepting, within certain limits – that is to say, in never entirely accepting – the givenness of a context, its closedness and its stubbornness [*sa fermeture et sa fermeté*].[3]

Deconstruction's double critical movement of preservation and transformation consists of undoing a system in order to understand it and reconstruct it on new bases. Like deconstruction, the reflexive method is a productive form of criticism, which generates new practices out of the aporias of established theories. As I practise it here, the reflexive method creates ~~foreignizing~~, responsive, hesitant and analytical translations out of the impossibility of performing the concepts of foreignization, dialogic translation, reflexive decision-making and self-reflexive analysis. In the reflexive method, like in Derrida's deconstructionist approach, theories are produced as responses to anterior theories: 'every text is a text upon a text (...) any theory is another text in an unstable network of texts in which every text bears the traces of all the others'.[4] The reflexive method develops on the basis of, and in distinction from, reflexive translation theories. It uses the conserving-and-negating movement of displacement characteristic of translation to unsettle translation theories that call for an ever-greater accumulation of reflexivity in translation. The reflexive method, as I have developed it here, displaces the theories it enacts, takes them beyond the realm of literary translation and nudges them towards a broader disciplinary context.

Using theory as praxis and praxis as theory, the reflexive method brings out the partial nature of performative translation endeavours, including my own. It shows that a reflexive performance of another text through translation cannot be achieved, in the sense of secured or sustained, for in its attempt to represent the other text a translation marks the absence of that text, displacing it into another context, subjecting it to the translator's stance. My attempt to fold a theory back on itself by translating it into another form indicates that reflexivity in translation can only be experienced negatively, as a partial and subjective performance, as an incomplete representation of one's own understanding of a text. And yet, as a method unable to provide a privileged viewpoint of heightened self-awareness or neutrality, the reflexive method is negatively self-reflexive and in that way illuminating. Embracing its own partiality as a subjective, critical enactment of a specific translation theory, the reflexive method enables a critical form of self-reflexiveness that highlights the unpredictability at play in translation processes. My experimentation with reflexivity in this book suggests that the major asset of a deconstructionist approach to translation is, ironically, its ability to make translators experience the limits of their own *self*-reflexivity.

Ultimately, the reflexive method indicates that an ethical translation practice can neither be systematised nor secured, but only intimated during the singular experience of attempting (and failing) to translate a text in a reflexive way. Translating reflexively shows that an ethical decision cannot be programmed, since it is incalculable, and the non-calculable is itself unpredictable. Translating reflexively takes place beyond established parameters, but also testifies to them, including those formulated by the author of the source text. In my deconstructionist redefinition of reflexivity, a decision taken in formulating a translation is reflexive, and thus ethical, when it involves uncertainty – when it acknowledges its own limits as a partial and partly intuitive choice that exceeds the translator's full understanding. The moment of reflexivity in translation is now a critical moment when the subject does not know what to decide but must decide nevertheless. It is the moment when, unable to follow a given translation theory or strategy, she must create something new, invent something which is *not* viable: a contradiction, like the ~~foreignizing~~ translation. In my reflexive method, like in Derrida's deconstructionist approach more broadly, from which it is drawn, 'the condition of possibility of the thing called responsibility is a certain *experience and experiment of the possibility of the impossible*'.[5] In this perspective, the translator becomes responsible when she experiences, practically and experimentally, the possibility that translating reflexively might be beyond the translator's reach. This moment is also, as I experienced while writing this book, one in which I submit myself to the unpredictable, to the viewpoint of that which I cannot know or foresee, calling upon the Other, the unknown reader, to take the reflexive method beyond its own limits.

The reflexive method is criss-crossed by many contradictions. It is a performative way of engaging with texts which stages the failure of its own effort to exhaustively perform another text. It is a form of theorising and a method of translating that highlights the limits of translation methodology itself. Like the deconstructive gesture that inspired it, the reflexive method is neither an analysis nor a critique. In 'Letter to a Japanese Friend', Derrida explains:

> [Deconstruction] is not an analysis in particular because the dismantling of a structure is not a regression toward a simple element, toward an indissoluble origin. These values, like that of analysis, are themselves philosophemes subject to deconstruction. No more is it a critique, in a general sense (...). The instance of *krinein* or of *krisis* (decision, choice, judgment, discernment) is itself, as is all the apparatus of transcendental critique, one of the essential 'themes' or 'objects' of deconstruction.[6]

The reflexive method in translation is not an analysis in the sense of discovering something pre-existing, but in the sense of formulating a new perspective on the text translated. It is not a critique of prior theories, nor does it seek to propose a definitive form that reflexivity should take in translation. Rather, the reflexive method in translation interrogates the possibility of achieving reflexivity itself. In other words, it is not defined in opposition to the non-reflexive, but delves into the viability of that opposition. However, as an instrument of critical and self-critical investigation, the reflexive method is itself subject to the exigencies of self-reflexivity. It recognises that no amount of experimentation can ensure self-awareness, or undermine the effects of self-identity, or establish a theory impervious to future challenge.

The reflexive method addresses rather than evades the aporias that it throws into relief: it strives to embrace its own contradictions, as an operation that simultaneously does and does not constitute a method. Systematically folding a theory back on itself by translating it constitutes a method to the extent that it proceeds according to a rule as to how the translator should approach the task of translating the theory expounded in the text itself. However, the translation method used and explored in the process varies depending on the text investigated and its approach to translation – foreignization, intimate dialogue, machine translation, productive criticism, etc. The reflexive method functions by displacement and digression, detour and re-contextualisation, rather than through automatic pursuit of equivalence or the repetition of a procedure. In fact, the reflexive process shows that repetition and reproduction themselves contain an element of digression and displacement, an element which resists measurement. The reflexive method operates according to a certain undecidability, challenging method itself. As a process embedded in the particular, its significance is constructed in the singularity of each translation task. It is a method which highlights, and allows us to experience, the impossibility of systematising an ethical practice of translation.

But the reflexive method in translation is not simply a systematised transgression. It is not an attempt to systematise displacement, criticism or interrogation, but is rather a process which demonstrates that displacement and critical engagement occur regardless of the translator's or the researcher's intentions. Paradoxically, reflexivity is also and inevitably unreflexive, partly unthinking and unconscious. It arises as a response to a singular encounter with a text, a contingent interaction with it, a particular translating experience. Reflexivity as such is not something that the subject can secure or direct, but a gesture, a movement, a process of interrogation which must be made to cease for any decision to take place. It is a mechanical operation which exceeds programming, in that paradox lies its pertinence. As a response to Derrida's deconstructionist approach to translation, it shows that translating concepts involves undoing them, transforming them. Unlike interpretations of Derrida's work that focus on the notion of untranslatability (defining translatability in terms of assimilation by the Other, as opposed to untranslatability, the experience of the Other as Other), my understanding of his thought suggests that untranslatability takes place *in the process of translating,* and in the attempt and simultaneous failure to translate without displacing, transforming and recontextualising the text being re-enacted in the other language. Like deconstruction, the reflexive method is above all a process of translation triggered by the impossibility of translating faithfully and transparently, of enacting a text in both its form and content, of performing it without making it different. The reflexive method shows that reflexivity is not something that can be inscribed in the translated text or secured through specific translation strategies, but is rather an experience of uncertainty that is integral to the process of translating. Ultimately, my experimentation with the reflexive method suggests that an ethical approach to translation is not something about which translators can learn cumulatively, applying that knowledge in the same way in different contexts; it is developed by each translator in the decisions she makes in the act of translation.

In *Exploring Translation Theories*, Anthony Pym devotes a full chapter to what he calls theories of 'indeterminacy'. At the end of the chapter, Pym recognises that, even though deconstructionist approaches to translation 'offer very few guidelines that might be of practical use to translators', they 'could be of some practical consequence for the way in which translators are trained'.[7] Pym does not go on to indicate how deconstruction could be used concretely in translator training. He does mention 'productive use of translation within philosophical discourses' as being 'one of the paradigm's most profound contributions' to translator education,[8] but he does not explain why, or what such 'productive use' would involve in practice. My exploration of the pedagogic applications of the reflexive method below seeks to address this question by providing a detailed account of the possible benefits and limits of a deconstructionist approach to training translators in higher-level education. The following section presents a summary of its main points.[9]

Pedagogic applications

My experimentation with the reflexive method suggests that it is in its capacity to allow an experience of its own limits that the reflexive method is at its most productive. For reflexivity is not something that can be conveyed or transmitted, passed on securely to another; rather, it comes about as a singular experience of uncertainty inseparable from the very process of translating. The reflexive method is an incomplete, process-driven approach embedded in the translator's point of view. For that reason, it provides a uniquely effective instrument for teaching the values and limits of self-reflexive decision-making in translation. The attempt is not to pass on precedent knowledge, but to allow students to experience the limits of (self-)reflexivity through and as a translation process.

The reflexive method offers an innovative, stimulating and playful way of engaging with theory. The gap between theory and practice has long been discussed in translation studies, particularly in the pedagogy of translation, by scholars such as Hanna,[10] Woodsworth[11] and Rogers.[12] While many academics in the discipline (including Pym,[13] Chesterman[14] and Baker[15]) recognise the need for theoretical knowledge, students often express a negative attitude towards theoretical training and tend to think that practice should be prioritised.[16] Combining theory and practice, the reflexive method provides stimulating exercises which enable students to engage with theory in a practical way by translating the theoretical texts themselves. Translating theory in a reflexive way encourages students to learn theory by practising it, in so far as translating a concept involves attempting to understand it. The reflexive method invites students to interact with theories in form as well as content, highlighting the fact that translating involves a degree of theoretical engagement, since translating a text also requires positioning oneself in relation to it, and developing one's own view of translation in the process.

Using the reflexive method in an educational framework helps to allow students to experience the challenges of fidelity in translation. Striving to fold a theory back on itself encourages them to rethink the demand of fidelity in translation not in opposition to unfaithfulness or betrayal, but in terms of performativity, simultaneously saying and doing what the source text says/does. The aspiration to be faithful to the source text is challenged in such a practice, since the translator cannot perform a theory or concept (e.g. increase awareness of the text's status as translation) without also negating it and/or going beyond it (e.g. in the act itself of pointing to translating). In accordance with a deconstructionist approach to performativity, the reflexive method shows that a performative translation of a theoretical concept involves displacing it, transforming it. Trying and failing to perform a theoretical text by simultaneously saying and doing what it says/does, students experience translation as a performative act rather than as 'the transport of a semantic content into another signifying form'.[17]

Attempting to translate translation theory reflexively throws into relief the limits, incompleteness and contingency of the attempt to theorise translation in an objective way. It shows that the endeavour to explain or predict translation phenomena is embedded in a view of translation with its own limitations, internal contradictions and blind spots. The reflexive method teaches students that while being familiar with an existing theory will help them make better-informed decisions, in order to make effective use of theory they also need continuously to interrogate it in light of their own practice. What constitutes a theory is that it remains partial, open to question, open-ended and vulnerable to refutation. The attempt to fold a theory back on itself allows students to experience the contingency of any given theory; it invites them to resist the temptation of applying theory unconditionally and indistinguishably from text to text. In other words, it encourages them to develop their own point of view and explore new possibilities of translation. As Pym explains, 'theories provide translators with valuable tools not just to defend their positions but also to find out about other positions'.[18] By getting students to translate translation theory reflexively, and making them experience the limits of such an ambition, the reflexive method helps them to develop a tangible form of theoretical vigilance.

The reflexive method teaches students that responsible decision-making takes place in the singularity of each translation event. It presents a responsible decision as the result of a moment of indecision, a moment of reflection on the rules of reflection. It proceeds from a questioning of the strategies that are spontaneously formed in the act of translating. When translating reflexively, a decision must be *made*, almost invented; it cannot be calculated or programmed. Through the reflexive method students experience the uncertain, interrogatory nature of responsible decision-making in translation. They are encouraged to explore their own proposed solutions. To that extent, however, the moment of the decision, even as experienced through the reflexive method, interrupts the indeterminacy that makes that method possible, for ultimately translators must choose a translation. The reflexive method is not just an analysis or an exploration of hypothetical translations; it requires that students *actually* make a decision; it obliges them to decide without and beyond certainty. Translating reflexively shows students that uncertainty is indispensable to responsible decision-making, and that simultaneously a decision transcends the paralysing moment of indecision. It teaches them that a reflexive decision is also, partly and inescapably, unreflective, instinctive and intuitive, exceeding the decision maker's prescription and intentions.

The reflexive method allows students to experience their own partiality in highlighting a concept within a given text and choosing to translate it in a certain way. It shows them that the manner in which a text is translated depends very much on the way the translator interprets it. By inviting students to translate a theoretical text according to their own understanding of that text, the reflexive method puts them face to face with their own role and agency as translators – emphasising the fact that translators are responsible for their translation, which necessarily reflects their own interpretation of a text, their subjective interaction with it and position in relation to it. As such, the reflexive method contributes to developing the students' awareness of their role as translators – a key objective of successful translator training, according to Donald Kiraly.[19] For Kiraly, this self-perception (or 'self-concept', as he calls it) is crucial for developing translator expertise because it provides translators with their own *point of view* to carry out the tasks.[20] The mechanism of reflexivity at play in the reflexive method does certainly enable a heightened sense of self-awareness, a grasp of one's own relation to and positioning toward the source text, but the self-awareness it brings about is incomplete and partial. The knowledge the reflexive method generates is the knowledge of partiality and opacity – of the impossibility of stepping outside one's own perception.

The reflexive method shows that translating involves a double risk: the risk of misunderstanding the author and the risk of being misunderstood by the reader. Through the reflexive lens, translating therefore becomes an experience of double uncertainty. On the one hand, translators realise that their interpretation of the text is inevitably partial and subjective, determined by factors that exceed the frame of their awareness. On the other hand, they recognise that their imperfect rendering will in turn be interpreted in a subjective, intuitive or uncritical way. Training translators who understand the risks involved in translating is essential in encouraging them to take responsibility for their decisions. By inviting students to acknowledge the partiality of translation tasks and the uncertainties involved, the reflexive method requires them to be all the more daring and experimental in the choices that they make. It encourages them to analyse the possible implications of their decisions all the more thoroughly; it also teaches them to be humble about their work, open to the criticism of others (clients, readers, collaborators, etc.) and forgiving towards the errors or contradictions of fellow translators or critics, starting with those of the texts translated critically and reflexively.

Interest in the ethical dimension of translation has boomed in the past decades,[21] and yet in most classrooms the ethos of neutrality still prevails.[22] For Baker and Maier, 'educators need to engage far more directly and explicitly with the issue of ethics and build it into the curriculum'.[23] In their view, in order to encourage students to take responsibility for their decisions, teachers must refrain from prescribing strategies or specific courses of action: 'Building ethics into the curriculum means opening up a space for critical reflection, training students to think through the consequences of their behaviour, rather than telling them what is right or wrong *per se*.'[24] The reflexive method closely responds to this approach. By showing that the ethical decision cannot be taught, programmed or calculated, but that it emerges in the moment of translating itself, the reflexive method enables a teaching practice which recognises that 'ethical decisions can rarely, if ever, be made *a priori* but must be understood and taught as an integral and challenging element of one's work'.[25] The reflexive method teaches ethics by showing that ethics cannot be taught. As such, it provides 'a space of experimentation and reflection' where students are free to explore any argument and encouraged to decide responsibly.[26]

As a method that changes according to the text it translates, the reflexive method also emphasises the singularity of translation tasks as unique events embedded in an individual, historical experience. The reflexive method highlights that performing a given strategy or concept to the letter is impractical, for the significance of the strategy or scope of the concept enacted is itself subject to change, fluctuating and contingent. Translating reflexively exacerbates the unpredictable nature of translation, the impossibility of anticipating every translation problem, of predicting one's own response to a particular challenge. When asked to translate translation theory performatively, students often realise that elements in their translation decisions exceed prediction.[27] They are thereby brought to recognise that as professional translators (of literature in particular) they will have to face situations for which they will not have been prepared.

Using the reflexive method means also, from an instructor's perspective, acknowledging that, however thoughtful and thorough our training might be, it is itself limited. This is so not only because it is informed to a certain extent by our own partial and subjective experience of translation, but also because it cannot predict every translation situation, or the state of translation in the future – something which has become all the more apparent in recent years, considering the rapid evolution and growing impact of technology on the way we translate. The question, then, is how can we prepare translators for something which does not yet exist? The possibility offered by the reflexive method is to teach translation not by providing ready-made solutions but by engaging in a process of interrogation and discovery. Students are inspired to constantly challenge their own approach to translation and to remain open to the possibilities offered by the specific context of the translations they undertake.

In its attempt to foster a translation practice that enables flexibility and openness to the unknown, the reflexive method provides a pedagogy which is itself flexible and open. In *Becoming a Translator*, Douglas Robinson stresses the importance of developing a learner-centred training which is adapted to its audience, and which respects the learning preferences of each student:

[T]ranslation is intelligent activity involving complex processes of conscious and unconscious learning; we all learn in different ways, and institutional learning should therefore be as flexible and as complex and rich as possible, so as to activate the channels through which each student learns best.[28]

The reflexive method allows students to engage with translation both theoretically and practically in their own and multiple ways. Translating a text reflexively will mean different things to different students. The reflexive method allows for plurality because it is a process-oriented pedagogy, which does not teach by showing, but through experience – the experience of failing to enact a translation theory exhaustively.

In 'Ethics in Interpreter and Translator Training', Mona Baker and Carol Maier describe the main objectives of effective translator education in the following terms:

> First, training should aim to provide students with the *conceptual tools* they need to reason critically about the implications of any decision. This means engaging with some of the theoretical literature on ethics that can provide a coherent terminology and a means of reflecting on the pros and cons of particular ways of justifying behaviour (...). Second, training should enable students to identify a range of *potential strategies* that may be deployed to deal with ethically difficult or compromising situations (...). And third, educators need to develop a set of *pedagogical tools* that can be used to create an environment in which students can make situated ethical decisions, rehearse the implications of such decisions, and learn from this experience.[29]

The reflexive method fulfils every aspect of the above description and more: it provides students with the conceptual tools they need not only to reason critically about the implications of their decisions, but also to think critically about the tools themselves. It invites them not only to identify a range of potential strategies for dealing with ethical issues, but also to interrogate the usability of these strategies in a different situation. It provides a pedagogic tool which invites students to reflect on possible consequences and learn from experience, and to consider that a responsible decision cannot be programmed or calculated. In other words, it teaches the importance of both vigilance and risk-taking.

As an educational tool, geared towards a flexible, learner-centred approach which celebrates student singularity and diversity, the reflexive method is itself traversed by contingency and uncertainty. In translator education, great emphasis is placed on determining teaching objectives and learning outcomes prior to a session.[30] However, if, as my experimentation with the reflexive method suggests, the effects of any reflexive project are contingent, then the benefits of the reflexive method itself are not entirely securable or sustainable. Teaching the limits of self-reflexivity is contingent, for educating is as much an encounter with the Other, the unknown, as the experience of translating itself. I can spell out learning outcomes to students so as to influence them, but how they understand them, interiorise them and transform them over time is not something that I, as a tutor, can ensure or control, even if I wanted to. This challenge, which applies to any teaching approach and not only to the reflexive method, does not mean that the pedagogic benefits listed previously are immaterial, but only that their emergence is subject to instability, change and uncertainty. From the translator trainer's point of view, the reflexive method makes evident the need for continual re-evaluation and readjustment of teaching objectives.

Just like non-reflexive approaches, the reflexive method does not provide, nor does it seek to provide, an absolute truth, or an ultimate approach to teaching translation theory. True, its experimental, innovative mode of operation seems to fulfil many key requirements of effective translator training, including combined theory and practice;[31] a process-driven approach;[32] a learner-centred pedagogy;[33] flexibility;[34] intuition;[35] self-perception;[36] critical thinking; [37] and incalculability.[38] However, these effects are themselves, in part, incalculable. If, as Lynch argues, 'attempting to be reflexive takes one no closer to a central source of illumination',[39] the benefits of the reflexive method themselves cannot be taken at face value. For, like non-reflexive approaches, the reflexive method is also flawed, imperfect and lacking. The experience of incompleteness that it triggers should therefore also be applied to itself, thereby drawing attention to the fact that parts of its learning outcomes may be irrelevant in certain contexts or proved wrong in particular situations. One of the dangers of such a reflexive pedagogy is that it can easily be misinterpreted as solving the contradictions that it raises, instead of being used to face them.

The open-endedness of the reflexive method (the fact that the form of critical engagement and self-interrogation it triggers is indefinite) is perhaps its greatest challenge. The aporias it highlights are insoluble (if they can be elucidated it is only to a certain extent, by producing new aporias in the process). As Biesta points out in 'Preparing for the Incalculable':

The main problem of deconstruction, which has been the cause of many 'misunderstandings' and 'misinterpretations', lies in what I propose to call its *reflexivity*, i.e., the fact that its conclusions (which are by no means endings) constantly subvert its assertions.[40]

Even the sense of incalculability of the decision (the impossibility of programming the event) can be misleading, according to Derrida. In *Without Alibi*, he explains:

> Will this be possible for us? Will we one day be able, and in a single gesture, to join the thinking of the event to the thinking of the machine? Will we be able to think, what is called thinking, at one and the same time, both what is happening (we call that an event) and the calculable programming of an automatic repetition (we call that a machine)? For that, it would be necessary in the future (but there will be no future except on this condition) to think both the event and the machine as two compatible or even indissociable concepts. Today they appear to us to be antinomic. Antinomic because what happens ought to keep, so we think, some nonprogrammable and therefore incalculable singularity. An event worthy of the name ought not, so we think, to give in or be reduced to repetition.[41]

Derrida acknowledges that, if in his philosophy an event or decision can only emerge beyond calculation, it may still become programmable.

My argument in this book has been that deconstruction in fact anticipates the emergence of a programmable event – of a system preparing for the incalculable and preparing to manage it. According to Derrida 'deconstruction is not a method' but a non-programmable 'event' deconstructing itself.[42] Equally, my reinterpretation of Derrida's approach to translation, and transformation of it into a method of critical interrogation and a translation pedagogy, suggests that trying to systematise the event might itself be a useful and productive endeavour, if only for investigating the scope, degree and various manifestations of its incompleteness. In realising that it is impossible to programme an event, it might be possible to prepare for it. As Biesta explains:

> Just education – if such a thing exists – has to be on the outlook for the impossible invention of the other. The other, Derrida writes, 'is not the possible.' The other is 'precisely what is not invented' (Derrida 1989: 59–60). This means that 'deconstructive inventiveness can

consist only in opening, in uncloseting, destabilizing foreclosionary structures so as to allow for the passage toward the other' (Derrida 1989: 60). But one should not forget that one does not make the other come. One lets it come by *preparing* for its coming. Education, in short, must prepare for the incalculable.[43]

With deconstructive inventiveness, the reflexive method destabilises translation theory as a whole, and in doing so opens a passage towards the Other, towards something which is yet to come, new concepts, new practices and new pedagogies. The reflexive method displaces, limits and partialises Derrida's performative translating endeavour in 'Des Tours de Babel' by attempting to systematise it. Moreover, the reflexive method itself can only move into different contexts, both within and beyond academia. Its effects cannot be fully predicted, nor secured, since every new interaction will occasion a different experience, a singular encounter. Further benefits and limitations of the reflexive method are yet to emerge from further acts of displacing, translating and re-contextualising – from experiences which I, in this moment of writing, can neither determine or foretell.

Notes

1   Jacques Derrida, *Politics of Friendship*, trans. George Collins (London & New York: Verso, 1994/1997), 67.
2   Jacques Derrida, *Margins of Philosophy*, trans. Alan Bass (Chicago: University of Chicago Press, 1978/1982), 23.
3   Jacques Derrida, 'Afterword', in *Limited Inc.*, trans. Samuel Weber (Evanston: Northwestern University Press, 1988), 152.
4   Geoffrey Bennington and Jacques Derrida, *Jacques Derrida*, trans. Geoffrey Bennington (Chicago: University of Chicago Press, 1991/1999), 92.
5   Jacques Derrida, 'Force of Law: The "Mystical Foundation of Authority"', in *Deconstruction and the Possibility of Justice* (New York: Routledge, 1992), 41.
6   Jacques Derrida, 'Letter to a Japanese Friend', in *Derrida and Différance*, ed. David Wood and Robert Bernasconi (Evanston: Northwestern University Press, 1987/1988), 3.
7   Anthony Pym, *Exploring Translation Theories* (London & New York: Routledge, 2010), 113.
8   Pym, *Exploring Translation Theories*, 114.
9   For a full account of my research on the pedagogic applications of the reflexive method, see Silvia Kadiu, 'Teaching Theory Through Practice: A Reflexive Approach', *Current Trends in Translation Teaching and Learning E* 4 (2017): 48–77.
10 Sameh Hanna, 'Exploring MA Students' Attitudes to Translation Theory and Practice', *The Sign Language Translator and Interpreter* 3, no. 2 (2009): 141–155.
11 Judith Woodsworth, 'Teaching Literary Translation: Integrating Theory and Practice in the Classroom,' in *Teaching Translation and Interpreting 4: Building Bridges*, ed. Eva Hung (Amsterdam & Philadelphia: John Benjamins, 2002), 129–138.
12 See Margaret Rogers in Christina Schäffner, *The Role of Discourse Analysis for Translation and in Translator Training* (Clevedon: Multilingual Matters, 2002).
13 Pym, *Exploring Translation Theories*.
14 Andrew Chesterman, *Memes of Translation: The Spread of Ideas in Translation Theory* (Amsterdam: John Benjamins, 1997).
15 Mona Baker, *In Other Words: A Coursebook on Translation* (London: Routledge, 1992).
16 See:
    – Mona Baker and Carol Maier, 'Ethics in Interpreter and Translator Training: Critical Perspectives', *The Interpreter and Translator Trainer 5*, no. 1. (2011): 1–14.
    – Michael Cronin, 'Deschooling Translation: Beginning of Century Reflections on Teaching Translation and Interpreting', in *Training for the New Millennium: Pedagogies for Translation and Interpreting*, ed. Martha Tennent (Amsterdam: John Benjamins, 2005), 249–265.
    – Mark Shuttleworth, 'The Role of Theory in Translator Training: Some Observations about Syllabus Design', *Meta: journal des traducteurs / Meta: Translators' Journal* 46, no. 3 (2001): 497–506.
17 Jacques Derrida, *The Ear of the Other: Otobiography, Transference, Translation*, trans. Avital Ronell and Peggy Kamuf (New York: Schocken, 1982/1985), 120.
18 Pym, *Exploring Translation Theories*, 4.
19 Donald Kiraly, *Pathways to Translation: Pedagogy and Process* (Kent and London: Kent State University Press, 1995), 110–112.
20 See Ricardo Muñoz Martín, 'Situating Translation Expertise', in *The Development of Translation Competence*, ed. Aline Ferreira, 2–56 (Newcastle: Cambridge Scholars Publishing, 2014), 31.
21 Peter Cole, 'Towards an Ethics of the Art', in *Translation: Translators on Their Work and What It Means*, ed. Esther Allen and Susan Bernofsky (New York: Columbia University Press, 2013), 3.
22 Baker and Maier, 'Ethics in Interpreter and Translator Training: Critical Perspectives', 3.
23 Baker and Maier, 'Ethics in Interpreter and Translator Training: Critical Perspectives', 3.
24 Baker and Maier, 'Ethics in Interpreter and Translator Training: Critical Perspectives', 4.
25 Baker and Maier, 'Ethics in Interpreter and Translator Training: Critical Perspectives', 4.
26 Baker and Maier, 'Ethics in Interpreter and Translator Training: Critical Perspectives', 4.
27 Kadiu, 'Teaching Theory Through Practice: A Reflexive Approach', 67.
28 Douglas Robinson, *Becoming a Translator* (London: Routledge, 2003), 49.
29 Baker and Maier, 'Ethics in Interpreter and Translator Training: Critical Perspectives', 5–6.
30 Dorothy Kelly, *A Handbook for Translator Trainers: A Guide to Reflective Practice* (Manchester: St Jerome, 2012), 20–41.

31 Donald Kiraly, 'Occasioning Translator Competence: Moving Beyond Social Constructivism toward a Postmodern Alternative to Instructionism', *Translation and Interpreting Studies* 10, no. 1 (2015): 30.

32 Daniel Gile, *Basic Concepts and Models for Interpreter and Translator Training* (Amsterdam: Rodopi, 1995), 10.

33 Kelly, *A Handbook for Translator Trainers: A Guide to Reflective Practice*, 17.

34 Robinson, *Becoming a Translator*, 49.

35 Kiraly, 'Occasioning Translator Competence: Moving Beyond Social Constructivism toward a Postmodern Alternative to Instructionism', 16.

36 Donald Kiraly, *Pathways to Translation: Pedagogy and Process* (Kent and London: Kent State University Press, 1995), 101.

37 Baker and Maier, 'Ethics in Interpreter and Translator Training: Critical Perspectives', 4.

38 Gert J.J. Biesta, 'Preparing for the Incalculable', in *Derrida and Education*, ed. Gert J.J. Biesta and Denise Eguéa-Kuhenne (New York: Routledge, 2001), 49.

39 Lynch, 'Against Reflexivity as an Academic Virtue and Source of Privileged Knowledge', 47.

40 Biesta, 'Preparing for the Incalculable', 47.

41 Jacques Derrida, *Without Alibi*, trans. Peggy Kamuf (Stanford: Stanford University Press, 2000/2002), 172.

42 Derrida, 'Letter to a Japanese Friend', 3–4.

43 Biesta, 'Preparing for the Incalculable', 51.

Bibliography

Alvesson, Mats, and Kaj Sköldberg. *Reflexive Methodology: New Vistas for Qualitative Research*. London: SAGE, 2009.

Anderson, Nicole. *Derrida: Ethics under Erasure*. London and New York: Continuum, 2012.

Apter, Emily. *Against World Literature: On the Politics of Untranslatability*. New York: Verso, 2013.

Arnold, Doug. 'Why Translation is Difficult for Computers.' In *Computers and Translation: A Translator's Guide*, edited by Harold Somers, 119–142. Amsterdam and Philadelphia: John Benjamins, 2003.

Arrojo, Rosemary. 'Postmodernism and the Teaching of Translation.' In *Teaching Translation and Interpreting 3*, edited by Cay Dollerup and Vibeke Appel, 97–103. Amsterdam and Philadelphia: John Benjamins, 1995.

Arrojo, Rosemary. 'Deconstruction, Psychoanalysis, and the Teaching of Translation.' *TranScribe: The Teaching Translation Journal* 1 (2005): 25–35.

Attridge, Derek. *Reading and Responsibility: Deconstruction's Traces*. Edinburgh: Edinburgh University Press, 2010.

Austin, John Langshaw. *How to Do Things with Words*. Oxford: Clarendon Press, 1962/1975.

Baker, Mona. *In Other Words: A Coursebook on Translation*. London: Routledge, 1992.

Baker, Mona. 'The Pragmatics of Cross-Cultural Contact and Some False Dichotomies in Translation Studies.' In *CTIS Occasional Papers*, edited by Maeve Olohan, 7–20. Manchester: UMIST, 2001.

Baker, Mona. *Critical Readings in Translation Studies*. London and New York: Routledge, 2010.

Baker, Mona, and Carol Maier. 'Ethics in Interpreter and Translator Training: Critical Perspectives.' *The Interpreter and Translator Trainer* 5, no. 1 (2011): 1–14.

Barthes, Roland. *Essais critiques*. Paris: Seuil, 1964.

Bassnett, Susan. *Translation Studies*. New York: Routledge, 2002.

Bassnett, Susan. 'Bringing the News Back Home: Strategies of Acculturation and Foreignisation.' *Language and Intercultural Communication* 5, no. 2 (2005): 120–130.

Bassnett, Susan. 'Writing and Translating.' In *The Translator as Writer*, edited by Susan Bassnett and Peter Bush, 173–183. London: Continuum, 2006.

Bellos, David. *Is That A Fish in your Ear?* London: Penguin Books, 2011.

Benjamin, Walter. 'The Task of the Translator.' Translated by Harry Zohn. In *The Translation Studies Reader*, edited by Lawrence Venuti, 75–85. London and New York: Routledge, 1923/2004.

Bennington, Geoffrey, and Jacques Derrida. *Jacques Derrida*. Translated by Geoffrey Bennington. Chicago: University of Chicago Press, 1991/1999.

Berman, Antoine. *L'épreuve de l'étranger*. Paris: Gallimard, 1984.

Berman, Antoine. *The Experience of the Foreign*. Translated by Stefan Heyvaert. New York: SUNY Press, 1992.

Berman, Antoine. 'La traduction comme épreuve de l'étranger.' *Texte*, 4 (1985) : 67–81.

Berman, Antoine. *Pour une critique des traductions*. Paris: Gallimard, 1995.

Berman, Antoine. *La traduction et la lettre, ou L'auberge du lointain*. Paris: Seuil, 1999.

Berman, Antoine. 'Translation and the Trials of the Foreign.' Translated by Lawrence Venuti. In *The Translation Studies Reader*, edited by Lawrence Venuti, 276–289. London and New York: Routledge, 2004.

Berman, Antoine. *L'Âge de la traduction: 'La tâche du traducteur' de Walter Benjamin, un commentaire*. Saint-Denis: Presses Universitaires de Vincennes, 2008.

Berman, Antoine. *Toward a Translation Criticism*. Translated by Françoise Massardier-Kenney. Kent: Kent State University Press, 2009.

Biesta, Gert J.J. 'Preparing for the Incalculable.' In *Derrida and Education*, edited by Gert J.J. Biesta and Denise Eguéa-Kuhenne, 32–54. New York: Routledge, 2001.

Boase-Beier, Jean, and Michael Holman, eds. *The Practices of Literary Translation: Constraints and Creativity*. Manchester: St Jerome, 1999.

Boase-Beier, Jean. 'Who Needs Theory?' In *Translation: Theory and Practice in Dialogue*, edited by Antoinette Fawcett, Karla L. Guadarrama García and Rebecca Hyde Parker. London: Continuum, 2010.

Bonnefoy, Yves. 'Translating Poetry.' Translated by John Wilmer. In *Theories of Translation: An Anthology of Essays from Dryden to Derrida*, edited by Rainer Schulte and John Biguenet, 186–192. Chicago and London: University of Chicago Press, 1992.

Boulanger, Pier-Pascale. 'Traduire Meschonnic en anglais.' Interview by René Lemieux and Caroline Mangerel. *Trahir*, 4 (2013): 1–7.

Boulanger, Pier-Pascale. 'Introduction.' In Henri Meschonnic, *Ethics and Politics of Translating*, 11–33. Amsterdam and Philadelphia: John Benjamins, 2011.

Bourdieu, Pierre. *Science of Science and Reflexivity*. Translated by Richard Nice. Cambridge: Polity Press, 2001/2004.

Bowie, Malcolm. *Lacan*. Cambridge: Harvard University Press, 1991.

Bush, Peter, and Susan Bassnett, eds. *The Translator as Writer*. London: Continuum, 2006.

Butler, Judith. *Giving an Account of Oneself*. New York: Fordham University Press, 2005.

Cahen, Didier. 'Derrida and the Question of Education: A New Space for Philosophy.' In *Derrida and Education*, edited by Gert J.J. Biesta and Denise Eguéa-Kuhenne, 32–54. New York: Routledge, 2001.

Calzada Pérez, Maria. 'Applying Translation Theory in Teaching.' *Perspectives: Studies in Translatology* 12, no. 2 (2004): 119–133.

Caminade, Monique, and Anthony Pym. *Annuaire mondial des formations en traduction et en interprétation*. Paris: Société des Traducteurs Français, 1995.

Camus, Albert. *The Stranger*. Translated by Matthew Ward. New York: Vintage International, 1966.

Caputo, John D. *Deconstruction in a Nutshell: A Conversation with Jacques Derrida*. New York: Fordham University Press, 1997.

Charron, Marc. 'Berman, étranger à lui-même?' *TTR: traduction, terminologie, rédaction* 14, no. 2 (2001): 97–121.

Chesterman, Andrew. *Memes of Translation: The Spread of Ideas in Translation Theory*. Amsterdam: John Benjamins, 1997.

Chesterman, Andrew. 'On the Idea of a Theory.' *Across Languages and Cultures* 8, no. 1 (2007): 1–16.

Chesterman, Andrew, and Rosemary Arrojo. 'Shared Ground in Translation Studies: Concluding the Debate.' *Target* 14, no. 1 (2002): 137–143.

Chesterman, Andrew, and Emma Wagner. *Can Theory Help Translators?* Manchester: St Jerome, 2002.

Cole, Peter. 'Towards an Ethics of the Art.' In *Translation: Translators on Their Work and What It Means*, edited by Esther Allen and Susan Bernofsky, 3–16. New York: Columbia University Press, 2013.

Crisafulli, Edoardo. 'The Quest for an Eclectic Methodology of Translation Description.' In *Crosscultural Transgressions: Research Models in Translation Studies II. Historical and Ideological Issues*, edited by Theo Hermans, 26–43. Manchester: St Jerome, 2002.

Critchley, Simon. *The Ethics of Deconstruction: Derrida and Levinas*. Edinburgh: Edinburgh University Press, 1992.

Cronin, Michael. *Translation and Globalization*. London: Routledge, 2003.

Cronin, Michael. 'Deschooling Translation: Beginning of Century Reflections on Teaching Translation and Interpreting.' In *Training for the New Millennium: Pedagogies for Translation and Interpreting*, edited by Martha Tennent, 249–265. Amsterdam: John Benjamins, 2005.

Cronin, Michael. 'The Cracked Looking-Glass of Servants: Translation and Minority Languages in a Global Age.' In *Critical Readings in Translation Studies*, edited by Mona Baker, 249–262. London and New York: Routledge, 2010.

Davis, Kathleen. *Deconstruction and Translation*. Oxford and New York: Routledge, 2014.

Delisle, Jean. *La traduction raisonnée: Manuel d'initiation à la traduction professionnelle de l'anglais vers le français*. Ottawa: Université d'Ottawa, 1993.

Derrida, Jacques. *Writing and Difference*. Translated by Alan Bass. Chicago: University of Chicago Press, 1967/1978.

Derrida, Jacques. 'Difference.' In *Speech and Phenomena*, 278–301. Translated by David B. Allison. Evanston: Northwestern University Press, 1968/1973.

Derrida, Jacques. 'Signature Event Context.' In *Limited Inc*, 1–24. Translated by Samuel Weber. Evanston: Northwestern University Press, 1972/1988.

Derrida, Jacques. *Positions*. Translated by Alan Bass. London: Continuum, 1972/2010.

Derrida, Jacques. *Margins of Philosophy*. Translated by Alan Bass. Chicago: University of Chicago Press, 1978/1982.

Derrida, Jacques. 'Living On/Borderlines.' In *Deconstruction and Criticism*, 75–176. Translated by James Hulbert. New York: Continuum, 1979.

Derrida, Jacques. *The Postcard: From Socrates to Freud and Beyond*. Translated by Alan Bass. Chicago and London: University of Chicago Press, 1979/1987.

Derrida, Jacques. 'Moi–La psychanalyse: introduction à la traduction.' *Meta: journal des traducteurs / Meta: Translators' Journal* 27, no. 1 (1982): 72–76.

Derrida, Jacques. *The Ear of the Other: Otobiography, Transference, Translation*. Translated by Avital Ronell and Peggy Kamuf. New York: Schocken, 1982/1985.

Derrida, Jacques. 'Des Tours de Babel.' In *Difference in Translation*, edited by Joseph F. Graham, 165–207. Translated by Joseph F. Graham. Ithaca: Cornell University Press, 1985.

Derrida, Jacques. 'Letter to a Japanese Friend.' In *Derrida and Différance*, edited by David Wood and Robert Bernasconi, 1–5. Evanston: Northwestern University Press, 1987/1988.

Derrida, Jacques. 'Afterword.' In *Limited Inc.*, 111–160. Translated by Samuel Weber. Evanston: Northwestern University Press, 1988.

Derrida, Jacques. *Memoires: For Paul de Man*. Translated by Cecile Lindsay, Jonathan Culler and Eduardo Cadava. New York: Columbia University Press, 1989.

Derrida, Jacques. '"Eating Well", or the Calculation of the Subject: An Interview with Jacques Derrida.' In *Who Comes After the Subject?*, edited by Eduardo Cadava, Peter Connor and Jean-Luc Nancy, 96–119. New York and London: Routledge, 1991.

Derrida, Jacques. *The Other Heading: Reflections on Today's Europe*. Translated by Pascale-Anne Brault and Michael Naas. Bloomington and Indianapolis: Indiana University Press, 1991/1992.

Derrida, Jacques. 'Force of Law: The "Mystical Foundation of Authority."' In *Deconstruction and the Possibility of Justice,* edited by Drucilla Cornell, Michael Rosenfeld and David Gray Carlson, 3–67. New York: Routledge, 1992.

Derrida, Jacques. *Points...: Interviews, 1976–1994*. Translated by Peggy Kamuf. Stanford: Stanford University Press, 1992/1995.

Derrida, Jacques. 'Nietzsche and the Machine.' *Journal of Nietzsche Studies* 7, no. 7 (Spring 1994): 37.

Derrida, Jacques. *Specters of Marx*. Oxford and New York: Routledge Classics, 1993/2006.

Derrida, Jacques. *Politics of Friendship*. Translated by George Collins. London and New York: Verso, 1994/2005.

Derrida, Jacques. *Monolingualism of the Other; or, The Prosthesis of Origin*. Translated by Patrick Mensah. Stanford: Stanford University Press, 1996/1998.

Derrida, Jacques. *Adieu to Emmanuel Levinas*. Translated by Pascale-Anne Brault and Michael Naas. Stanford: Stanford University Press, 1997/1999.

Derrida, Jacques. 'What Is a "Relevant" Translation?'. Translated by Lawrence Venuti. *Critical Inquiry* 27, no. 2 (1998/2001): 174–200.

Derrida, Jacques. *Without Alibi*. Translated by Peggy Kamuf. Stanford: Stanford University Press, 2000/2002.

Derrida, Jacques. 'Above All, No Journalists!' Translated by Samuel Weber. In *Religion and Media*, edited by Hent de Vries and Samuel Weber, 56–94. Stanford: Stanford University Press, 2001.

Derrida, Jacques. *For What Tomorrow... A Dialogue*. Translated by Jeff Fort. Stanford: Stanford University Press, 2001/2004.

Derrida, Jacques. *Paper Machine*. Translated by Rachel Bowlby. Stanford: Stanford University Press, 2001/2005.

Derrida, Jacques, *Negotiations: Interventions and Interviews, 1971–2001*, edited by Elizabeth Rottenberg. Stanford: Stanford University Press, 2002.

Derrida, Jacques. *Traces, archives, images et art*. Paris: INA, 2014.

Dizdar, Dilek. 'General Translation Theory.' In *Handbook of Translation Studies Volume 3*, edited by Yves Gambier and Luc van Doorslaer. 52–58. Amsterdam and Philadelphia: John Benjamins, 2012.

Du Bellay, Joachim. *Défense et illustration de la langue française*. Tours: Centre d'Études Supérieures de la Renaissance, 1549/2009. http://www.bvh.univ-tours.fr/Epistemon/B751131015_X1888.pdf.

Forcada, Mikel L. 'Machine Translation Today.' In *Handbook of Translation Studies Volume 1*, edited by Yves Gambier and Luc Van Doorslaer, 215–223. Amsterdam and Philadelphia: John Benjamins, 2010.

Freud, Sigmund. *Interpreting Dreams*. Translated by Jim Underwood. London: Penguin, 1899/2006.

Gadamer, Hans-Georg. *Truth and Method*. Translated by Joel Weinsheimer and Donald G. Marshall. New York: Continuum, 1991.

Gentzler, Edwin. *Contemporary Translation Theories*. Clevedon: Multilingual Matters, 2001.

Gile, Daniel. *Basic Concepts and Models for Interpreter and Translator Training*. Amsterdam: Rodopi, 1995.

Gile, Daniel. 'Integrated Problem and Decision Reporting as a Translator Training Tool.' *Journal of Specialised Translation* 2 (2004): 1–20.

Godard, Barbara. 'L'Éthique du traduire: Antoine Berman et le virage "éthique" en traduction.' *TTR: traduction, terminologie, rédaction* 14, no. 2 (2001): 49–82.

Godard, Barbara. '"Windows" and "Fenêtres."' In *One Poem in Search of a Translator: Rewriting 'Les Fenêtres' by Apollinaire*, edited by Eugenia Loffredo and Manuela Perteghella, 195–205. With an introduction by Timothy Mathews. Oxford: Peter Lang, 2009.

Graham, Joseph F., ed. *Difference in Translation*. Ithaca: Cornell University Press, 1985.

Hanna, Sameh. 'Exploring MA Students' Attitudes to Translation Theory and Practice.' *The Sign Language Translator and Interpreter* 3, no. 2 (2009): 141–155.

Hatim, Basil, and Ian Mason. *Discourse and the Translator*. London: Longman, 1990.

Hatim, Basil, and Ian Mason. *The Translator as Communicator*. London: Routledge, 1997.

Hatim, Basil. *Teaching and Researching Translation*. Harlow: Longman, 2001.

Hermans, Theo, ed. *The Manipulation of Literature*. New York: St Martin's Press, 1985.

Hermans, Theo. 'The Translator's Voice in Translated Narrative.' *Target* 8, no. 1 (1996): 23–48.

Hermans, Theo. *Translation in Systems*. Manchester: St Jerome, 1999.

Hermans, Theo. 'Paradoxes and Aporias in Translation and Translation Studies.' In *Translation Studies: Perspectives on an Emerging Discipline,* edited by Alessandra Riccardi, 10–23. Cambridge: Cambridge University Press, 2002.

Hermans, Theo. *The Conference of the Tongues*. Manchester: St Jerome, 2007.

Holmes, James S. 'The Name and Nature of Translation Studies.' In *Translated! Papers on Literary Translation and Translation Studies*, edited by James S. Holmes, 67–80. Amsterdam: Rodopi, 1972/1988.

Holmes, James S., ed. *Translated! Papers on Literary Translation and Translation Studies.* Amsterdam: Rodopi, 1988.

Hutchins, John. 'Multiple Uses of Machine Translation and Computerised Translation Tools.' International Symposium on Data and Sense Mining, Machine Translation and Controlled Languages–ISMTCL, 2009. http://www.hutchinsweb.me.uk.

Jakobson, Roman. 'On Linguistic Aspects of Translation.' In *The Translation Studies Reader*, edited by Lawrence Venuti, 137–143. London and New York: Routledge, 1959/2004.

Kadiu, Silvia. 'Teaching Theory Through Practice: A Reflexive Approach.' *Current Trends in Translation Teaching and Learning E* 4 (2017): 48–77.

Kelly, Dorothy. *A Handbook for Translator Trainers: A Guide to Reflective Practice*. Manchester: St Jerome, 2005/2012.

Kenny, Dorothy, and Stephen Doherty. 'Statistical Machine Translation in the Translation Curriculum: Overcoming Obstacles and Empowering Translators.' *The Interpreter and Translator Trainer* 8, no. 2 (2014): 276–294.

Kiraly, Donald. *Pathways to Translation: Pedagogy and Process*. Kent and London: Kent State University Press, 1995.

Kiraly, Donald. 'Occasioning Translator Competence: Moving Beyond Social Constructivism toward a Postmodern Alternative to Instructionism.' *Translation and Interpreting Studies* 10, no. 1 (2015): 8–32.

Koehn, Philipp. *Statistical Machine Translation*. Cambridge: Cambridge University Press, 2010.

Kruger, Jean-Louis. 'Translating Traces: Deconstruction and the Practice of Translation.' *Literator* 25, no. 1 (2004): 47–71.

Lacan, Jacques. 'The Mirror Stage.' In *Écrits: A Selection*, translated by Alan Sheridan, 1–6. London: Routledge/Tavistock, 1949/1977.

Lacan, Jacques. *Écrits*. Translated by Bruce Fink. New York: W. W. Norton, 1966/2007.

Ladmiral, Jean-René. *Sourcier ou cibliste: les profondeurs de la traduction*. Paris: Belles Lettres, 2014.

Lecercle, Jean-Jacques. *The Violence of Language*. London and New York: Routledge, 1990.

Lederer, Marianne. 'Can Theory Help Translator and Interpreter Trainers and Trainees?'. *The Interpreter and Translator Trainer* 1, no. 1 (2007): 15–35.

Littré, Émile. *Dictionnaire de la langue française*. Paris: Hachette, 1863–1877.

Levinas, Emmanuel. *Humanism of the Other*. Translated by Nidra Poller. Urbana and Chicago: University of Illinois Press, 1972/2006.

Levinas, Emmanuel. *Ethics and Infinity: Conversations with Philippe Nemo*. Translated by Richard A. Cohen. Pittsburgh: Duquesne University Press, 1982/1985.

Lewis, Philip E. 'The Measure of Translation Effects.' In *Difference in Translation*, edited by Joseph F. Graham, 31–62. Ithaca: Cornell University Press, 1985.

Loffredo, Eugenia, and Manuela Perteghella, eds. *Translating and Creativity: Perspectives on Creative Writing and Translation Studies*. London: Continuum, 2006.

Loffredo, Eugenia, and Manuela Perteghella, eds. *One Poem in Search of a Translator: Rewriting 'Les Fenêtres' by Apollinaire*. Oxford: Peter Lang, 2009.

Lynch, Michael. 'Against Reflexivity as an Academic Virtue and Source of Privileged Knowledge.' *Theory, Culture and Society* 17, no. 3 (2000): 26–54.

Marmontel, Jean-François. *Œuvres complètes de Marmontel*. Paris: Belin, 1787/1819.

Massardier-Kenney, Françoise. 'Introduction'. In *Toward a Translation Criticism*, i–xxi. Translated by Françoise Massardier-Kenney. Kent: Kent State University Press, 2009.

Meschonnic, Henri. *Critique du rythme*. Paris: Verdier, 1982.

Meschonnic, Henri. *Poétique du traduire*. Paris: Verdier, 1999.

Meschonnic, Henri. *Éthique et politique du traduire*. Paris: Verdier, 2007.

Meschonnic, Henri. *Ethics and Politics of Translating*. Translated by Pier-Pascale Boulanger. Amsterdam and Philadelphia: John Benjamins, 2011.

Meschonnic, Henri. 'Traduire au XXIè siècle.' *Quaderns: Revista de traducció* 15 (2008): 55–62..

Munday, Jeremy. *Introducing Translation Studies: Theories and Applications*. London: Routledge, 2001.

Munday, Jeremy. 'Translation Studies.' In *Handbook of Translation Studies Volume 1*, edited by Yves Gambier and Luc Van Doorslaer, 215–223. Amsterdam and Philadelphia: John Benjamins, 2010.

Muñoz Martín, Ricardo. 'Situating Translation Expertise.' In *The Development of Translation Competence*, edited by Aline Ferreira, 2–56. Newcastle: Cambridge Scholars Publishing, 2014.

Nasio, Juan-David. *Five Lessons on the Psychoanalytic Theory of Jacques Lacan*. Translated by David Pettigrew and François Raffoul. Albany: SUNY Press, 1992/1998.

Newmark, Peter. 1981. *Approaches to Translation*. Oxford: Pergamon.

Newmark, Peter. *A Textbook of Translation*. New York: Prentice-Hall International, 1988.

Nichols, Bill. *Representing Reality*. Bloomington: Indiana University Press, 1991.

Nikolaou, Paschalis and Maria-Venetia Kyritsi, eds. *Translating Selves: Experiences and Identity between Languages and Literatures*. London and New York: Continuum, 2008.

Nord, Christiane. *Text Analysis in Translation*. Amsterdam: Rodopi, 1991.

Nord, Christine. 'Training Functional Translators.' In *Training for the New Millennium: Pedagogies for Translation and Interpreting*, edited by Martha Tennent, 209–223. Amsterdam: John Benjamins, 2005.

Nouss, Alexis. 'Preface.' In Henri Meschonnic, *Ethics and Politics of Translating*, 1–10. Amsterdam and Philadelphia: John Benjamins, 2011.

O'Sullivan, Carol. 'Multimodality as Challenge and Resource for Translation.' *Journal of Specialised Translation* 20 (2011): 2–14.

Oxford English Dictionary. Oxford: Oxford University Press, 2011.

Peirce, Charles Sanders. *The Essential Peirce: Selected Philosophical Writings*. Bloomington: Indiana University Press, 1992.

Petrilli, Susan. 'Translation and Semiosis.' In *Translation Translation*, edited by Susan Petrilli, 17–37. Amsterdam: Rodopi, 2003.

Petrilli, Susan. 'The Intersemiotic Character of Translation.' In *Translation Translation*, edited by Susan Petrilli, 41–53. Amsterdam: Rodopi, 2003.

Polezzi, Loredana. *Translating Travel: Contemporary Italian Travel Writing in English Translation*. Ashgate: Aldershot, 2001.

Popovič, Anton. 'Aspects of Metatext.' *Canadian Review of Comparative Literature* 3, no. 3 (1976): 225–235.

Pym, Anthony. *Translation and Text Transfer: An Essay on the Principles of Intercultural Communication*. Frankfurt am Main: Peter Lang, 1992.

Pym, Anthony. 'Venuti's Visibility.' *Target* 8, no. 2 (1996): 165–177.

Pym, Anthony. *Exploring Translation Theories*. London and New York: Routledge, 2010.

Robinson, Douglas. *The Translator's Turn*. Baltimore and London: Johns Hopkins University Press, 1991.

Robinson, Douglas. *Translation and Taboo*. DeKalb: Northern Illinois University Press, 1996.

Robinson, Douglas. *Becoming a Translator*. London: Routledge, 2003.

Robinson, Douglas. '22 Theses on Translation.' *Journal of Translation Studies* 2 (1998): 92–117.

Robinson, Douglas. *Who Translates? Translator Subjectivities Beyond Reason*. Albany: SUNY Press, 2001.

Rovira-Esteva, Sara, Pilar Oreroa and Javier Franco Aixelá. 'Bibliometric and Bibliographical Research in Translation Studies.' *Perspectives: Studies in Translatology* 23, no. 2 (2015): 159–160.

Ruby, Jay. 'Exposing Yourself: Reflexivity, Anthropology and Film.' *Semiotica* 3, no. 1–2 (1980): 153–179.

Ruby, Jay. 'Speaking For, Speaking About, Speaking With, or Speaking Alongside: An Anthropological and Documentary Dilemma.' *Visual Anthropology Newsletter* 5, no. 1 (1991): 50–67.

Sakamoto, Akiko. 'Translators Theorising Translation: A Study of Japanese/English Translators' Accounts of Dispute Situations and its Implications for Translation Pedagogy.' PhD diss., University of Leicester, 2013.

Scott, Clive. *Translating Baudelaire*. Exeter: University of Exeter Press, 2000.

Scott, Clive. *Translating Rimbaud's 'Illuminations.'* Exeter: University of Exeter Press, 2006.

Scott, Clive. 'Translating the Art of Seeing in Apollinaire's "Les Fenêtres": the Self of the Translator, the Selves of Language and Readerly Subjectivity.' In *Translating Selves: Experiences and Identity between Languages and Literatures*, edited by Paschalis Nikolaou and Maria-Venetia Kyritsi, 37–51. London and New York: Continuum, 2008.

Scott, Clive. *Literary Translation and the Rediscovery of Reading*. Cambridge: Cambridge University Press, 2012.

Scott, Clive. *Translating the Perception of Text*. Cambridge: Cambridge University Press, 2012.

Schäffner, Christina. *The Role of Discourse Analysis for Translation and in Translator Training*. Clevedon: Multilingual Matters, 2002.

Schleiermacher, Friedrich. 'On the Different Methods of Translating.' Translated by Susan Bernofsky. In *The Translation Studies Reader*, edited by Lawrence Venuti, 43–63. London: Routledge, 1813/2004.

Schneider, Monique. 'À l'origine de la psychanalyse, l'étranger.' *Filigrane* 1, no. 5 (1996): 8–17.

Schulte, Rainer, and Biguenet, John, eds. *Theories of Translation: An Anthology of Essays from Dryden to Derrida*. Chicago and London: University of Chicago Press, 1992.

Shuttleworth, Mark, and Cowie, Moira. *Dictionary of Translation Studies*. Manchester: St. Jerome, 1997.

Shuttleworth, Mark. 'The Role of Theory in Translator Training: Some Observations about Syllabus Design.' *Meta: journal des traducteurs / Meta: Translators' Journal* 46, no. 3 (2001): 497–506.

Snell-Hornby, Mary. 'Translation Studies: Art, Science or Utopia?' In *Translation Studies: The State of the Art*, edited by Kitty M. Van Leuven-Zwart and Tom Naaijkens, 13–23. Amsterdam: Rodopi, 1991.

Spivak, Gayatri Chakravorty. 'Preface.' In Jacques Derrida, *Of Grammatology*, translated by Gayatri Chakravorty Spivak, ix–lxxxvii. Baltimore: Johns Hopkins University Press, 1976/1997.

Susam-Saraeva, Şebnem. *Theories on the Move*. Amsterdam and New York: Rodopi, 2006.

Toury, Gideon. *Descriptive Translation Studies and Beyond*. Amsterdam and Philadelphia: John Benjamins, 1995.

Tymoczko, Maria. 'Translation and Political Engagement: Activism, Social Change and the Role of Translation in Geopolitical Shifts.' *The Translator* 6, no. 1 (2000): 23–47.

Tymoczko, Maria. 'Trajectories of Research in Translation Studies.' *Meta: journal des traducteurs / Meta: Translators' Journal* 50, no. 4 (2005): 1082–1097.

Tymoczko, Maria. 'Translation: Ethics, Ideology and Action.' *Massachusetts Review* 47, no. 3 (2006): 442–461.

Tymoczko, Maria. 'Translation Theory.' In *The Encyclopedia of Applied Linguistics*, edited by Carol A. Chapelle, 1–7. Oxford: Blackwell, 2013.

Venuti, Lawrence. *The Translator's Invisibility: A History of Translation*. First edition. London and New York: Routledge, 1995.

Venuti, Lawrence. *The Translator's Invisibility: A History of Translation*. Second edition. London and New York: Routledge, 2008.

Venuti, Lawrence. *The Translator's Invisibility: A History of Translation*. Second edition. London and New York: Routledge, 2017.

Venuti, Lawrence. *The Scandals of Translation: Towards an Ethics of Difference*. London and New York: Routledge, 1998.

Venuti, Lawrence. 'Introduction.' In Jacques Derrida, 'What Is a "Relevant" Translation?' Translated by Lawrence Venuti. *Critical Inquiry* 27, no. 2 (2001): 174–200.

Venuti, Lawrence. 'Translating Derrida on Translation: Relevance and Disciplinary Resistance.' *Yale Journal of Criticism* 16, no. 2 (2003): 237–262.

Venuti, Lawrence. *The Translation Studies Reader*. London and New York: Routledge, 2004.

Venuti, Lawrence. 'Translation as Cultural Politics: Regimes of Domestication in English.' In *Critical Readings in Translation Studies*, edited by Mona Baker, 65–79. London and New York: Routledge, 2010.

Way, Andy, and Mary Hearne. 'On the Role of Translations in State-of-the-Art Statistical Machine Translation.' *Language and Linguistics Compass* 5, no. 5 (2011): 227–248.

Williams, Jenny, and Andrew Chesterman. *The Map: A Beginner's Guide to Doing Research in Translation Studies*. Manchester: St Jerome, 2002.

Wills, David. *Matchbook*. Stanford: Stanford University Press, 2005.

Woodsworth, Judith. 'Teaching Literary Translation: Integrating Theory and Practice in the Classroom.' In *Teaching Translation and Interpreting 4: Building Bridges*, edited by Eva Hung, 129–138. Amsterdam and Philadelphia: John Benjamins, 2002.

Young, Robert J. C. 'Freud on Cultural Translation.' In *A Concise Companion to Psychoanalysis, Literature, and Culture*, edited by Laura Marcus and Ankhi Mukherjee, 367–384. Chichester: Wiley-Blackwell, 2014.

Žižek, Slavoj. *Interrogating the Real*. London and New York: Bloomsbury Revelations, 2005.

Index

truth 74, 95, 132, 158
Tymoczko, Maria 12

uncertainty 17, 42, 66, 68, 75, 79, 83, 87–92, 133, 135, 139, 141, 146, 148, 149, 152, 154, 158; *see also* hesitation; indeterminacy
unconscious, the 9, 16, 114, 118, 131, 132, 135, 136, 144, 151, 157
undecidability 66, 72, 73, 86–90, 91, 92, 135, 138–9, 145, 146, 151
unknown, the 88–9, 145, 146, 156, 158 *see also* unknowingness; unknown reader
unknowingness 135, 136, 138–41, 151
unknown reader, the 66, 68, 141, 150
untranslatability 3, 16, 61, 62

Venuti, Lawrence
  domestication 23, 36, 41, 42
  ethics of translation 17, 21–6, 30, 35, 36, 41
  fluency 21–5, 27–9, 30, 33, 38, 42
  foreignization 10, 17, 21–6, 30–42, 61, 146, 147, 148, 151

The Translator's Invisibility 1, 10, 17, 21, 22, 26, 30, 32, 35, 37, 40, 41, 42
visibility 1, 15, 17, 21, 22, 30, 39, 41, 96, 97, 145; *see also* invisibility; invisible translator
violence, ethnocentric 1, 2, 22, 36, 37, 40, 97, 105, 132; *see also* ethnocentrism
voice, and translation 45, 47, 48, 56, 58, 60, 63, 67, 132

Wills, David 64, 65
Woodsworth, Judith 153
writing 1, 2, 35, 4, 45, 46, 47, 48, 55, 59, 61, 63, 64, 66, 71, 122, 131, 148
  rewriting 47, 57, 118, 135
  'Writing and Translating' 1, 17, 45, 46, 47, 48, 55, 59, 62, 63, 67
  writing 'under erasure' 40–1; writing under influence 63
  writing subject, the 45

Žižek, Slavoj 95

Lightning Source UK Ltd.
Milton Keynes UK
UKHW050029020419
340286UK00002B/5/P